THE ELEGANCE CODE

Nina Gates

Published by Boheme Eclat Press LLC, Austin, Texas. First printing, May 2026, copyright

ISBN: 979-8-9952330-0-8, 979-8-9952330-1-5

Library of Congress Control Number: 2026911010

BOOKS BY NINA GATES

The Elegance Code

Be an Artist or Just Live Like One

The Roses of Ainsworth Manor

The Gilded Talisman

Contents

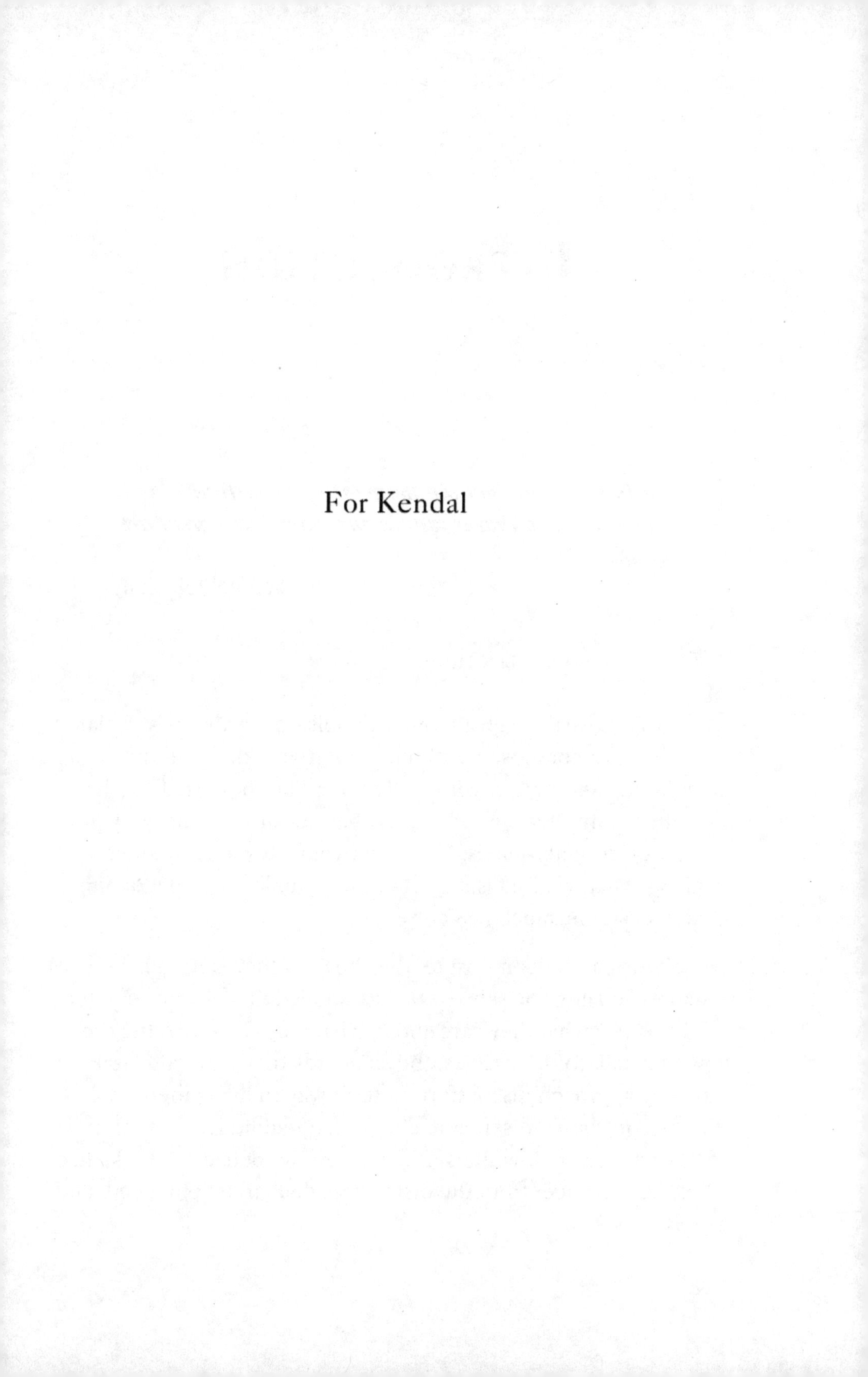

For Kendal

INTRODUCTION

To improve the golden moment of opportunity and catch the good that is within our reach is the great art of life.

Samuel Johnson

YOU'VE PROBABLY SEEN THEM.

They move through a room with poise and a kind of soft glamour. They are composed without being rigid, kind without being ingratiating, and stylish without looking like they tried too hard. They have a mysterious "it" factor that doesn't depend on youth, wealth, or designer labels. You catch yourself watching them and thinking, whatever that is, I want it. The trouble is, it's maddeningly hard to describe, much less copy.

The charisma, the composure, the "how do they stay so calm and gracious?" quality you sense is the accumulation of dozens of internal decisions: what they care about, what they allow to rattle them, how they talk to themselves, the standards they maintain, and the way they approach discomfort on their way to living their dreams. The reason their presence is elusive (and addictive) is that most of this happens below the surface. From the outside, it looks like effortless elegance; from the inside, it is deliberate, practiced, and deeply personal.

It's tempting to chalk it up to good genes or good luck, but it's not an accident; *it's an operating system. I call it an Elegance Code.*

I use public figures in this book as examples, but I'm just as interested in fictional characters because the writer reveals the character's operating system in ways that are easy to see.

Icons and Trends

Not everyone, real or imagined, has a sustainable inner code. Some people (and some fictional characters) are merely popular in the moment. They arrive with a trend and fade when society's mood shifts. The truly original figures on screens, pages, or in real life are iconic because their reference point is inward, not outward. They are guided not by "What is everyone else doing?" or "What does everyone want from me?" but by "What do I stand for, what is my vision for my life, and how do I want to make my way in this world?"

That inward reference point makes all the difference.

This is not a book about how you look to others; it is a book about becoming structurally calm inside your own life. I'll show you how to build an elegance code of your own, so you can live from a composed, graceful center and let the surface take care of itself.

You Are the Expert

You'll see me poke gentle fun at "the grown-ups in the room" and the invisible committees we strive to please. That's not because expertise is bad, or because I ignore it. Quite the opposite. I turn to professionals for many things I am not qualified to do.

Nothing here is a substitute for medical, legal, financial, or mental health advice. This isn't a manual for logistics, childcare, or eldercare, and it won't rearrange your external obligations. If you are facing illness, trauma, addiction, depression, or other challenges, please pause here. Skip what feels heavy, and reach for professionals who can help you feel safe, supported, and well. Use what resonates. Leave what doesn't. Adapt everything to your season, health, obligations, faith (or lack thereof), and constraints. As always, you remain the expert on your life.

A Note About Belief

When I write about vision, values, and centering yourself in your own life, I'm not asking you to abandon God, faith, or any sacred tradition that sustains you. Many philosophies and religions place the divine or a greater purpose at the center, and if that's true for you, let it remain so. My point is simpler: within whatever you believe, you are the one making the choices, phone calls, and plans; saying yes or no; and bearing the consequences that follow. If some ideas in this book harmonize with your faith, use them. If others don't, release them. The Elegance Code is yours to shape so it supports, never competes with, what you hold sacred.

Your Code

What follows is an exploration of something I know to be true: the elegance you admire in others is not out of reach. You can build it. Turn the page and let's begin.

With love and peace,

Nina Gates

1

THE ELEGANCE CODE

Thus, reader, I am myself the matter of my book.
Michel de Montaigne

THIS BOOK HAS BEEN a very long time in the making, arguably since I was about five and first realized that the world I'd been dropped into as a timeless little soul was both dazzling and bizarre. I could sense, even from a child's-eye view, that much of what passed for "The Way Things Are" was make-believe. I didn't have the words yet, but I could see the seams. What fascinated me then, and still does, is how willing we all are to play along.

Humans want to believe that somewhere out there exists a leather-bound manual, smudged with 4.54 billion years of coffee rings called How to Do Life Correctly, and that people wiser than us have read it. If they have it all figured out, the rest of us can just relax and copy their homework. But there is no such manual. There never has been. Humanity has been winging it all along.

Our species survives on spectacular improv. We invent fire, language, mathematics, and the classic white kitchen, then lose half of what we have made and congratulate ourselves when we "discover" it again centuries later. So it was with Aristotle, Euclid, Galen, Archimedes, and others: their works slipped out of Western circulation, only to return through Arabic and Byzantine copies, as though civilization had stumbled on something new. We habitually mistake recovery for progress, and memory for invention.

Humans once knew how to make Roman concrete strong and self-healing enough to outlast empires, then let that recipe fall out of the collective brain until it had to be reverse-engineered from ruins nearly 2,000 years later. The ancient Greeks built the Antikythera mechanism, a shockingly sophisticated astronomical calculator sometimes called the world's first analog computer, and the knowledge behind it disappeared for centuries. Hypocaust underfloor heating, large-scale aqueducts, and elaborate public baths—along with the personal hygiene that went with them—also vanished from most of Western Europe and only much later found modern equivalents. If there really were a universal instruction book, you'd think we'd have managed not to lose the chapter titled How to Keep Your Best Ideas.

The Myth of the Right Way

So when our brains insist there is a correct way to be happy, elegant, or successful, that's not truth speaking. That's fear scanning the room for an officious-looking person in a blazer. He may be no smarter than we are, but fear says, "If he has a flashlight and a name badge, he must be the authority."

The myth is that there is a universal Right Way to do things and that we, tragically, were absent the day this knowledge was handed out. We mistake pockets of legitimate knowledge—like math that keeps bridges standing and medicine that keeps hearts beating—for proof that someone, somewhere, has all the answers. So we wait. We wait for the permission slip. We wait to do or be or have whatever we want to do or be or have, until we are certain we're allowed to be it or have it, and that we're doing it correctly. Since no permission is forthcoming, we can, in theory, wait forever.

This is why the idea of deciding, "I am an author," or "I am a founder," or "I am going to put my face on YouTube," can feel shockingly out of line, almost rude, as if we skipped several forms and an approval process. There is nothing wrong with following the masses; it's just expensive. The cost is not only a kind of perpetual low-grade anxiety but, more importantly, that we may never fully occupy our own lives or bring our brilliant ideas, insights, and talents to a world that sorely needs them.

The people we idolize are making it up too. Their great advantage is the willingness to act without a crystal ball or proof that they are doing it "right." They learn to tolerate the discomfort of uncertainty and move forward anyway. When we accept the slightly tipsy, sparkling freedom at the heart of our dreams, we can stop searching for The Manual and start writing our own.

This is not about becoming an outlaw, walking away from the life you've built, or making dramatic speeches to your friends and family. Elegance is not what you wear; it's a quality of lucidity. It's the ability to navigate a chaotic, nonsensical world with precision, economy, and grace. It's the mental equivalent of Ferris Bueller's Day Off: slipping through daily drama like it's an amusing obstacle course and still getting home in time for dinner.

Following Your Compass

I was fortunate—thoughtful, loving parents and a life that would generally be labeled "privileged," with no Dickensian hardships to report. But I was also what is now termed a highly sensitive person, and it often felt as though there was very little buffer between my inner, eternal self and the rough-and-tumble of the world outside.

I realized very early that if I did not navigate by my own compass, I would be endlessly buffeted by the whims of a fickle public. Somehow I knew the solution lay in adopting a private philosophy: a set of principles that could shape my behavior, mindset, manners, and even personal style. As I grew older and began dealing with relationships, jobs, institutions, and the peculiar rituals of adulthood, this ceased to be a charming childhood theory and became a survival skill.

This book is for anyone who, like I once did, suspects our conventions are largely invented but still has to live within them, and wants to do so by their own design as much as possible. It is not written from above, not a prescription for a correct life, and not permission to break the rules and laws that govern us. It is a companion for those who have looked around and thought, Surely there must be a more graceful way to be a person than whatever this is, and who might secretly crave an elegance manifesto, even if they would never use that phrase out loud.

The project is serious, but it need not be solemn: to craft a personal elegance code: a private, off-the-record, non-spectacular way of living, choosing, and caring for oneself that feels serene and coherent when the world seems to have gone off its rocker.

Why Now

In its current form, this book began with a very practical problem: there were simply too many piles of books. They were stacked on nightstands, teetering on chairs, colonizing corners of the house. It became clear that if proper bookshelves were not forthcoming, I would eventually be sleeping on an unstable fortress of paperbacks and hardcovers instead of a bed.

When the shelves were up, I began the slow work of migrating the wayward books. In the process, I pulled out volumes that had followed me from childhood bedroom to dorm room, to storage units, to various houses. As I opened them, little avalanches of paper fell out: notes, lists, and folded scraps in my handwriting at ten, fifteen, twenty-five.

They made me laugh because they were all strangely familiar. My elementary-school self had written things like "organize Barbie house" and carefully itemized what should go into her overnight bag. My teenage self saved lists of horse names, clothing and accessories torn from Vogue, and "Ways to Improve My Handwriting." A page from my military officer basic course held notes from a logistics lecture and painstaking measurements of the slope of a hill—proof that even the most romantic souls can calculate gradients under duress.

As a beginning artist and later a professional, the lists morphed into creative practices and attempts to understand the art world. Spread out across the floor, these scraps looked like a small archaeological dig. The handwriting changed, the circumstances changed, the stakes certainly changed, but the theme did not. Again and again, I found traces of the same impulse: to be prepared, to create balance and order from turmoil, and to live beautifully.

At some point, sitting there on the rug amid half-shelved books and forty years of lists, it occurred to me that I had been writing this book in fragments my entire life. I had simply been slipping the pages into margins and between chapters instead of giving them a spine of their own.

Whether the world really has come unmoored lately or is revealing more of what was always there, there is something deeply relieving about saying, Here is what I have learned so far about living with elegance and sanity on this planet, and offering that to anyone who recognizes themselves in the girl making lists on the back of a napkin.

What This Book Is (and Isn't)

This is not a glow-up or etiquette book. It will not teach you about fish forks or the difference between demitasse and dessert spoons (though both are remarkably useful to own). It is not about learning how to look elegant on the outside. It is not about impressing anyone but yourself, buying new clothes, changing your hair, fitting in with your supposed betters, or chasing status that only exists if others approve of you. Those things may or may not happen as side effects of having an elegance code, but they are not the point.

In the feeds and ad campaigns that shape modern taste, elegance is treated as a product: a look you can purchase, a dress, a bag, a hairstyle, a house. This book argues something different. Elegance is not a thing. It cannot be manufactured or bought. It is a living state of inner calm, poise, and refinement that, though observable, is built from the inside out.

In The Elegance Code, you will learn how to build that inner state deliberately. You will create a personal protocol for navigating a tumultuous world in your own style, on your own terms.

Your elegance code weaves together four elements: your vision (where you are heading), your values (what matters most to you), your center of balance, and your ethos (how you live, whether anyone is watching or not). When created thoughtfully, it becomes a set of private operating instructions you carry inside you. A standard you choose to answer to in service of the life you most want to live.

2

VISION

Your vision will become clear only when you can look into your own heart. Who looks outside dreams; who looks inside, awakes.

Carl Jung

A FRIEND TOLD ME recently that she has spent hours down the internet rabbit hole searching "how to be elegant." What she found, she said, was a lot of rules. Apparently, the consensus is that elegance requires a long list of non-negotiables: wear this but never that; always do this, but for heaven's sake, stop doing that. She sighed and said, "If I followed all of that advice, I'm not sure who I'd wake up as, but it wouldn't be me."

She is right, of course. Those ideas are irresistible because they promise an easy shortcut through complicated territory. When life feels messy, uncertain, or vaguely disappointing, a good "do this, don't do that" list is soothing. It offers the hope that if we just follow the steps, our lives will fall into place.

But deep down, we know it does not work. Copying someone else's version of elegance (or confidence, or success) is like borrowing their prescription glasses. You can see something, but the world looks slightly distorted, and after a while you get a headache. At best, you get a blurry approximation of a life that is not yours.

The Ready-made Identity

Modern culture makes prescriptive style very tempting. It keeps handing us ready-made identities to choose from, like flavors at a frozen yogurt bar: "Old Money," "It-Girl," "Clean Girl," "Boss Babe." Just pick one and voilà—you, optimized. No need to sit alone asking awkward questions like, "Who do I want to be, really?" "What do I care about?" and "What are my preferences?"

I'll just go ahead and say the thing you probably already know: trying to change your life from the outside in almost never sticks. Outwardly, you can wear the pleated white linen wide-leg trousers, master an impeccable calligraphed thank-you note, and balance a champagne coupe on your head, but when your toddler is melting down, your boss is impossible, or your partner is having a bad day, that applied persona vanishes faster than the last double-fudge brownie.

Grace, equilibrium, and arresting style are powered from within. Picture a spring that bubbles up because the underground source is full. Your behavior and your image are the water at the surface. Your vision, values, preferences, and philosophy are the source.

When you get a chip in your brand-new windshield the same day your dog throws up on your antique Aubusson rug and you discover that someone you thought was a friend has said something unkind behind your back, you do not have to re-evaluate your entire existence. You schedule the windshield repair, clean the rug, ignore the gossip, treat yourself to an early evening and a bubble bath with a stack of interiors magazines, and let your code remind you who you are.

Let's get one thing out of the way: I know I have just spent several pages making fun of lists that tell people how to live. And here I am, writing one. Hypocritical? Maybe. But this is not that kind of list. The numbers are here only so you do not lose your place if you drop the book in the bathtub, which, frankly, is where most good thinking happens anyway.

An Invitation to an Elegant Life

Have you ever received a large, thickly padded invitation to a wedding or gala? Maybe it was edged in gold and arrived in a double envelope. The ivory paper was smooth and heavy, the words engraved in gorgeous looping script. You picked it out of the pile of bills and ads, ran your fingers across your name on the front, turned it over slowly, and felt the weight in your hands before slipping a letter opener or your finger under the flap.

In this chapter, you are a secret agent of elegance, and your vision for your life is classified—for your eyes only. You do not have to tell anyone or justify it, and you certainly do not need a committee to approve it. Your vision does not require changing anyone else, nor does it need anyone's buy-in or cooperation.

This is your invitation.

1. MAKE SOME NOTES

Look at your life right now and ask yourself:

When and where do I feel most energized and content? When and where am I not at my best? What do I love about my life right now? Who do I enjoy spending time with, and who exhausts me? Which habits are helpful, and which ones get in my way? Do I have work that I love? Do I have interesting hobbies? What am I making time for?

Your notes might be:

I am happiest doing something creative. I am spending too much money eating out. I open the fridge every twenty minutes as if something new will appear. I complain about being exhausted, but rarely go to bed before midnight. I talk to my dog in a more encouraging tone than I use with myself. I rehearse arguments in my head with people I have not spoken to since 2014. I am bored and I do not know why. I reward myself for doing one adult task by not doing the next four. I love working at home. I need to get out more.

Now step back and read your notes aloud the way you would if you were a clear-eyed coach working with a friend. What are the themes? Which habits, people, places, and patterns reliably leave you feeling more alive? Which ones reliably drain you?

When I step outside myself and observe my life like a subject in a lab, I see more clearly what I like and dislike, and what serves me and what does not. Psychologists sometimes call this creating "psychological distance."

2. THE NOISE AND THE SELF

In 1841, Ralph Waldo Emerson published an essay called *Self-Reliance* that opened with an observation so pointed it has never stopped being true: "Society everywhere is in conspiracy against the manhood of every one of its members." He was not speaking of enemies. He was speaking of the ordinary, relentless pressure that civilization exerts on every person within it. This is the pressure to conform, to perform, to want what is sanctioned, to become what is legible to others. The conspiracy he described was not malicious. It did not need to be. It worked precisely because it was invisible, woven into every expectation, opinion, and social arrangement a person encountered from birth.

That pressure has not diminished. It has multiplied.

For most of human history, the forces acting on an individual came from a defined radius. Your family told you who you were and what you were worth. Your village told you what was possible and what was shameful. Your religion told you what to want and what to suppress. Your class told you your station and your ceiling.

These were powerful forces, and they shaped the interior lives of everyone they touched. But they had a perimeter. A woman with enough courage or desperation could leave the village, change her religion, cross a class line, put an ocean between herself and everything she had been told to be. There is no edge now.

The woman trying to hear her own thoughts in the twenty-first century is not contending with only a village. She is contending with an algorithm designed by some of the most sophisticated engineers alive, whose explicit purpose is to capture her attention and hold it. She is contending with a media apparatus that has discovered, and repeatedly confirmed, that anxiety and outrage keep people watching longer than contentment does. She is contending with a consumer economy that, in order to function, requires her to feel perpetually insufficient because a woman who is satisfied with who she is doesn't buy as much.

Add to that, the curated highlight reels of people she has never met, presented to her as evidence of what a life can look like, what a body should look like, what success looks like at thirty, forty, fifty. Then pile on the opinions of her colleagues and friends, all arriving on the same pocket-sized device, at all hours, with equal urgency.

This is why elegance must begin from the inside. Not because the outside world is irrelevant, but because a woman who has not first located her own center, and does not have a firm grasp on her personal values and vision, has no stable ground from which to evaluate what the outside world offers her.

Marcus Aurelius, writing in the second century to no audience but himself, returned again and again to a single distinction: the things within his control, and the things outside it. He was the most powerful man in the known world, and he wrote daily notes to remind himself that his personal peace must not depend on the latter.

Crafting your vision requires setting aside, temporarily, everything you have been told to want. The credentials your parents valued. The body your culture approves of. The career that would finally make a certain person proud of you. The version of success that photographs well.

As you make notes, sit with this question: *Whose voice am I hearing when I imagine the life I want?* If the answer is your mother's, your partner's, your industry's, your Instagram feed's, note that, and set it aside. Not with resentment. Just with clarity. Those voices have had their say. This opportunity belongs to you.

3. WRITE IT DOWN

What you write next is the anchor for everything else in this book. We will circle back to it constantly. Another prompt:

If my days were more curated, true, and satisfying to me, what would that look like? What would the most beautiful version of my life feel like?

Don't edit. Don't worry about how on earth you could ever possibly live in France, start a business, lose ten pounds, buy a house, or meet the love of your life. How is for later.

If you get stuck, one technique is to start with a feeling and build from there: I want my days to feel calm and connected, or I want to approach my work with energy and integrity. Imagine what a day feels like when it aligns with what you believe in. Who surrounds you? Do you know them, or are they people you have not met yet? What do you do on weekends, and what does Monday morning look like when it begins on your terms?

Use your imagination without apology. Let yourself want what you want. A rough, honest vision is enough. The rest of this book is written as if you have something down on the page.

Here's an example:

I wake up early without an alarm, in crisp white sheets, to the sound of waves. I do gentle stretches, yoga, or Pilates overlooking the ocean, then shower, dress, and journal before making a pot of strong black coffee and writing for two uninterrupted hours before I look at my phone. The house is filled with sunlight, abundant flowers, soft morning jazz, and cheerful voices. My assistant arrives, and we plan the day over a brunch of quiche, fruit, and fresh-squeezed orange juice. I spend a few more hours in deep work with words: writing, editing, shaping ideas, then step away to take meetings, return calls, and talk with people I love. Income from my work arrives steadily enough that bills are paid, savings grow, and I can be generous with the causes I care about. The day ends with a light, delicious dinner, great conversation with creative friends, a little spa time and reading, and lights out before ten.

And another:

My ideal day begins just before the rest of the family wakes up. I make a mug of green tea in the kitchen, clear yesterday's dishes, and sit for a few minutes at the table by the window while the sky lightens over the city. The morning is unhurried and organized: kids' lunches are packed, the dog is fed, and everyone leaves home with what they need. Once the house is empty, I have a protected block of time for my work without notifications pulling at me. In the afternoon, I run a few errands, prep dinner, and take a short walk through the neighborhood, saying hello to neighbors and noticing trees, sky, and window boxes instead of only my phone. Evenings are calm: a meal at the table, then a bit of reading or a show with my partner while the pets snore at our feet. The day ends in a reasonably tidy house and a bedroom that feels like a retreat, with a stack of good books and asleep early enough that tomorrow does not start with regret.

These are just examples. Keep in mind also that you are not signing a contract. You can revise it tomorrow, share it or keep it entirely to yourself, and want something completely different by next year.

4. BE SPECIFIC

Be specific. Vague visions produce vague results. “I want to live beautifully” is a wish. “I wake up in shell-pink sheets, in a white clapboard house in the tropics, make an iced mocha latte, and sit on the porch for an entire hour before anyone wants something from me” is something your brain can work with.

You may be surprised, looking back in a year or two, by how much of it has come true.

5. YOUR VISION PROTECTS YOU

Your vision statement guides you when culture tries to sell you another trend, when Instagram makes someone else’s life look like the one you should live, or when opportunities arrive and you have to decide quickly whether they belong in your life.

Consider what happens without one. Someone texts “You in!?” and your only criteria are (1) you are not in pajamas yet and (2) they used an exclamation point. The next thing you know, you are three bars, two tequila shots, and one tearful bathroom conversation deep, wondering how this became your life.

On the other hand, if your vision for this season is to roll with whatever comes, affirming that keeps you in the right frame of mind. Now the same night is not “I don’t know how I ended up here.” It is “This is exactly the spontaneity I chose on purpose.”

The moment you imagine the life you want, and name the people, places, and things you want in it, you begin to assemble a reliable internal compass. Think of your vision as your personal gravity field: just as you do not walk around consciously aware of being held to the ground, your vision pulls your choices, relationships, and habits into alignment with very little effort on your part.

In doing this, you might be surprised to discover you want to learn Portuguese, move abroad, or fall in love. Even if you do nothing with it immediately, it works like a seed put into the ground in autumn: forgotten until spring, when it opens into something you did not plan for and could not have forced.

The next time the same invitation arrives, all you have to do is check in with yourself. Your vision is to save for a trip to Costa Rica, or finish a book this year, and you have to be up early tomorrow to write before work. You text back: "Not tonight, but I would love a coffee this weekend." Then you make tea, wash your face properly, and read the travel book you have been looking forward to instead of re-living someone else's drama. The evening is not a sacrifice. It is a choice you own.

6. YOU BECOME WHAT YOU BELIEVE

The vision you just wrote is not wishful thinking. There is solid research behind what you did on that page.

Psychologist Hazel Markus spent years studying what she called "possible selves," the future versions of ourselves we hold in our minds, both the ones we hope for and the ones we fear. Her findings were straightforward: people who carry a vivid, specific image of a desired future self make different choices today than people who don't. Your vision statement functions as inspiration and as a behavioral regulator, pulling your daily decisions toward what you have imagined.

The stories we tell about ourselves shape who we become. We are not passive characters in our own lives, waiting to see how the plot resolves. We are the authors. When you write a forward-looking account of your life and make a claim about what comes next, your brain takes that seriously. This is not journaling for its own sake. It is identity construction. You are not describing a fantasy. You are building the self who will live it.

Pure positive visualization, on its own, is less effective than pairing it with a vivid description of the life unfolding hour by hour. In other words, "I want to feel more at home" is a starting point. Gabriele Oettingen's research suggests that the mind needs something more specific to work with: the smell of the coffee, the hour you sit down to work, the feeling of the evening when it ends the way you wanted it to. When you imagine that level of detail, you give your brain a working map.

7. ONE THING

Read back what you wrote. Sit with it for a moment.

If there is one change in how you think, live, or spend your time that would bring you closer to that vision, what is it? Not a complete overhaul. One thing. The change that, if you made it, would make the others more possible.

Name it. Write it down beneath your vision statement. You do not have to act on it today. For now, acknowledging it is enough.

8. WHEN VISION MEETS VALUES

Vision gives you direction. Values give you substance. Without values, vision can drift into vanity. Without vision, values remain abstract and never touch your life. But when you pair them, you get something both sturdy and luminous.

The next chapter will show you how to find your values. You have them. They are living inside the paragraph you just wrote.

3

VALUES

The greatest elegance is kindness.

Deborah Kerr

FROM THE BEGINNING, THERE was nature. Not in a vague, "I like trees" way, but in an elemental sense, as if the boundary between me and the living world was thinner than advertised. I never really doubted that I was in it and it was in me; this seemed obvious in the way breathing is obvious until someone asks you to explain it and you realize there are no tidy words.

Animals were my first great confidantes. My dog and I appeared to share a similar outlook on life: observant, mildly perplexed, and unconvinced by many of the human arrangements around us. We watched things together. I cried if an animal, a bug, or a fish was harmed or even looked unhappy. I took it personally when I saw children and elders, those most dependent on the care of others, left lonely, frightened, or despondent. Their vulnerability felt like an alarm bell only I could hear, which is a dramatic job for a small child.

For a long time, this level of introverted sensitivity felt like too much: too porous, too easily moved, too overreactive for a world that prizes both being an extrovert and having thicker skin. I now see it as one of my best virtues. To feel that much is not a flaw; it is a way of honoring the fact that other beings are real, that their experience matters, and that none of us are separate from one another or from the living world, no matter how we try to behave as though we are.

There is a name for that ache I carried around as a child—the one that flared when an animal was hurt or a lonely elder sat ignored at the edge of a room. It was not dramatics (though I am sure it looked like that at times); it was my earliest evidence that certain things were non-negotiably important to me: gentleness, protection of the vulnerable, a sense that all living beings are kin rather than props. What I did not know then was that these values were my first, untrained glimpses of a personal code.

Before I had any language for "values," I had that visceral yes and no in my body. Yes to care, to tenderness, to beauty, to loyalty. No to casual cruelty, to humiliation, to waste, to treating anything living as disposable. Those reactions were not random; they were the outlines of an inner moral landscape.

This is where values begin, not as lofty words on a page, but as deep, often inconvenient sensitivities that have been with you for as long as you can remember. In the next pages, we will name them: the qualities of character you admire, return to, and want to embody, so that your choices are aligned with what you have loved (or could not bear) all along.

9. ELEGANCE AS A MORAL COMPASS

Elegance is self-control and self-direction in a messy world that flip-flops from headline to headline. Before you worry about how your life looks from the outside, get clear inside. Decide what matters to you. Decide what doesn't. Decide who you are off-camera. That's your compass. Without it, you're the average person pushed around by news and circumstance. With it, you're thinking for yourself, and moving by design, not by reflex.

10. DON'T GET HACKED

What you care about—your values—is essentially the cipher for your life. Without strong personal values, your thoughts, words, and actions can be hacked by distraction, peer pressure, and clever marketing.

Most people operate in plaintext. They react. Their decisions follow the vicissitudes of the media, the opinions of their tribe, and whoever is lobbying them hardest. Their boundaries are porous. To the world, they are an open book; to opportunists, they are a book that can be conveniently edited.

11. YOUR FOUNDATION

Your values are the axiomatic beliefs that underpin your behavior. When you value, for example, self-respect over approval, you become much harder to read or exploit. When you value restraint over attention, external events can no longer so easily find a frequency to trigger you. This matters not only because it reduces stress and increases your daily pleasure, but because, with a vision and clear values, you accomplish more of what is right for you instead of allowing everyone else to determine how you spend your time and energy. Values plus vision help you create an elegant life.

12. VALUES ARE SEXY

A by-product, for anyone interested in being extremely attractive to others regardless of physical appearance, is that a person who is values-directed has an almost magnetic pull. When a person knows their true north and follows their own path, they stop leaking energy through indecision or the constant need for external validation.

When your values and your vision are deeply satisfying to you, you become more opaque. That opacity is a mystery, and mystery is like catnip to a cat. The important distinction is that the mystery is real, not manufactured. You are not hiding a void; you are protecting a treasure.

13. WHY "DIRECTIONLESS" IS NOT SEXY

Elegance requires both selection and rejection. If you do not know what you value, you cannot consistently select what is best for you. Instead, you try to be everything to everyone, which creates a noisy, frantic presence that feels more scattered than sophisticated.

Directionless is not the same as open and easy-going. Your vision might be a life that is carefree and easy, and your values might encompass words like: freedom, connection, fun, peace, creativity, relaxed, mellow, unflappable, unfazed, good-humored, or happy-go-lucky. Your motto might be that variety is the spice of life, or easy come, easy go. This is a laid-back way of living, but it isn't lacking direction. You know what you want, what you're true to, and you have a code that allows you to choose people, places, and things that move in the same groove you do.

Standing Instructions

In his book In Pursuit of Elegance, Matthew E. May describes elegance as achieving maximum impact with minimal input, emphasizing simplicity, subtraction, and sustainability as three defining features. A personal elegance code works the same way. By pre-deciding what you will not chase, you subtract static from your thinking and free your attention to read situations with your inner barometer. You gain the ability to notice small, aligned openings that clutter and overcommitment would otherwise hide.

Little by little, you stop living like someone guessing on the fly and start moving through your world with the assurance of someone following private internal operating instructions. Your values are those instructions. They are the clauses in your private dossier: what must be protected, what may be ignored, what is never worth the cost.

Another of May's criteria for elegance is sustainability: a solution is not elegant if it cannot abide ongoing use or changing conditions. When your code is simple and value-based, rather than a haphazard list of rules, it can endure across many life changes, because only the expression must adapt, not the values themselves.

Coherence

Your elegance code is not about achieving fragile perfection. It is about coherence. Coherence is harmonizing your beautiful inner world with your actions on the outside. When you know what you care about most deeply, your daily choices arrange themselves around that center, strengthening your balance.

When you are centered like this, you can do things that would otherwise feel impossible. Think of Luke in the trench run in the first Star Wars film: at the crucial moment, he turns off the targeting computer and trusts the Force within himself instead of all the chatter in his headset. He does not grow new superpowers in that instant; he lines up his actions with what he already believes and knows. That coherence lets him make the one shot that changes everything. Your values work the same. When you are strong and balanced, you can do remarkable things.

14. THE MORE GOOGLY EYES THE BETTER

This is a hard concept, so bear with me for a moment. Most people cannot effectively process criticism. It either pierces right through them and confirms their worst fears, or it bounces off completely because they decide it is too false, too painful, or too something else to consider. Without a values filter, any "negative" comment feels like a verdict on who we are, not information about what we did.

To protect ourselves, we reject all of it. This is not especially smart because we need the information. We know the saying, "Knowledge is power." When we block out criticism, we block out information. We block knowledge, and we block power. Criticism, handled well, can be a superfood for growth.

There is almost always a small piece of truth or usefulness hidden inside something "negative." When we know what matters to us, we can take in criticism without collapsing. This makes us very calm and very difficult to manipulate. We are not dependent on outside approval, but we are also not blind to the ways we can change or adapt.

Imagine that every time something pokes us—a sharp comment, an awkward moment, a so-called mistake—we get to add another pair of eyes there. Think of the little googly eyes from the craft store. We stick them (metaphorically) on the tender spots instead of armoring over them. Suddenly we are not walking around with only the two viewpoints we had at age sixteen; we have a hundred small eyes helping us see ourselves and the world more clearly. That is what happens when you use your values as a filter: discomfort becomes information you can use to your advantage.

15. LISTENING IS NOT SURRENDER

There is a common fear: "If I really listen to what they say, I will lose my right to choose." So we protect ourselves by tuning out completely. We treat criticism like a trap: if I let it in, I must stay, fix myself, and keep everyone else comfortable.

Your values give you another option. You can decide in advance that you will listen for information without handing over your authority. Hearing someone out does not cancel your right to act on your own behalf, or to make a choice for no other reason than it delights you.

You can stay rooted in what matters to you, even while you turn your attention outward long enough to learn a thing or two.

Think of it this way: committing not to tune out is not submission, it is your power move. Knowledge is still power. The more you are willing to notice about yourself, about others, and about the dynamics you are in, the more clearly you can see your options. Listening adds tools to your toolkit; it does not add chains to your wrists.

You are free. If the people around you are cruel, careless, or not for you, you do not owe them your presence. You can hear them out, keep the one or two useful grains of truth, and leave the room, the job, or the friend group if that serves your life. You may take the information and walk away.

16. LISTENING WITHOUT LOSING YOUR LICENSE

Think about how James Bond handles his boss. M hauls him into the office, tells him he is reckless, arrogant, and one disaster away from losing his license to kill. He does not crumple into a puddle of shame, and he does not storm out with his fingers in his ears. He listens, smiles that annoying little Bond smile, pockets the parts that might keep him alive, and then goes right back to doing his job in his own infuriatingly stylish way.

In real life, you can let people talk, collect any useful intel, and still walk out of the room free to make your own choices. You do not have to become the person they would prefer; you are allowed to be the secret agent of your own life, not their obedient side character.

You can let the information land without letting it define you. You are always free to walk away from a bad situation, or keep your own style, or to choose pleasure and self-respect over compliance. Hearing someone out does not mean you now owe them your life.

17. AUTHENTICITY

When you are sure of your values, you move through the day with the sangfroid of a character like James Bond. Knowing what he values does not make every day easy, but it spares him from re-deciding who he is every time something goes wrong.

His choices match his values, so he comes across as authentic to others. Psychologists routinely find that living in line with your values increases authenticity, trust, and life satisfaction, which is what Bond models on screen. Because he spends less time measuring himself against others and more time attending to what genuinely delights him, his life is richer and more pleasurable, even in a highly dangerous job.

Although James Bond and other characters I mention are fictional, they are useful for our purposes because they embody certain traits in a concentrated, almost exaggerated form. We borrow them the way an intelligence analyst might use a simulation: not because it is "real life," but because it makes the underlying pattern easier to see. That shared understanding is part of what makes Bond and other characters so effective—and so much fun—as examples in this book.

18. WHY GOOD VALUES MAKE YOU LESS PREDICTABLE AND MORE TRUSTWORTHY

As a side note, a friend and I were talking about this book, and he wondered whether Bond's rogue behavior and unpredictability made him untrustworthy. My answer is that predictability does not make someone trustworthy. What makes someone trustworthy is character: the integrity that comes from embodying good values consistently.

Bond operates by his own values, whether or not they are convenient for anyone else, including the British government; but M trusts him because she knows he has character, is authentic, and has proven that he has committed his life to his values. She might not be able to name his values on command, but she has watched him fight to defend them.

Predictable, interestingly, is usually what the villains are. Bad guys almost always value power, money, fame, or revenge. Those are all flavors of the same traits: self-enhancement at any cost: power, control, dominance, gratification, getting even. They are crude, blunt motives, so they look very similar from the outside: grab more, protect ego, get even, win.

"Good" values, by contrast, span many different motivations: care, creativity, freedom, beauty, excellence, justice, loyalty, wonder, and so on. They can combine in endlessly different proportions. That makes embodied goodness feel more varied and nuanced, because there is not just one way to live out courage, benevolence, or integrity.

When someone is driven by power, money, or revenge, you can usually predict their next move: whatever increases power, money, or revenge. The value is narrow; the behavior is linear.

When someone lives from a constellation of "good" values, say, self-respect, compassion, beauty, and truth—their choices must honor all of those at once. That means they sometimes surprise you: they may walk away instead of "winning," tell the truth instead of people-pleasing, choose rest instead of more status. Their behavior is consistent with their inner compass, but not always convenient or easily read or controlled from the outside.

That is what makes them (and Bond's character) feel authentic. Their actions are not optimized for approval; they are optimized for coherence with who they are. Values like dignity, love, freedom, and fairness multiply possibilities instead of narrowing them, so they naturally generate surprising alliances, new ideas, and unexpected forms of courage. In short, goodness is a lot more interesting and harder to figure out.

19. CHOOSE YOUR WORDS

When you think about your vision statement, what words, phrases, or moments feel especially meaningful?

Look back at what you wrote in the last chapter and circle the parts that make you feel relaxed, contented, inspired, and energized. Those feelings are clues to your values.

If your vision statement includes calm, tidy spaces, it might point to values like serenity, order, or beauty. If your vision includes time to talk to your family in the morning before everyone scatters, that might hint at intimacy, connection, or generosity. A vision statement that describes meaningful work might point to contribution, creativity, mastery, or service.

20. YOUR VALUES WORDS

The following list of sample value words is not a test or a complete catalog. It is just here to spark ideas and help you find language for what matters to you. If you like a particular word, but it does not quite fit, check a thesaurus; there might be a similar word that feels just right.

Abundance, Acceptance, Accessibility, Accountability, Active, Authenticity, Achievement, Admiration, Adventure, Aliveness, Allure, Ambition, Animals, Appreciation, Art, Assertiveness, Athletics, Authority, Autonomy, Awe, Balance, Beauty, Bohemian, Boldness, Books, Bravery, Business, Calm, Caring, Casual, Celebration, Celebrity, Challenges, Character, Charity, Charm, Cherish, Chic, Children, Choice, Citizenship, Clarity, Color,

Comfort, Communication, Community, Compassion, Competition, Competency, Composure, Confidence, Connection, Consistency, Constructive, Contentment, Contribution, Cosmopolitan, Courage, Cozy, Craft, Craftsmanship, Creativity, Culture, Curiosity, Dance, Delight, Democracy, Design, Determination, Devotion, Dignity, Duty, Earth, Ease, Eccentric, Education, Elegance, Enchantment, Encouragement, Endurance, Energy, Equality, Etiquette, Experiences, Exploration, Expression, Fairness, Faith, Faithfulness, Fame, Family, Fashion, Feminine, Fitness, Food, Freedom, Free Speech, Friendliness, Friendships, Forgiveness, Fun, Future, Fusion, Gardening, Generosity, Genius, Genuine, Gentility, Gentleman, Gifts, Giving, Goodness, Grace, Grandeur, Gratitude, Growth, Happiness, Harmony, Health, History, Home, Honesty, Honor, Humor, Illumination, Imagination, Independence, Inclusion, Influence, Ingenuity, Inner Peace, Innovation, Integrity, Intellectual, Intelligence, Joy, Justice, Kindness, Knowledge, Lady-like, Land, Leadership, Learning, Legacy, Light, Listening, Logic, Love, Loyalty, Luxury, Magic, Manners, Masculinity, Meaningful Work, Mentoring, Modernity, Money, Motherhood, Movies, Music, Natural, New Ideas, Nobility, Nostalgia, Nurturing, Open-mindedness, Openness, Optimism, Opulence, Organic, Originality, Outdoors, Painting, Passion, Patience, Peace, Performance, Perseverance, Philanthropy, Play, Playfulness, Plants, Pleasure, Poise, Polish, Popularity, Possibility, Presence, Professionalism, Prudence, Purpose, Quality, Quiet, Radiance, Recognition, Refinement, Relationships, Reliability, Religion, Reputation, Resilience, Respect, Responsibility, Safety, Sea, Seasons, Security, Self-Discipline, Self-Respect, Sensuality, Service, Simplicity, Sincerity, Single, Smart, Social, Solo, Space, Spirituality, Stability, Stealth, Strength, Style, Success, Sustainability, Status, Structure, Taste, Teaching, Theater, Timelessness, Touring, Transparency, Travel, Trustworthiness, Truth, Understated, Value, Warmth, Wealth, Welcome, Wilderness, Wildness, Wisdom, Wonder, Work, Workmanship, Worship, Writing, Zen

21. CORE VALUES

Look at your list of values and without overthinking, put a star next to three to five that feel like they have the most resonance in your body. If it helps, ask yourself: If I could only protect a few things in my life, which do I believe in? Which would I be heartbroken to lose? Which ones do I most want to share with the world through my words and actions? What do I most want to receive from the world?

One self-test you can perform to see if your values belong to you or someone else is to ask yourself, If I could perform an act related to this value, but **no one would ever know** I did it, would I still do it?

Imagine Charlotte from Charlotte's Web and her core values of friendship and service. Over and over, she spends her time and energy weaving words into her web to save Wilbur, even when she is tired and no one is watching her or praising her for it. If you asked her, "Would you still help Wilbur if no one ever knew you did it?" the answer would be yes. In fact, even though it is obvious that a spider wove the words into the web, Wilbur is the one who gets the credit. That is what a real value feels like: you would live it without recognition.

22. YOUR PRIVACY

You do not have to share this list with anyone. You are allowed to choose words that feel unfashionable, unfeminine, un-spiritual, or un-Instagrammable. If you genuinely value luxury, or romance, or ambition, there is nothing wrong with that; it is better to name it openly than to pretend your foundation is something else.

Your words will have personal meaning for you. "Luxury" might mean space, time, and quiet, or it might mean a beautifully made, high-quality wardrobe. As long as your values are not causing harm to you or to others, they belong on the page.

Others may never know the details of your elegance code, and that would serve little purpose anyway. On the outside, it might look like good manners, a calm voice, or a well-made bed. On the inside, it is more like a private creed, a set of promises you have made to yourself. It is very much in the spirit of the old Stoic idea: you carry your principles with you, without fanfare, as your own source of stability. At the heart of an elegance code is the person you are when no one is looking.

4

CENTER OF BALANCE

At the center of your being you have the answer; you know who you are and you know what you want.

Lao Tzu

WHEN I SAY I belong at the center of my life, I can hear the objections already: What about the children, the partner, the aging parent, the disabled friend? Surely they come first. The truth is, we can run our lives for a surprisingly long time with ourselves at the far edge of our own circle. Many loving, responsible people do. But finding our center of balance is not just about surviving this week or this year; it is about living the entire span of a life in a way that is healthy, fulfilling, and sustainable. Only you can know what that looks like for you.

It is part of being human that we are cared for and that we give care throughout our lives. When we are children, someone takes care of us; later we take care of children and elders, and later still, someone takes care of us again. This is the beautiful rhythm of life, and it has been going on, in one form or another, for thousands of years. In the middle of all that caregiving, humans have managed to grow, learn, work, and play.

In our relatively short lives, we have a responsibility to keep ourselves safe, healthy, and centered so we can be the best human we were put on earth to be. It serves no one if we become casualties of our own neglect.

If I am always the last one I consider—the last one to sleep, the last one to have time to think, breathe fresh air, eat a decent meal, or enjoy a little unstructured time—I know that my generosity will eventually sour into exhaustion and resentment. For example, you might announce to the family, "I'm going to take a bath and read for twenty minutes. Unless the house is on fire or someone is actively bleeding, please pretend I am in another country." Five minutes later, a small hand appears under the bathroom door with a worksheet and the words, "I know you said not to disturb you, but... what's a parallelogram?"

Putting myself at the center does not mean neglecting my people. It means recognizing that my energy, my health, my attention, and my values are the soil in which everything and everyone connected to my life is growing. If the soil is depleted, nothing in the garden thrives for long.

> A note: managing time, family, and caregiving responsibilities are complex situations. When we are in the thick of them, what we often require is not another idea but help: support from partners, relatives, friends, professionals, or community resources. If you are in a season of intensive caregiving or acute crisis, your first task is not to implement an elegance code; it is to get yourself more support wherever you can find it.

23. ARRANGE YOUR LIFE

People we think of as elegant tend, almost without exception, to live as if they are responsible for the quality of their personal soil. They have a vision for their life, or at least for their current season, and they are honest with themselves about what matters to them. As far as reality allows, they arrange their lives to support their dreams and values. In effect, they stack the deck in their favor right from the start.

Most of us are not taught that we are allowed to do this. Instead, we find ourselves dragged along by life until one day it is over. Clinicians and caregivers in end-of-life settings often hear a version of the same regret: "I wish I'd had the courage to live a life true to myself, not the life others expected or demanded of me." This is not a selfish wish; it is profound grief over having sidelined one's values and gifts for too long.

24. CENTERED IS NOT SELF-ABSORBED

There is an important distinction between living from your center of balance and being self-obsessed. Self-obsession is not balanced. It is the opposite. It tilts everything into a projection of yourself, and once that happens, you stop seeing other people and events clearly. You no longer observe; you assume. You no longer learn; you react.

Centeredness does the opposite. It gives you enough ground under your feet that you can see what is in front of you. A mentor of mine used to say that when you are down in the weeds, you miss the predators and cannot read the terrain. Living from your center of balance is what lifts you out of the weeds. You are stable enough inside that the world outside comes into focus.

25. CHOICES

I remember standing in formation at zero dark thirty during my Army Officer Basic Course. We were exhausted, and it was raining hard. Water dripped off our helmets and soaked our boots. Our trainer, a tough old master sergeant, stood in front of us and said, "You have two choices today. You can be cold, wet, and unhappy..."

We all perked up, sensing a much better alternative was coming.

"Or," he continued, "you can be cold, wet, and happy. Either way, you are going to be cold and wet."

This caused a laugh and a collective groan, but the lesson has stayed with me all these years. We may not always be able to choose our circumstances, but can always choose how we meet them. We're the only ones who can. That is the essence of an elegance code: actively choosing a positive mindset, again and again, even when the weather outside is less than ideal.

26. TENSION AND PRESSURE

Tension and pressure exist all around us. They are woven through the universe down to the subatomic level because nature balances itself with opposing energies. This is another fundamental truth most of us are not taught. Once we grasp it, life becomes less frightening. We can learn to work with and direct opposing energy instead of assuming it means something has gone wrong.

When most people hear the word "tension" or "pressure," their automatic response is to reduce it or escape it as quickly as possible. In physics, tension means something very different: it is how energy, as a pulling force, is carried through objects. When you stretch a rubber band, for example, you put it under tension; you ask the material to carry a force along its length and fill it with internal stress. That tension allows the rubber band to hold a ponytail, keep a bundle of pens together, or secure a stack of 3×5 cards. Without tension and stress, the rubber band is not more enlightened; it simply cannot do anything useful.

Once you start looking for tension and compression, you see them everywhere. A suspension bridge only stands because its steel cables are under enormous, continuous tension, carrying the weight of the road and cars into the towers and then down into the ground.

The bridge does not survive because there is no strain; it survives because the strain is organized, with cables in tension and towers in compression, each taking the stress it handles best.

A guitar string can make a note only when it is pulled tight between two fixed points. Tightening or loosening the string changes its vibrational frequency, which alters the pitch. Tension is not a problem to eliminate with a stringed instrument; it is the precise condition that makes music possible.

Think of a bow and arrow. When you pull back the string, you bend the bow and stretch the string away from its natural shape, loading both with potential energy stored in the tension and internal stress of the materials. To a casual observer, it might look like nothing is happening. In reality, the system is charged. The instant you release the string, the stored tension turns into motion. No tension, no stored energy; no stored energy, no flying arrow.

Pressure is everywhere in nature as well. In physics, pressure is a pushing force spread out over a surface such as skin or the ground. Gravity creates pressure constantly: the weight of the air above you creates atmospheric pressure, and differences in that pressure drive winds and weather. Inside a tree, nutrients move because of pressure and tension working together. Water is pulled upward through tiny tubes while gravity and the weight of the fluid push back. The tree does not interpret this tension and pressure as a problem. It is how a living system functions.

27. A MORE PERFECT UNION

In the United States, a healthy democracy was never supposed to feel like a spa day. It was built to create deliberate tension between branches of government. From the very beginning, the people drafting the Declaration of Independence and the Constitution argued fiercely over how much power each branch should hold and how they would restrain and balance one another; the system was born in productive disagreement, not blind consensus.

Our checks and balances are a kind of civic tug-of-war, where the executive, legislative, and judicial branches each have enough strength to pull back when another branch pulls too far. The arguments and delays this creates are frustrating for citizens sometimes, but checks and balances are not signs of failure. They are the political version of a suspension bridge's cables and towers: the opposing forces that keep the whole structure standing.

Your Checks and Balances

Your inner life has its own checks and balances that create tension and pressure. Again, this is designed into the system: part of you wants security, another part wants adventure; one part wants to save, another wants to spend or give; one part craves harmony, another insists on independence. These "branches" of you push and pull against each other, and that can feel like something has gone awry. But just as a constitutional system uses tension between branches to prevent any one branch from taking over, the tension between your values and desires keeps a single impulse from ruling your entire life. Your goal is not to silence the conflict between your "branches," but to listen to it and let each part have a say, so your final decisions are stronger and feel more stable to you.

Healthy tension and pressure are not signs that something is broken. They are not forces to fear or outrun. Many times, tension and pressure mean things are working exactly as intended. Without the steady pressure of gravity holding us to the ground, we would drift off into space. Without tension in our muscles, tendons, and ligaments, we could not stand up, reach for anything, or even smile. Elegance begins when you recognize tension and pressure as natural conditions of a living, moving, thinking human life, and find your center of balance inside them instead of wanting them to disappear.

This idea is 180 degrees from conventional thinking, but the ancient

Greeks had the right idea. The pre-Socratic philosopher Heraclitus famously argued that the most powerful things in the world depend on a "harmony of tension" between opposing forces. In practical terms, you can use the tension and pressure inherent in life to propel yourself toward your dreams.

28. RUBBER BAND THEORY

If you have a rubber band handy, go get it. I'll wait here. It will make the next idea much easier to understand.

Take your rubber band and pull on it a little. Imagine your vision for your life and your goals are pulling on one end, and your current reality is pulling on the other. Feel that stretch between your hands? That's tension, and it's doing exactly what it is supposed to do. It's trying to pull your hands closer together—in other words, it's trying to bring your current reality closer to your vision.

Notice something else: you're probably not freaking out about this tension. You didn't gasp, drop the rubber band, and decide this experiment was too emotionally overwhelming. You are probably standing there playing with it a little, feeling the springiness, maybe bouncing the band between your hands and thinking, "Gee, this is kinda fun." That bouncy, playful tension trying to pull your hands together is the same energy that pulls you from where you are to where you want to be. Exactly. The. Same.

Think about that. Your vision, dreams, and goals create energy just by existing at a distance from your current life. You know how people get upset when the space between themselves and their goals seems really far? Well, try this: pull your hands farther apart. What happens?

That's right. When the distance between you and your goal is large, the tension in the rubber band increases. The greater the distance, the more energy is created by the tension. That means the tension in the band is "helping" you even more. So the bigger your dreams, the more potential energy there is to help you get there.

The stretch is not proof that you will never reach your dreams; it is the very energy that will pull you forward if you learn how to work with it instead of fighting it. When you think of tension as your helper, wrestling with it feels a little silly.

29. WAIT-Y, WEIGHTY GRATITUDE

If you would like to lose weight, I'm going to guess you have not been telling yourself how lucky you are. If you have a lot to lose, you are probably not standing in front of the mirror thinking, "I am so grateful for all this untapped potential." You are more likely looking at your goal weight thinking, "Ugh. This is impossible." But go back to your rubber band. When your hands are far apart, the tension is higher. There is more energy stored in the system, not less. In the same way, a sizeable gap between where you are and where you want your weight to be means there is more potential energy available for change.

The early stages of a diet often prove this. The first ten or twenty pounds come off faster, not because you suddenly became a morally upgraded human being, but because the system is under more tension and even modest changes release a lot of stored energy. Later, as you move closer to your goal, the "rubber band" slackens a little. The visible changes slow down, the urgency fades, and it can feel harder to stay committed—not because you are weaker, but because the tension has decreased and your body is adapting. Your brain reads "less distance" and downgrades the project from emergency to "nice if it happens."

Seen through this lens, having a lot to lose does not mean the situation is hopeless. It means you are holding an exciting amount of potential energy. Very much the opposite of hopeless.

So you can see when you're doing something that matters to you, whether that is losing weight, starting a business, painting a portrait, writing a book, dating, or cleaning your closet, the question is not "Why is there so much tension?" but "How do I aim it? How do I use it?" Instead of seeing that stretch as a reason to despair, you can treat it as a friendly force that wants to help you achieve anything you desire.

30. IT IS ALL JUST ENERGY

Let's pick a complex centering challenge this time with a lot of moving parts. Imagine a public figure whose name you know well. She might be a celebrity or high-profile leader with a clear mission: she genuinely cares about service and wants to use her platform to open doors for others. The media, unfortunately, has decided she is a symbol. Every outfit, every project, every imperfect decision becomes a headline and comment war.

There is constant tension between her vision ("use my visibility and gifts to build something generous and lasting") and the daily racket of public opinion ("you are too much, not enough, and wrong in this new way"). As a public figure, she likely cannot reduce that tension and pressure. It seems to come with the territory. But she can decide how she will use the energy.

First, she names the gap between her vision and her current reality with honesty. Perhaps some of her decisions have landed badly. Some media criticisms are fair; others are not. On one end of the rubber band is what exists: messy rollouts, misunderstood choices, people who like her, and some who don't. On the other end is her vision: real kindness, empathy, and a body of work that leaves people feeling more seen, respected, and better off.

Instead of collapsing that gap by either shrinking her vision or denying reality, she allows the tension in her rubber band to exist. That stretch between "what is" and "what I am building" can become her source of fuel.

Next, she needs to separate the useful data from the commotion. Her team reads the media coverage through the filter of her values and vision. Which media criticism touches something real? Where did she fall short of her own ideals, and where is she merely bumping into other people's opinions? The media coverage, rather than being only a source of pain, becomes valuable free research which she can use as prompts to improve her business: her products, policies, and communication.

If she has a strong internal elegance code, she and her team can create a way forward that strengthens her code instead of wasting time chasing media approval. When something truly goes wrong, she responds clearly and without drama. She acknowledges the problem, takes specific corrective action, and shows what will be different next time. When the criticism is static about her being herself, she calmly re-states her mission and keeps going. In both cases, she uses the positive and negative energy surrounding her to refine her alignment on the inside.

You may not have headlines, but you have your own version of this tension every time other people talk about you, misunderstand you, or decide you stand for something you did not say. Your family group chat, office politics, your social circle, and your corner of the internet can feel like a very opinionated press corps. The same elegance code that would center a public figure can center you too. You do not control the commentary, only how you translate that tension into information you can use.

31. NEGATIVE OR POSITIVE ENERGY IS ENERGY

Here's an extreme example, because we now see excessive negative energy in the news almost daily. A failure to use this kind of brash, unruly publicity constructively can turn destructive very quickly.

Imagine a woman who works in fashion and communications. For years, she has helped build an iconic brand around clean lines, elegant clothes, and a certain pared-back glamour. Then her personal life becomes public, and overnight there are twenty photographers outside her door every time she leaves the house. She once moved confidently through studios and fittings; now she is being chased down sidewalks and boxed in by cars. It is pure harassment and a complete invasion of privacy. It makes perfect sense that she is angry and afraid.

Within the gap between her reality and the outcome she wants (let's say that's peace and quiet, and the ability to walk down the street like a normal human being), she sees four possible choices.

- She can hide in her apartment and almost never leave.
- She can exit the building with her head down, feeling hunted and accidentally feeding the predatory machine every time she flinches, because those are the photos they can sell.
- She can spend half her life in court, trying to swat every annoying fly, one lawsuit at a time.
- Or she can do something unexpected.

She is beautiful, intelligent, charismatic, and articulate. These are gifts that not everyone has, and she is dedicated to doing good work. She has strong personal values and a broad vision for both her company and her philanthropic projects. Rather than running from the paparazzi machine, she sees potential for operating it. Using her gifts, values, and vision, she decides to take all twenty "units" of wild, destructive human energy and point them where she wants them to go, illuminating her work instead of her worst fears.

The energy we are talking about is raw, rowdy, unfocused, and calamitous to be sure. But the combined energy of twenty humans looking for something to do every day could also be very useful to her, her business, and her charities.

Taking Control of the Script

She decides she will step out of the house each day grounded with a calm intention and a slightly mischievous sense of humor. As the photographers shout at her, she pauses, turns on her own cordless mic, and says, "Good morning! Since you're all here, let me tell you about our new collection," or "Here is what's happening with the children's charity right now and how you can help. Since you're filming anyway, here are all of the details at length." Then she talks and walks, slowly, taking her time, never rushing. By the time she gets to her office, she has used all of that unfocused energy to promote her business or her charity. What the photographers don't realize on day one is that they are going to get bored with her very quickly because she will do this every single time they follow her.

If the paparazzi get too close, she hires four capable bodyguards to provide a respectable amount of space, and dresses them in her own fashion brand. As she walks to work, she can point out the newest pieces her team is wearing. She will answer questions, but circles every question or comment back to her work and her causes. With a bit of moxie and a grounded elegance code, she refuses to be the hunted object and starts acting like a director who has inherited a chaotic but free media crew. She realizes she is receiving millions of dollars in free publicity.

The dynamic changes surprisingly quickly. Day after day, walk after walk, event after event, every time paparazzi jump in front of her and ask for a comment, she gives them the same presentation: a relaxed, graceful plug for either her business or her charity. Yes, the media still gets photos, because they were going to get photos anyway, but what they do not get from her is fresh drama.

Eventually, just as she expected, the photos and commentary become unsellable as "scandal" and unusable as "news." No magazine is going to run free advertisements for her brands and causes day after day.

She does not have to like the situation, approve of the press, or agree with their motives. But if they are going to follow her anyway, she can raise the bar for everyone by treating herself, and them, with respect and dignity. She can refuse to endanger herself or others by running. If these photographers have volunteered to be an unpaid media crew, she will make lemonade out of lemons and use their energy to promote something positive.

This is what having an elegance code can do for us. It shows us where our problems are a source of power. There may be unwanted energy swirling around us, but our elegance code shows us how to harness it. As Marcus Aurelius said, "The impediment to action advances action. What stands in the way becomes the way." The energy that exists in the space between our current reality and where we'd rather be is ours to use.

You may not have photographers waiting outside your door, but you have your own forms of unwanted attention and criticism. Use your intelligence, creativity, talents, vision, and values to point that energy toward something positive. You cannot stop people from looking at you or talking about you, but you can decide who you will be when they do.

32. YOUR CENTER OF BALANCE

There is a philosophy at the core of elegance that places an individual at the practical center of her life because this is the place of balance. Without it, poise is impossible. With inner balance, we can feel graceful and composed even when the world is anything but.

This is a blessing because it gives us freedom, but it is also a nuisance because it assumes that we are responsible for keeping ourselves centered, even while we are surrounded by people, circumstances, or media we can't control. Tempting as it is, we cannot draft an employer, a partner, or the situation itself to stand in the middle of our lives and hold us upright. If you've ever tried, you may have noticed that it does not work.

In the previous section, I talked about directing negative energy and positive energy as if they were equally useful. Is it fair to be famous and have twenty paparazzi outside your door every morning? I do not know. Is it fair to be a complete unknown who has to struggle in poverty every day? Or to be an average person, in an average job, with an average amount of influence, and the average wage to go with it?

There is no such thing as fair in the way we wish there were. There is only whether we are centered, and whether we use our energy, and the energy surrounding us productively.

Paradoxically, once we accept we can control nothing except our own thoughts and responses, a great weight is lifted. We have permission to stop trying to manage the entire universe and focus our attention on what we can affect: what we think, what we say, and what we do next.

33. "YES, BUTS" ARE MAPS

By now, you might think, "Yes, but my situation is different. I am dealing with something entirely unique with my family, friends, neighborhood, finances, or marriage." Those thoughts matter because they are often where our sense of being off-center really lives. Instead of arguing with your "yes, buts," you can treat them as maps. Ask yourself: Where, exactly, do I feel unbalanced, off-center, or convinced that life is unfair to me? Is it at work, at home, in money, in my friendships, in my body, online?

Pick one situation and write it in a sentence: "This is where I feel off-center." Then ask a second question: "If I refused to wait for fairness or perfect understanding, how could the situation I find myself in propel me even one step closer to my vision and my values?" You are not asked to like the circumstances. You are asked to look for one way to let the energy in those circumstances push you a little closer to the person you want to become. That may mean you leave the situation you're in, hire help, or seek guidance from professionals. When you take your thoughts and ideas seriously, you practice the freedom that underlies this entire chapter.

34. MISUNDERSTOOD BUT CENTERED

One unvarnished truth of adult life is that no one ever feels understood. Not by the public, the government, their spouse, their friends, their children, their parents, their clients, or their social media followers. This might be why we love dogs so much.

There are a few reasons it is unlikely we'll ever be fully understood. First, everyone else is busy feeling misunderstood themselves, so it's hard to get them to focus on us properly. Second, no one except us lives inside our exact history, body, temperament, and circumstances. Third, when we try to explain ourselves, we quickly hit another limit. To make someone truly "get" us, we'd have to narrate every moment of our thinking, every nuance of our motives and fears, and every small context that shaped our choices.

We can explain ourselves in exacting detail, but after ten minutes the person listening is glancing at the clock. If we were to make this a habit, people would avoid sitting next to us at parties. Being fully explained is not only impossible; it is unbearable to everyone involved, including us, because we have way better things to do with our time.

This is, incidentally, why our heroine's paparazzi technique above works so well. We do not argue with every misconception or try to make the world see us from the inside out.

We accept that people project their issues onto us, and we decide calmly what behavior we will give them to point their literal and figurative cameras at. We trade the fantasy of being known and understood for the reality of knowing ourselves, and being internally balanced in our own center. This is why we develop an elegance code.

READING THE GREAT MINDS

Human beings have been asking "How should I live?" for as long as we have had language. Philosophy is the long, ongoing conversation about that question and all its companions: What is a good life? What is real? What is just? What matters? People have been writing and arguing about these things for thousands of years, across cultures and centuries, and there is a whole library of minds you can invite into your own thinking. Some are austere and rigorous, some are mystical, some are playful and skeptical.

Whether you feel drawn to the clear ethics of the Stoics, the searching questions of the Greeks, the devotional intelligence of religious thinkers, or the sharp, restless critiques of more modern voices, it is worth spending time with a few of the great minds of history. Reading philosophy will not hand you a finished elegance code, but it will enlarge the room you are thinking in.

In the back of this book, you will find a short list of writers and books you might enjoy exploring if you want to deepen this part of the journey.

STARTING NOW

5
Start Where You Are

If you can't be James Bond in a t-shirt, you'll never be James Bond in a dinner jacket.

Nina Gates, The Elegance Code

There comes a point in any conversation about vision, values, and balance when real life says, "Uh, Ahem." It usually sounds like a notification from your bank, a child asking for a snack, or the uncomfortable crunch of a credit card bill. Vision is intoxicating. Reality is sometimes... well... whatever the opposite of champagne is.

This is where many people bail out. "After I lose the weight." "When I have more money." "Once I move." "As soon as things calm down." The fantasy is that a future, more polished version of you will show up unbidden, and that version will finally be qualified to live elegantly. Until then, you're in a holding pattern of sweatpants and self-loathing.

Let's gently, lovingly ruin that idea.

The Elegance Code is a radically different philosophy. Most books, posts, and videos about elegance center on how you look, but I am not especially interested in whether you are pretty, symmetrical, thin, polished, or on-trend. It does not matter what you wear, whether you know how to accessorize, or whether you are the slightest bit attractive by conventional definitions. So let's start by throwing out everything we've been taught about elegance and build an ethos we can use right now.

35. OBSESSION WITH HOW WE LOOK IS THE GREATEST THIEF OF HAPPINESS IN HUMAN LIFE

Studies find that dissatisfaction with appearance is tightly linked to anxiety, depression, and lower overall life satisfaction. The more importance we place on looking a certain way, the worse we feel. It is a trap. No one ever thinks they look as good as they could, and there is always someone to compare ourselves to and come up short.

The trap is so tight that even the women chosen as the beauty standard are caught in it. Research on professional fashion models shows high levels of body-image concern and relentless pressure to stay extremely thin, despite already embodying the cultural ideal. In interviews and essays, models have said openly that they are "the most physically insecure women on the planet," and that being paid to set the example of beauty for the rest of us does not give them peace about their looks. If tall, thin, gorgeous women feel not-enough, we can safely assume that chasing that kind of perfection will never give us the ease we imagine.

The Elegance Code is both a relief and a higher order. It is a self-created internal code of genteel, deliberate poise. The power of your code is that it moves from the inside outward, not from the outside in. Your vision, your values, and your center of balance are not abstract ideas; they are the coordinates from which you live. As you circle closer to them, the way you dress or present yourself may change almost incidentally, but elegance itself has nothing to do with your face, your age, your bone structure, or your clothing size. It is not an aesthetic upgrade; it is a way of being.

Here is the wild heresy that, embraced, just might change your life: one could be, by some cruel universal ranking, the "ugliest" person on earth and still be the most elegant person in any room: the happiest, the most at peace, the most magnetically engaging. Because the key to happiness and true elegance is not physical beauty. It is an internal lucidity and serenity that can inhabit any body, any face, any age.

36. THE ELEGANT LIFE OF NERO WOLFE

Nero Wolfe, Rex Stout's great armchair detective, is famously large, sedentary, and uninterested in physical exertion. He is obese, middle-aged, and spends most of his life inside a New York brownstone he almost never leaves. He loves food to the point of ritual: elaborate meals prepared by his chef, eaten at fixed times, never rushed. He keeps an orchid room on the roof where he tends thousands of rare plants according to a strict schedule. His days are governed by routine: breakfast at a certain hour, orchids at another, clients only at specific times. No one is allowed to disturb his order. He moves very little, but his mind is in constant, precise motion. Seen through The Elegance Code, Wolfe is a case study in inner values, vision, and balance.

His values are clarity, order, beauty (expressed in orchids and cuisine), and intellectual honesty. His vision for his life is pure and unwavering: to live comfortably and intelligently on his own terms, solving problems that interest him and refusing everything that violates his standards. His balance comes from knowing exactly who he is and what he will and will not do. He does not chase clients; they come to him. He does not roam the city; he sends Archie Goodwin. He solves crimes not because he is glamorous or physically impressive, but because his mind is organized and his judgment is calm, logical, and elegant under pressure.

Nero Wolfe demonstrates that elegance is not a matter of being slim, young, or visually refined. It is the way you order your world, the integrity of your routines, the pointed nature of your attention, and the consistency with which you inhabit your own life, even if you rarely, if ever, step outside your front door.

37. THE BRILLIANT ELEGANCE OF COLUMBO

The Los Angeles homicide detective is famous for his shabby beige raincoat, scuffed shoes, unkempt hair, cheap cigar, and battered Peugeot; he looks like a man who dressed in the dark and never once consulted a mirror. Suspects write him off instantly. They see a disorganized, mumbling civil servant with coffee stains and a bad car. What they miss is his internal code. Columbo is exquisitely courteous, patient, and almost eerily calm. He listens more than he talks. He lets powerful people underestimate him on purpose, then uses careful observation, attention to detail, and relentless, logical questions to pull their lies apart thread by thread. His elegance is based on humility that is partly performance, moral clarity about right and wrong, and a refusal to be rushed, rattled, or impressed by money. He is living proof that a person can look like a walking laundry pile and still embody a finer, steadier way of being than almost anyone around him.

38. THE COMMANDING ELEGANCE OF JAMES T. KIRK

Captain James T. Kirk is a superb illustration of someone who lives almost entirely by an internal elegance code rather than by surface aesthetics. He wears the same neat Starfleet uniform every day; the "look" is almost irrelevant. What defines him is how he occupies the captain's chair. Kirk is guided by a very specific constellation of values: curiosity, a spirit of adventure, integrity, and goodwill. He is fascinated by other worlds and will risk himself to explore them; his sense of adventure is tied to discovery and connection, not mere thrill-seeking. His values mean he will bend rules but not his core sense of decency, and when Starfleet's regulations collide with that inner code, he chooses his own, because he trusts it and lives at the center of his own life. For all his bravado, he is fundamentally generous: he treats his crew as people, not equipment, and his quick, dry humor defuses tension. Under pressure, he becomes more focused; he listens, gathers what he needs, then commits to a course of action with unhurried decisiveness. He takes the greatest risks himself and accepts the consequences. Kirk's elegance lives in the way he handles crises: calm voice, direct orders, refusal to humiliate subordinates, and the willingness to act from his own inner code even when the ship is literally shaking under his feet.

39. THE SURPRISING ELEGANCE OF MISS MARPLE

Miss Marple is an almost perfect Elegance Code exemplar: visually unremarkable, internally precise.

Miss Jane Marple is introduced as a "fluffy" old lady in soft cardigans and sensible shoes, often with knitting in her lap and weeds under her fingernails. She is the last person anyone would pick as glamorous or even particularly noticeable. That is exactly why she is so powerful. Her elegance has nothing to do with presentation and everything to do with how she inhabits her age, her village, and her mind.

Her vision is simple and unwavering: to keep her little corner of the world truthful and in order. She does not dream of escape or reinvention; she dreams of things being as they ought to be: just, considerate, and sane. Her "big picture" is St. Mary Mead and the human heart. Her values are just as clear. She believes deeply that the truth matters, even when it is uncomfortable or socially awkward, and she will risk being dismissed as a nosy old woman if that is what it takes to name what really happened. Her sense of justice is tempered by mercy: she understands weakness and motive, but she does not confuse understanding with excusing. She is almost ceremonially courteous; she thanks people, apologizes when she intrudes, and keeps the social fabric intact even as she tears lies apart. Above all, she prizes observation over showmanship. She values seeing, not being seen, and her attention goes outward rather than toward worrying about how others perceive her.

Miss Marple is perfectly centered in her own small life. She has no career to defend, no reputation as a "great detective" to manage, no need to prove that she is clever. She gardens, she knits, she listens. That ordinariness is her ballast. Because she does not require recognition, she can afford to be patient. Because she is not showing off how smart she is, she can use her intelligence effectively.

When things become frightening, she does not thrash; she thinks. She watches more than she speaks, and when she speaks, it is to ask a deceptively simple question or tell a seemingly irrelevant village anecdote that, in fact, maps perfectly onto the situation at hand. She uses gentleness as a deliberate tool: the soft voice, the harmless appearance, the knitting needles—all of it lowers other people's defenses so that the truth has space to emerge. She remains composed in proximity to ugliness: murder, greed, and vulgarity. She refuses to mimic the hysteria around her. Instead, she absorbs it, sifts it, and then points to the thread that matters.

Seen through The Elegance Code, Miss Marple is the opposite of what women have been taught to chase. She is not young or fashionable. She would vanish instantly from an Instagram feed. Yet she is profoundly elegant: internally ordered, ethically serious, attentive, and calm. Her "look" is almost camouflage; the real elegance is the still, exacting mind behind the ball of yarn.

40. THE COOL ELEGANCE OF FERRIS BUELLER

Ferris Bueller is a beautiful example of how an inner elegance code can make someone magnetic long before you get to his clothes or looks. Ferris's vision for his life is astonishingly clear for a teenager:

he does not want to be a passive object moved through systems; he wants to experience his own life. "Life moves pretty fast. If you don't stop and look around once in a while, you could miss it" is not just a quip; it is his operating thesis.

Everything he does in the film bends back toward that vision: stepping out of the script to break the "fourth wall," refusing to let fear, schedules, or other people's dreary expectations dictate what this one day will be. He is not trying to burn everything down; he is trying to be alive inside the life he has.

His values are unexpectedly specific. He values presence: he wants to be in the day, not just accruing gold stars for having attended it. He values loyalty and friendship; for all his mischief, the emotional center of the movie is his insistence that Cameron, who is frozen in anxiety and resentment, be pulled into motion. He values joy and beauty: the art museum, the parade, and the city itself are not backdrops for him to show off; they are things to be delighted in, touched, and absorbed. He also values a kind of rebellious integrity. He lies about being sick and manipulates systems, but not for ego or power; he does it to create a day that feels worthy of being alive.

Ferris's center of balance is what people read as "cool." He is rarely rattled. When things go wrong, his first move is not collapse but improvisation. He trusts himself to think on his feet, talk his way through, and come up with something. That faith in himself lets him stay loose and playful instead of tense and self-protective. He does not waste time worrying about whether people will like him; he lives as if that question has already been settled, which is paradoxically what makes people like him. Even when he is scared for Cameron's relationship with his father, or for getting caught, he does not hand the wheel to fear. He keeps steering.

The way his code moves outward is what reads as elegance. He navigates the day with an almost choreographed lightness: borrowing the car, orchestrating the restaurant scene, the museum visit, and the parade, all with a sense of timing and grace. He is good-natured, not cruel. His jokes punch up (the pompous maître d', the bullying principal, the joyless systems) rather than down. He notices Cameron's internal state, Sloane's feelings, and even his sister's deeper frustration under her surface hostility.

Most people think they want Ferris's clothes, his one-liners, his ease. What they really crave is his internal structure: his vivid vision for his life, values that favor experience, loyalty, and joy over numb compliance, and a center of balance that does not fly apart under pressure. That is why he feels universally loved and strangely enviable, because at seventeen he is more together than most of the adults in the film. The "cool" everyone remembers is the outer trace of an inner elegance code.

41. THE PHILANTHROPIC ELEGANCE OF AUDREY HEPBURN

Audrey Hepburn possessed all the externals people worship: she was breathtakingly beautiful, impeccably dressed, soft-spoken, and globally famous. She became a style icon through her collaboration with Hubert de Givenchy, favoring pure lines, high-quality fabrics, and a "less is more" simplicity that made everything she wore look definitive. Yet those who knew her insist that her style expressed her inner beauty. She did not follow trends or reinvent herself every season. Once she found a way of dressing that felt good to her, she kept it for life.

Her vision shifted over time from acting to public service. After her film career, she became a UNICEF Goodwill Ambassador and devoted her later years to visiting famine-stricken and war-torn regions, advocating for children with the same seriousness she once gave to her movie roles. She articulated her values directly in quotes attributed to her: "The beauty of a woman is not in the clothes she wears...it is reflected in her soul." She believed in altruism, quality, respect, and hope; people who worked with her described her as disciplined but gentle, and reserved but deeply humane.

Her center of balance was stable despite her fame. Friends and biographers consistently describe her as grounded, almost shy, with a strong sense of privacy and an instinct to protect her inner life from the machinery of celebrity. As an Oscar-winning actress, she preferred a small circle of trusted people to constant publicity, and used her visibility to raise money and attention for children, rather than as an end in itself. Seen from The Elegance Code, Audrey Hepburn had beauty, designer clothes, and charm, yet insisted, in word and deed, that elegance is internal.

42. THE FIERCE ELEGANCE OF LARA CROFT

Lara Croft is a useful example for this chapter because she operates from an elegance code, but also has exaggerated beauty. Lara as a character is written to be unforgettable: tall, athletic, and beautiful. Her signature tank top, shorts, and dual holsters make her one of the most recognizable figures in gaming and the movies that followed. What keeps her culturally alive, however, isn't her appearance; it's the way she lives.

Lady Lara Croft comes from privilege and aristocratic comfort, yet in most versions of her story, she rejects the safe, curated life offered her and chooses risk, discomfort, and the unknown. Those are value choices disguised as an adventure plot. Her vision is to be an active agent in the world, not an ornament in a drawing-room. Depending on the story iteration, her vision crystallizes as the desire to uncover lost histories, protect powerful artifacts from exploitation, and understand the mysteries buried under ruins and legends. She is not searching for fame, romance, or status. She travels the world seeking knowledge.

She is a lifelong, self-taught learner who values intense inquisitiveness over safety and approval. She values independence and refuses to let family expectations, institutions, or villains decide who she is. In later characterizations, she also values responsibility: she learns that taking artifacts for sport has consequences, and shifts toward protecting sites and people rather than collecting trophies. She values loyalty and risks herself for friends and allies. She has a hard, almost stubborn value about justice for those who exploit the vulnerable or desecrate sacred places.

Lara's center of balance makes her elegant rather than merely reckless. She has normal emotions that most of us can relate to, like panic, grief, and self-doubt. Fear does not get the last word though, she keeps moving toward what matters to her. Lara is creative and improvises constantly. She is self-contained but is not a woman averse to asking for help when she needs it. This tells me that her curiosity is bigger than her ego. She has an exciting life but isn't into drama. She recovers quickly from shock and focuses on the next foothold, the next puzzle, and the next decision. She is intuitive but rarely paralyzed by overthinking. Instead, she combines action with a long memory for patterns and clues. That blend of physical composure and mental focus under pressure directly results from living through her elegance code.

The way her code moves outward from her inner core is what audiences and other characters find so engaging. She has a sense of humor, and while she is capable of ruthlessness toward enemies, there is nearly always a protective motive under it: saving someone, stopping a catastrophe, preventing a weapon from being misused. She accepts the consequences of her choices. If a tomb collapses, a relic is lost, or an ally is hurt, she does not waste time blaming others. She adjusts, grieves if needed, and then tries again.

She can be covered in mud, and blood, hair half-destroyed, clothes torn and improvised, but those are the moments she is at her most compelling. Her elegance is not dependent on her clothes; it is in the unwavering trajectory of her decisions. She is visually iconic, but that is not why people aspire to be like her. What they admire is her internal grace: her vision for her life, values that favor truth and responsibility over comfort, and a center of balance that stays intact when the ground falls away.

43. BUILDING YOUR ELEGANCE CODE

I hope that by the end of this book you feel easier in your own skin: relaxed, free, and confident about living from your code. I hope, most of all, that you set aside the constant, distractive surveillance of your appearance. The world has trained us to stand outside ourselves, judging how we look from an imaginary audience's point of view, and to treat our bodies as problems to be fixed. The Elegance Code invites us back inside.

Start where you are, exactly as you are this moment, and begin building a life that is balanced, gracious, and luminous from the inside. The outer details can catch up later of their own accord.

44. ELEGANCE DOES NOT REQUIRE BEING STATIONARY

We are meant to grow and turn through different seasons, events, and roles. If you have ever watched a spinning-plate act, you know the most important thing is not the pole or the performer; it is the plate's center. As long as the plate is balanced on that point, it can spin and move with surprising freedom without flying off. An elegant person is like that plate.

Elegance does require that, even in motion, we remain close to our center of balance. When we drift too far from our center, we become like a plate that has slipped off its balance point. No matter how strong the pole or how skilled the performer, it will wobble and eventually fall.

Since we've used the elegant and decidedly movement-oriented James Bond as an example, let's think of him in the field. Headquarters might send him off with a sleek car and a gadget or two, but ten minutes into the mission he's usually leaping off something using a tablecloth as a rope and a ballpoint pen as a weapon. He does not pause mid-chase and say, "You know, I really wish I had my better outfit on and more in savings. I'll save the heroics for when conditions are ideal." He uses what is in front of him and commits, even when his pants are far too tight for charging around rooftops.

45. SOCIETY WILL NOT HELP

Society is not designed around the flourishing of any one person; it is mostly organized around its own survival, interests, and efficiency. This can be directly at odds with the individual. A large company will praise "dedication" and "going the extra mile," but what it really wants is consistent output and reliability. If an employee regularly answers emails late at night, skips lunch, and never uses vacation days, the system does not intervene to say, "Go home Bill, we're worried about your health and relationships." It absorbs the extra labor and, when the numbers change or a reorganization demands it, lays off that same worker with a form letter. The system's primary obligation is to its own continuity.

Society will not admit this, because in many ways we are all implicated in keeping the story going. It approves of whatever is safest for its own interests: whatever keeps things stable, predictable, and easy to manage. Society does not naturally encourage each individual to step back, question, and radically re-center her life around her own values.

Meaningful growth in a life or a culture usually begins when one person does something different: starts a business in her garage, writes a book no one asked for and publishes it without an agent, leaves a respectable path that is killing her, or chooses a gentler way of living for herself and her family. Those choices do not come pre-approved by society. They start as decisions made from the center of one life. Our own.

When we are centered in our code, the news, the paparazzi, the gatekeepers are just weather going on around us. We do not need to fight the world; it is just scenery.

46. LIBERTY AS A WAY OF LIFE

Society is organized around its own survival, not yours, yet even governments and political philosophers have had to concede that the individual has inherent worth and sovereignty. Society can't fully own you because the philosophical tradition it built itself on says it can't.

In the ancient world, "freedom" mostly meant the freedom of the city, or of citizens as a group, to govern themselves; the individual was usually seen as secondary to the polis. The idea that each person has inherent moral rights and worth of their own emerges much later, especially in the Western tradition. You can see early glimmers of it in documents like the Magna Carta (1215), which limited the king and acknowledged certain liberties for "free men."

There was a bigger leap during the Renaissance, Reformation, and Enlightenment, when thinkers began arguing that every human being possesses inborn rights that even governments are meant to respect, and that rulers who violate those rights can be challenged. By the late 1600s, philosophers like John Locke were explicitly describing "natural rights" like life, liberty, and property belonging to each person.

In the modern era, we can see how essential this idea of freedom is for the quality of everyday life. Across the world, societies that broadly protect individual dignity and basic rights tend to be wealthier, more stable, innovative, humane, and livable than those that do not. Democratic systems are associated with stronger economic growth and higher income per person. If a single life is held to be that valuable in principle, it follows that each of us has both the permission and the responsibility to live as if our individual freedom is worth honoring.

47. EMERGENCIES, PREFERENCES, AND INCONVENIENCES

We do not ignore emergencies. Genuine emergencies take priority. A facet of building an elegance code is deciding what in your sphere counts as an emergency, what counts as urgency, what is merely a preference, and what is only an inconvenience. When a real crisis appears, you interrupt your plans. When someone is uncomfortable that you have a boundary, you may decide that is different. Only you can decide whether to treat every raised voice, every reminder email, or every disappointed look as a summons.

This matters because your code lives or dies on how you spend your days. Most of us have less control over our official work hours than we would like, but we do have some control over how we use the margins of our time—early mornings, evenings, breaks, the small unclaimed pieces. If we hand those over to everyone else's urgency, there will be nothing left for our own vision. To live with one's vision and values at the center is to ask, privately and regularly: "Does this request, this habit, this use of an hour belong in a life built around what I say I care about?" If the answer is yes, make room. If the answer is no, you may choose to hesitate, renegotiate, or decline. This is stewardship. It is how you ensure that when you say yes, there is a whole person behind that yes, not a hollow shell following someone else's schedule.

At some point, your elegance code stops being theoretical and collides with the clock. The way you use those loose half-hours will either nourish it or leak it. You do not need four uninterrupted hours at a stretch to honor your code. You need a few protected pockets of attention that you treat as non-negotiable: reading something that refines your taste instead of scrolling the news; taking one concrete step toward completing your project instead of consuming social media images of other people completing theirs; sitting in silence on the porch watching the birds long enough to hear your own thoughts instead of watching television. Over time, these investments in the edges of your day shape the center of your life.

48. YOUR CODE WILL NOT WAIT

It is not in a future bank account. It is not locked in a storage unit with the furniture you will buy for the "right house." It is meant to carry you through the life you have today: your current body, your current schedule, your people, your clutter, your phone battery percentage.

49. YOUR CODE IS FREE

It costs nothing, and it is ready for you to shape now, as you are. It is powered by your vision and values, your creativity, your resourcefulness, and a little self-discipline. It does not require unlimited time, money, or higher cheekbones.

50. WHAT IF IT'S TOO LATE?

There is a particular flavor of shame that whispers, "I let myself go, so I am not allowed to feel beautiful now. I should have thought of this ten years ago." That shame is not noble. It will not help you. It is not even a stern coach; it is an indifferent bouncer blocking the door, "Not you," to someone who is absolutely on the list.

Shame has no authority. It is just in your way.

If you feel you have "ruined" yourself and it is too late for elegance, let's be clear about something: the elegance code is not a prize awarded to people who managed their lives correctly. It is not a reward for good behavior, a trim figure, or a decade of excellent decisions. It was never that. Which means you were never disqualified.

You are a person who has been through a considerable amount, in a culture that taught you to measure yourself by surfaces and other people's opinions. That is a lot to carry. But your history is not a debt you have to pay off before you may begin. It is the road that brought you here, which is where your code starts.

Your elegance code works for you. You do not work for it. It asks only one thing: stop using your past as a reason to withhold care from yourself today.

51. WE ARE NOT WAITING FOR LATER

We are beginning now, exactly where we are, with exactly what we have, and with the inner code we are building. Let's go!

A Radical Plan

If you haven't already, write your three to five core values words in a notes app on your phone, or in a notebook. Then write your vision statement again; the paragraph we wrote in chapter 2. Draw a circle with your name in the middle, and jot a few words about what it feels like when you are centered in your life. Do you feel calm, balanced, energized, relaxed, capable? Do you feel like the CEO of your days, or rooted in something larger, like nature itself?

When I'm centered, it feels like my natural state. I have tons of energy, but am relaxed and content. I get a lot done with minimal effort, and everything seems to just work out like magic. I am mystified to note that I run into the people I need to see, and connections I was about to make come to me. The information I need shows up when I need it.

Then note how it feels to be off center. What are the micro-indicators that things are tipping? We do not have to fall down completely or wait until we are so depleted that we snap at people we love. What have you noticed are your first small moves away from your center?

For me, it usually starts with my schedule getting completely full. I may want to do something kind for myself, like schedule a manicure, sleep in on Saturday, or have coffee with a friend, but see no time available. Those warning signs tell me I need to make corrections ASAP.

I find that I'm in my best flow state when there is breathing space in my days, and around my appointments, so that when something pops up at the last minute, my entire schedule doesn't collapse.

52. ELEGANCE LEAKS

We will talk about leaks in the next chapter, but I want to introduce this big concept here. Elegance leaks are slow drips that drain energy and attention. Identifying and plugging our elegance leaks is exciting, because stopping obvious leaks almost magically restores equilibrium and peace. The best part: you don't have to do more. You just stop doing what drains you.

What Constitutes a Leak?

Think of the rug you always trip over, or the jeans you tug at all day. The bra strap that constantly falls down, the friendship that offers nothing but bewilderment, the conversations that leave you tired. Anything you regularly notice, wince at, then ignore is a leak, and it costs you more than you think.

Usually no single item is huge, which is why we can tolerate leaks for years, but each one takes a small toll on our focus, our mood, and our sense of ease.

53. YOUR ELEGANCE CODE IS NOW

Anyone can feel elegant when they are rested, confident, and having a good hair day. Your code is not being tested then. It is tested when you are tired, heavier than you planned, marked by illness or stress, or disappointed in how you have treated yourself lately. Those are exactly the conditions under which an internal philosophy earns its keep, because an external one would have already quit.

You are not late. You are here, which is the only place your code ever starts.

54. THE STUFF ELEGANCE COULDN'T CARE LESS ABOUT

Remorse says, "If I had started earlier, I could have been elegant. Now I am ruined." It inventories your sagging skin, your soft places, your wrinkles, your exhaustion, and presents them as evidence for the prosecution. The verdict: hide and apologize.

Elegance is not interested in that case. It does not recognize the court.

An elegance code is not handed out at the finish line to people who maintained their figures and never made a mess of anything. It is the way you carry the life you have, in the body you have, starting from the moment you decide to pick it up. That moment can be now. It can be this paragraph. You don't have to do preliminary preparations, and there is no earlier appointment you missed.

55. DIGNITY

You may not like what you see in the mirror. You may feel betrayed by your body, or angry at yourself. If you can't love every inch of yourself, that's fine. You do not have to love yourself in order to treat yourself with a basic level of dignity.

Let's make a brief, practical agreement. Dignity doesn't require certain feelings. We only need a place to begin. Treating yourself with dignity means you commit to a minimum: you are clean, comfortable, and clothed in a way that does not add extra shame. Each day, you give yourself the chance to rest, drink water, and eat something nourishing.

That's it. Not social media-ready, just no longer punished. We can start here.

56. MOVES THAT COUNT

Think in terms of one-step upgrades: from brushing your teeth over the sink while scrolling, to brushing your teeth while looking at your own face. From collapsing into bed fully dressed, to placing your clothes on a chair and washing your face with warm water. From eating over the kitchen sink, to putting your food on a plate and sitting down, even if it is for five minutes.

None of these changes will get you a magazine spread, but they tell your heart and mind, "I am worth caring for." Elegance begins here.

57. ELEGANCE IS ALWAYS IN PROGRESS

Embarrassment tells you to hide until you are "fixed," which is a moving target you do not control and will never hit. Elegance starts now and is always in progress, which means the door is open at any hour, in any size, or at any age, with any history.

If you have picked up this book and are willing to think about these ideas, you are more elegant than you give yourself credit for. You do not need permission to go for a walk at your current weight, wear clothes you like, or take care of your skin as it is rather than as it was. Elegance is not a reward you must unlock. It is available now and always was. You were just told otherwise.

58. NO ANNOUNCEMENTS ARE NECESSARY

You do not need to declare anything to your friends or family. No manifesto, no explanation, no formal launch of the new you. Just begin acting with slightly more consideration for yourself than you did yesterday.

A useful rule: if you would extend grace to a friend in your situation, you are required to extend at least that much to yourself. You do not get to be the one person in your life who receives none.

59. STAY PRESENT

At some point, you will be tempted to look ten steps ahead at the ideal body, the ideal home, the ideal life. That can be useful, but when it tips into "how far I have to go," come back to a better question: What is one elegant thing I can do right now, for the person who is here right now?

You do not have to turn the Titanic in one dramatic move. You only have to nudge the wheel a few degrees at a time, so please stop standing on the deck shouting at yourself while the ship continues to drift. Take the wheel. Even now. Especially now.

6

The Elegance Audit

One can have no smaller or greater mastery than the mastery of himself.

Leonardo da Vinci

An elegance code is, foremost, a declaration of sovereignty. It may take time to arrive here, but once you decide to live by your own design, you gain a distinct advantage in a frenzied world. You have watched the systems long enough to see how often words and deeds part ways. You have learned the games, seen the false incentives, and read the generic, repetitive scripts. Instead of conforming, rebelling, or despairing, you choose something more powerful: you resolve to shape your own experience and curate your own life.

The woman who found her way to this book is done waiting for the world to agree that she is right. She may wish many external things were different, but she knows that trying to change other people is futile, and in the attempt, she loses her time and peace of mind. She can champion her causes fiercely, work to make a better world, and still maintain her center of balance. She no longer needs permission to take care of herself. She does not need the approval of friends to act on her own behalf. She reclaims her peace by changing her mind, and she can change it as often as she likes.

60. BACK YOURSELF FIRST

Elegance is private work. It happens in the pauses between thoughts, when you choose not to abandon yourself again. This matters more than it might seem, because most of us have learned over many years to be our own last priority. We wait for someone else to validate us or our work before we stand behind it. We wait for permission to take up space, to have opinions, to want what we want, to prefer what we prefer. When that permission does not arrive, we go out into the world half-formed, already apologizing, already braced, already leaking our self-esteem and authority. That is where leaks begin: not in the meeting room or at the dinner table, but long before that, when we neglect to get behind ourselves.

It is not easy to be out there. Whether you are putting creative work into the world, building a business from scratch, going back to school, or teaching yourself something you were told required a gift you do not have, the exposure is real and the fear is legitimate.

Frederick Douglass was a towering nineteenth-century figure, renowned as one of America's greatest orators and a brilliant writer. He delivered over two thousand speeches, published four influential newspapers, and wrote three autobiographies. He taught himself to read in secret while enslaved, knowing that literacy was a path to freedom and also knowing that discovery could cost him his life. Grandma Moses took up painting at seventy-eight when arthritis made embroidery impossible. Her work was discovered in a local shop, and she went on to become internationally celebrated, painting until she was one hundred and one. Neither of them waited for permission or a guarantee. Both of them backed themselves before anyone else did.

The Search Is Mutual

When I taught myself to paint, and later made the pivot from painter to writer, I had to learn something that did not come naturally: the people who love you are not always your audience, and that is not a verdict on your work or on them. The question is whether you keep going anyway. Getting behind yourself is not arrogance. It is the minimum requirement for doing anything worth doing.

Your audience is out there, and your most enthusiastic supporters will likely be strangers who love what you do. You have to find each other though, and that takes time, so you must be your own most reliable backer first. Each time you return to your center, you become more resolute. The result is a tranquil self-command that does not depend on anyone else's approval.

There is much to practice, of course, but we begin where all serious work begins: by plugging the leaks.

61. WHAT IS AN ELEGANCE LEAK?

As we mentioned earlier, an elegance leak is a small, persistent drain on your energy and attention. Individually they are small, which is why we pay little attention to them—but over time, they disrupt your focus, mood, and sense of ease.

What counts as a leak? It's the quick call you haven't made, the favor you regret agreeing to, the closet filled with clothes you avoid wearing, the task you keep deferring.

Leaks show up in behavior. Any habit that unsettles your composure qualifies: fidgeting, tugging at clothing, picking at cuticles, apologizing reflexively, filling silence, arguing, trying to control what is not yours to control, helping when no one asked, worrying, nagging, pleading, over-explaining, rushing, or reacting before you are ready—if at all. Each one may seem harmless on its own, but as they accumulate, your equilibrium and confidence begin to erode.

Most people assume self-transformation requires dramatic effort, so it may come as a surprise to discover that, in building an elegance code, the fastest way forward is to stop. If your bathtub is leaking, the solution is not to pour in more water. First, you plug the leak. The useful thing about this work is that once you notice leaks in your elegance code, you see them everywhere. Try not to hand out towels.

Leaks Cause Us Problems

Think of a time when you most wanted to be calm and self-possessed, but it did not go quite the way you planned.

Let me start with one of my less-than-elegant personal moments. I arrived at an Important Grown-Up Meeting—boss, diplomats, stakes higher than my shoe budget—wearing brand-new platform heels and clutching a stack of papers I hoped looked appropriately serious. The nervous choreography had started before I walked through the door and went downhill from there. You know: nodding too brightly, smiling at nothing in particular, adjusting my blouse, and shifting my weight from foot to foot like a show pony in a pencil skirt. Then my foot slipped just a fraction off the edge of my shoe, and suddenly I was in an "I Love Lucy" episode.

I flung my stack of papers into the air, which rained down like so much bureaucratic confetti, lurched into a desk, ricocheted off a row of chairs, and careened toward the window, grabbing for the curtains like a life raft. One dignitary did a quick courtly sidestep to avoid a flying memo, then froze again. It all happened so fast, and so absurdly, that they could only watch as I orbited the office like a rogue satellite.

When I finally stopped moving, the room was rearranged, my documents were everywhere, and I stood breathlessly cocooned in drapery. The pièce de résistance was my boss, who cleared his throat without missing a beat and said, "Sir, may I introduce my new assistant. She handles the advance work for our VIP visits."

You may have your own version of this story. Hopefully it did not involve swinging from office curtains, but you know the feeling: an important dinner, a first date, an interview, or a presentation in which your composure vanished at precisely the wrong time. My disaster did not begin with the stumble, though. It began earlier, with my mindset, and getting dressed in a way that pulled me off center.

62. WE KNOW A LEAK WHEN WE SEE IT

We recognize elegance leaks before we have language for them. Someone says, "No worries, it's fine," while their foot jack-hammers under the table. Their words are smooth, but their shoulders are up by their ears, their laugh is a little too loud, and their sentences come out in a rush. On the surface, nothing is wrong, yet we notice: she is not okay.

Exterior Effects

A leak is an unintentional outward sign of a hidden emotion or thought. When nonverbal signals and words do not match, it can confuse or unsettle others. We are wired to read the body before we trust the words, so these leaks can make us seem insincere or evasive, even when we are just nervous or trying to be polite.

Our nonverbal elegance leaks do more than confuse people; they drain our power. When we mix jittery body language with apologetic phrases like "I just think, maybe..." or "This might be a stupid idea, but...," we broadcast self-doubt, and people notice. The brain loves a mystery, so when we look uneasy, others wonder what is wrong. Are we hiding something? Are we overwhelmed?

Psychologists call this emotional leakage: feelings you think you have hidden seeping out through tone, posture, and small repetitive gestures. An elegance leak is my term for what that leak costs you in the moment: your calm, your authority, and your ease.

Consider this your first field mission: before we turn inward, do a bit of secret reconnaissance and see how many leaks you can spot in the wild now that you know they exist.

63. ENERGY-DRAINING HABITS

Once you see how little leaks drain your energy and focus, it is easier to understand why some days leave you feeling wiped out. Leaks live in behavior, but they also live in your environment. Both deserve attention. As you begin your audit, notice:

- Chronic exhaustion from over-committing. Ignoring basic needs or self-care. Saying yes when you mean no. Being late.
- Compulsively checking notifications. Scrolling instead of resting. Letting phone pings take priority over the person in front of you. Over-sharing to fill silence. People-pleasing. Laughing along at things that hurt you, or at tasteless jokes that hurt others. Replaying interactions on a loop and beating yourself up with what you "should have" said.

There are also the leaks that surround you:

- Unfinished tasks, visual clutter that makes it hard to relax in your home, car, or workspace, broken items you work around daily, and surfaces covered with undecided objects. Clutter and constant reminders of "things undone" that drain focus and mood.

Beneath the surface, there is impulse buying to manage feelings. This deserves its own look. When you reach for a purchase to soothe discomfort, you are not resolving the feeling; you are postponing it. We will return to this.

And then there are internal leaks:

- Harsh self-talk, catastrophizing, dismissing your own preferences, not saying what you mean, apologizing for taking up time or space, apologizing for your appearance, possessions, or home, and letting other people's moods dictate your own.

64. A GENTLE WAY AHEAD

As you refine your elegance code, you notice a new poise. The more leaks you plug, the more calm remains within, and the more your feelings reflect that self-assurance. Psychologists call this behavioral activation, but the principle is simple: action shapes feeling. What matters most is not the appearance of composure, but a deeper ease within yourself.

Once you have made your notes, do not scatter your attention. Choose one leak at a time, ideally the smallest or easiest one to notice, and stay with it until it no longer controls you. Sometimes the remedy is substitution: a new behavior where the old one used to be. Sometimes it is awareness, and slowing down long enough to see the impulse before it carries you away. The point is not self-improvement in the abstract. It is creating comforting stability for yourself, one habit at a time.

If filler words are your leak, treat them as a drill. Slow down. Let silence do some of the work. Pause before you answer. Breathe. Think in complete units before you speak. The more rushed your speech, the more likely you are to fill the space with "um," "like," and other verbal padding. Record yourself if needed. Notice where the filler appears. Then practice shorter, cleaner answers until the pause no longer feels dangerous.

If you bite your nails or pick at your cuticles, give your hands another job: apply hand cream, hold a pen, or treat yourself to regular manicures so your hands feel cared for and you are less willing to damage them. If you over-explain, consider allowing shorter sentences and room for the other person to think and respond. The goal is not to be someone else's version of perfection. It is stopping the leaks that matter to you. Someone else may label a behavior of yours a leak that you experience as a charming quirk. You get to decide, and you can work on as many or as few as you need to support your elegance code.

Think of finding leaks as exploration and experimentation. Exploration teaches you how to notice. Experimentation turns that noticing into change. Once you uncover a leak, the next one is no longer hidden in the same way. After you have done this once, you begin to see the pattern behind the behavior, not just the behavior itself.

65. YOU CHOOSE

Changing how you think and changing what you do may arrive together, or one may show up first. Both matter. When you work consciously with cause and effect, you shape your experience from the inside and the outside at once. Your elegance code draws from both worlds: it aligns your intentions with your actions so your mind and body move together, finally pointing in the same direction.

This elegance audit applies to this book as well. My job is to point out what most people will not. Your job is to decide what belongs in your life and what does not. In a very real sense, you are not here to follow this book; you are here to edit it. You are writing your own code and your own story; this is just a pile of pages to mark up.

66. DIGITAL AND SOCIAL MEDIA LEAKS

We are immersed in the age of digital. In this age, anyone, at any hour, can request a piece of your attention. Group threads, DMs, tags, and notifications all send the same message: Be here. Respond. Be available. It is not unreasonable to feel restless, anxious, or discomposed in these circumstances. An elegant life cannot survive on that diet.

In the past, there were all sorts of boundaries: natural, technological, and social, that protected privacy and peace. If you did not have household staff and you were not at home, it was impossible to receive a caller or a telephone call. (That is how "phone calls" got their name; it was considered a visit by telephone.)

Businesses were open during working hours, which is when customers called on them. Many shops and offices closed early in the evenings and were not open every day of the week. Social convention followed suit: one did not telephone people about business outside regular business hours. Before technology intervened, social protocols recognized that people needed to sleep, rest, work, think, and spend time with their families.

If you had staff at home, a visitor would leave her calling card with whomever answered the door, often with a note or an artfully folded corner to indicate the purpose of the visit. Specific folds signaled whether the caller had come in person or sent a servant on her behalf, and could convey congratulations, condolences, or farewells.

It was perfectly acceptable for a housekeeper or butler to answer the door and say, "Madame is not at home." What this sometimes meant, of course, was that Madame was not at home for that particular call. She might be upstairs with her hair in curlers, in bed with a cold, or reading a book. None of that was communicated to the caller. One was either "at home" or "not at home." Calling days and calling hours were recognized. Access ran on a schedule, not on demand.

The answering machine was, in a sense, the first technological butler. It intercepted calls, took messages, and allowed a household to decide when and whether to respond. Then came the mobile phone, text messaging, and social platforms, and the idea of ever being unavailable was thrown out the window. The default became: if you could be reached, you should be reachable.

You are not required to accept that premise.

Technology has changed, but human needs have not. You need not open your private life to one hundred percent access, even if those around you do. Access to you is not a human right; it is a privilege you may offer selectively and proportionately. You may decide how, when, and where you will be fully present.

Knowing Is Not Innate

By the time we have understood one digital landscape, new mediums, platforms, and apps arrive, designed to pierce—overtly or subtly—whatever limits and boundaries we had in place. They may offer ways to opt out or to screen ads and interactions, then "update" the platform and reset our carefully chosen parameters.

Some women joyfully participate in every new online space. Others prefer a more deliberate approach. You might decide to use none, one, or just a few social media platforms. Social media can be a wonderful way to connect with clients, readers, or distant friends and family. It is equally acceptable to decide that your greatest presence is in person and to limit your digital communication.

Protecting your digital privacy and sanity is not something you are born understanding, nor something you should have "figured out" by now. If you find it frustrating, you are responding normally to a system built to keep you perpetually distracted and available. But do spend a bit of planning time to decide intentionally how you want to handle access to you. That might mean separate lines on the same phone, or separate phones entirely. With multiple phones or lines, you can decide who receives your business number, your general number, and your private number. You may decide to have separate email addresses and social media accounts: public accounts, business accounts, personal accounts, and strictly private accounts.

Many of us would never have imagined, even ten years ago, that we would need so many layers to safeguard our privacy. The good news is that we can now create mini-protocols for how we—and, if applicable, those who assist us—respond within each layer. You might set times on your phone when you are unavailable for certain notifications. You can also mute alerts and check calls and messages at predetermined times of day that are convenient for you. You may enjoy group texts, or you may decide that group texts and invitations are informational only, not prompts you are obliged to engage with.

None of these choices are inherently right or wrong. What matters is that your digital life is governed by your code, not by other people's expectations.

7

THE SOVEREIGN WARDROBE

The only real elegance is in the mind; if you've got that, the rest comes from it.

Diana Vreeland

ELEGANCE MAY BE STYLISH, but style is not elegance. One can be an elegant person without ever being stylish, because elegance begins in the mind. It is a way of seeing yourself and thinking about how you want to relate to the world around you.

This chapter is about creating your wardrobe, but it is not about capsules or following rules. There are thousands of terrific books on closet organization that women mostly don't follow, because while the ideas work on paper, women cannot translate them to how they shop, dress, and live. What I want to give you is a different way of thinking about your clothes.

Principles and Techniques

When I was in ROTC in college, a mentor explained tactics to me this way. "You can use any techniques you want to accomplish your goals," he said, "as long as you don't violate the principles." Principles are fundamental truths that remain constant regardless of the situation. They are like laws of nature: not guidelines to consult when convenient, but the structure beneath every sound decision. In military doctrine, there are nine of them, including objective (define a clear, attainable goal) and simplicity (keep plans straightforward and clear).

The principle does not dictate how; it only determines what cannot be compromised. Techniques, on the other hand, are the choices you make within a principle's boundaries. There is no single correct technique. You can be as creative, unexpected, or unconventional as you want, as long as you do not violate the principle itself.

There are principles and techniques for everything in life, from playing golf to cooking to raising children. This is why two people can be successful achieving a similar goal using very different techniques, as long as neither violates the underlying principles. There are principles and techniques in building a wardrobe, too. As long as a garment honors the principles below, it does not matter whether you are wearing goth-punk or preppy-chic.

This is where most style advice gets it wrong. It tries to herd every woman into a category: Sporty, Natural, Classic, Dramatic, and so on. This places all the focus on technique, which is most flexible, and little or none on principles. It is why a wardrobe built on technique alone is so hit or miss. Sometimes an outfit comes together and feels exactly right. However, if a woman does not understand the underlying principle, she cannot explain it or reproduce it.

Wardrobe principles turn a lucky morning into a repeatable one.

SOVEREIGN WARDROBE PRINCIPLES

Utility: your clothes serve your life.
Fit: your clothes are made to fit your body, not the other way around.
Quality: every garment must earn its place.
Foundation: trusted neutrals form the base; variety lives on top.

Color and Cognition: what you wear shapes how you feel and think.
Readiness and Appropriateness: for the occasions life will deliver.

What follows is a walkthrough of each principle, with techniques you can use to honor them. If a technique I suggest does not suit you, find another that does. If you mind the principles, you will be well-dressed regardless of your personal style.

67. THE PRINCIPLE OF UTILITY

Clothes cover us, protect us, and can speak for us without us having to say a word. When they do their job, they support your life and strengthen you. When they fit your body, feel good against your skin, please your eyes, and align with your elegance code, they become allies in living that code. When they do not, they create drips that erode your aplomb as surely as a leaking roof ruins a ceiling.

How do clothes leak elegance? They leak when they are uncomfortable, distracting, or annoying to you. They leak further when they chip away at your confidence or make you second-guess your body. Each leak violates the principle of utility.

Your clothes exist for one purpose only: to serve you. They are meant to keep you warm, keep you cool, and help you move confidently through the day. It is reasonable to expect them to work as hard for you as you worked to pay for them. Every piece, from a pair of socks to a ball gown, should feel good, look pleasing to your eye, and function for what your life demands.

A Higher Bar

Starting today, expect better support from your hard-earned

wardrobe. You are under no obligation to "make it work" just because an influencer or retailer wants to make a sale. No one will care more than you do if your closets and drawers are overflowing with indifferent, "meh" items. You should feel fantastic in every single garment you own. Your clothes do not need to be expensive or fancy; they need to be chosen with intention.

Shoes that pinch, heels so high you need help walking, straps that slip, waistbands that dig, underwear that slides down, or socks that refuse to stay up are no longer welcome. Garments with rips, holes, stains, snags, or pills must be repaired or removed. Underwear that is faded, sagging, or stretched out goes too. Not because anyone else will notice, but because you will. Every time you tolerate a damaged or uncomfortable garment, you send a message to your brain that you do not deserve better. That is a leak because it costs energy to overcome.

Define Your Day

A wardrobe that violates the principle of utility is one built for a life you don't have. Create a wardrobe that serves your life today, not the life you had five years ago or the life a magazine claims you should want.

What percentage of your day is spent in each activity? Ask yourself:

The Commute: Do I sometimes walk six blocks in the rain or snow, catch a subway, or sit in a climate-controlled car? Does my "commute" involve a school carpool followed by a grocery run? Is it from the bedroom to the kitchen to make coffee? Do I get dropped off, or do I park and walk?

The Desk vs. The Field: Does my day involve sitting at a computer, or am I bending, lifting, and chasing little ones? Am I in a sleek office, a retail shop, or working outdoors? How much of the day am I on my feet? Do I need any specialized clothes or uniforms?

The Public Face: Am I leading boardroom presentations with people in suits? Do I have to interact with clients? Am I invisible behind a screen? Do I have pets that shed? Do I have hobbies or sporting activities like golf, pickleball, or horseback riding requiring sportswear? Do I exercise at home or in public?

The Temperature Factor: Am I oscillating between a freezing office and humid air? How many seasons are there in my area? Do I need primarily warm-weather clothes, cold-weather clothes, or a balance of both?

The Evening Pivot: Do I change for dinner, or does my outfit need to pull a double shift until 9:00 PM?

The Wind-Down: When do I transition from daywear to loungewear? Does my evening attire need to be presentable for family and guests, or is it strictly private?

The Accessories Edit: Do I need a hat, scarf, sunglasses, reading glasses, belts, or jewelry to make my outfits work for me? Do I need pockets? Do I wear a badge or lanyard? Do I carry or transport objects or equipment?

A woman who collects clothing as a hobby will have different objectives from one who needs a dependable wardrobe for daily life. A woman who earns a living through social media unboxing new pieces or modeling clothes for brands has a different purpose still. There is nothing wrong with this, but it is important to know that those wardrobes are part of a business model. The variety you see on your screen is inventory provided for content. If your goal is to dress quickly without a lot of fuss, do not measure yourself against someone who is paid to showcase endless outfits.

68. THE PRINCIPLE OF FIT

Your wardrobe is not a storage unit for a retailer's idea of an "average" person. You are a living, complex being, with the shapes and proportions that make you beautifully yourself, qualities no size label can capture. A tailor might say "short-waisted" or "low bust." That is shop talk; it is not identity. There is no such thing as an ideal body, regardless of whatever nonsense is out there, and you are not a collection of parts like an automobile. Your arms, legs, bust, and waist are just as they should be. What you need are clothes that fit and flatter you.

Have you noticed that when clothes do not fit our bodies, we rarely blame the garment? The blouse is not wrong; we are. "My arms are too long." "My butt is too big." "My body is the problem."

People are always more important than things.

You are not the problem; the cut, the pattern, or the design of the garment is. If a blouse does not fit you, it does not deserve you.

The Fitting Room Audition

A garment might look impeccable on a model in a catalog. It might carry a celebrated label. But before you exchange your hard-earned money for it, put the candidate through its paces.

The Mobility Test: Do not just stand still and admire the silhouette. Sit down. Cross your legs. Do your thighs feel strangled by the denim? Does the waistband dig into your stomach? Reach up as if grabbing a folder from a high shelf. Squat as if picking up a package or a toddler. Does your underwear show? Do the sleeves pinch your shoulders? Does the hem come untucked? If you cannot move naturally, you will never feel graceful in that piece.

The Seat of Authority Check: Sit in a few different chairs and look at yourself in the mirror. Does the skirt ride up? Can you get in and out of your vehicle? I once tried to drive to an event in a slim skirt and literally could not get into my Jeep. If you will be photographed coming or going from events, will you reveal anything you would rather not? If you have to spend your meeting tugging at your hemline or smoothing your bustline, this candidate is a leak waiting to happen.

The Texture Touch: Close your eyes and feel the fabric against your neck and inner arms. If there is even a hint of a scratch, a prickle, or a plasticky heat, the interview is over.

The Quality Qualifier: Are the seams finished and do they lie flat? Look for a high number of stitches per inch. Look at the buttons and button holes. Are the buttons smooth and sewn securely and is an extra button provided? Are the button holes neat with no loose threads? Check for bar tacks on pockets, belt loops, and zipper bases to prevent tearing. Patterns should align perfectly at the seams, indicating careful cutting and assembly. High-quality garments hide raw fabric edges with neat finishing.

The 360-Degree Review: Use a hand mirror or a three-way to check the back. Does it pull across the shoulder blades? Does the collar lie flat? Are the pockets lying flat or bulging? A dress should hang level and even all the way around. Does the vent gape on a jacket?

The Values & Vision Test: Does this represent the world I want to live in, or the world I am trying to escape? Research on enclothed cognition, which we will return to shortly, shows that what we wear influences how we think, feel, and behave—especially when the clothing matches an identity we care about.

The Verdict: If the garment requires you to lose five pounds, wear a specific uncomfortable undergarment, or never sit down to look good, do not buy it. You are looking for an ally, not a high-maintenance project.

Tailoring Is Not Optional

If a garment passes the audition in every other way: the fabric is divine, the color is radiant, the core fit is sound, but the sleeves are an inch too long or the waist has a slight gap, do not dismiss it. Unless your clothes are custom made, they will need to be adjusted for you. That is not a flaw in you; it is a flaw in the industry's sizing model.

An $80 blouse with $20 of tailoring will look and feel better than a $200 blouse that fits badly off the rack. When you buy a garment that needs adjustment, you are not fixing something wrong with your body; you are shaping the clothing to fit your beautiful self as you are now. Buy the size that fits today, and have it fitted to you today.

69. THE PRINCIPLE OF QUALITY

Right now, you probably own enough clothes to avoid having to go naked. You can check that box. From this point forward, whatever enters your wardrobe is wonderful, not merely passable. You are done with passable.

Retailers want space in your closet, but most have not earned that coveted real estate. If a garment behaves like a high-maintenance acquaintance, touchy, fragile, always one wrong move from a clothing malfunction, it is not a treasure. It is a leak. Think of it this way: you are not just buying a shirt; you are hiring a personal representative for the next ten hours. If it wrinkles, itches, pokes, or demands constant reassurance, it is not up to the job. If you have a closet full of clothes but nothing to wear, stop buying more and start expecting more from the items you buy.

Someone, it may have been Helen Gurley Brown, observed that ninety percent of what is out there is dreck, and that you must still choose very selectively from the remaining ten percent. That is a sobering statistic, but a useful one. It is not that you have poor taste or weak willpower when you come home with something disappointing. It is that the odds were against you from the start. Knowing this changes how you shop: more slowly, more skeptically, with a considered list and higher standards. The dreck is the default. Fabulous is what you are hunting for, and it requires patience, because it is rare.

When every item in your wardrobe makes you look and feel extraordinary, the daily fatigue of getting dressed vanishes. Your elegance code is not built on okay. If a garment is not an absolute *Yes*, it is a *No*.

70. THE FOUNDATION PRINCIPLE

Most women dress in a way that is neither different every day nor consistently great, because they have not made the choice between the two. They buy throwaway fashion that looks dated or shapeless within a season, and without a steady stream of fresh pieces coming in, they feel restless. So they shop for the moment: the one-off piece that looked right under the dressing room lights but doesn't work with anything they already own. The result is a closet bulging with items that felt exciting once and now just take up space, and a woman who stands in front of the mirror every day feeling like she is throwing money at looks that are just okay.

Style Wisdom

Few style books will tell you the truth: if you want to dress beautifully, unless you have an unlimited budget, unlimited closet space, and unlimited time to manage your clothes, you will have to prioritize. You can have endless variety, or you can have a wardrobe that always works. You cannot have both at full strength.

The good news is that the wardrobe that always works is built over time on a handful of well-chosen neutrals: a base of two or three colors that flatter you, in fabrics and silhouettes you love. Variety is not sacrificed; it is relocated to accessories. Years ago the J. Crew catalog under Jenna Lyons was an inspiring guide to dressing with basics but using unexpected accessories. They would pair yellow suede ballet flats with green capri pants and a navy and white sailor top, or a monochromatic camel outfit with a chunky lucite necklace and bracelet in bright magenta. There are endless clever ways to wear a pair of chinos: a tee with a man's necktie as a belt, a green tweed blazer and a denim shirt; black cropped pants with a matching top and sandals, coral red lipstick, and big white sunglasses. What they showed so well—and you can still search for 90s J. Crew inspiration—is that if you crave variety and a fun closet, you can get there with timeless pieces that last more than a season.

Style + Freedom

This is not confining; it is freeing. The woman who accepts the foundation principle stops fighting her closet every morning. She knows what is in there; she can pull an outfit together in minutes. She looks as stylish as she wants to be because her wardrobe is built on a principle, not on a series of impulse purchases. And because she is not buying twenty fresh pieces every season, she may be able to buy a few wonderful ones.

What Jenna Lyons proved at J. Crew is that the classic piece is not the safe choice; it is the patient one. It waits. It works with what comes next. The trendy piece makes one appearance and then becomes a problem you have to solve.

A Closet That Honors the Foundation

I once watched a movie where the filmmakers wanted to show that a character was rich, elegant, and selective. They opened his closet. Inside hung a row of the same perfectly cut suit in black, navy, and gray; a row of the same perfectly cut shirt in white and in blue; a row of the same shoe in black, brown, and oxblood. He had a stack of the same cashmere sweater in various colors and a stack of the same khaki pants. You could easily imagine his underwear and sock drawers as row upon row of the same pairs.

It was surprisingly soothing, even delightful. At no point did I think, *I bet this guy is really boring.* I was intrigued. What I wanted to do was wander around in his closet and look through the other drawers. Would there be a stack of the same gym shorts, the same bathing trunks, the same perfect pajamas?

The filmmakers chose repetition to signal decisiveness, self-knowledge, control, confidence, and refinement. That tells us something important: elegance reads as consistency, not constant novelty. Novelty is what retailers work hard to sell us. Refinement is a choice.

71. THE PRINCIPLE OF COLOR AND COGNITION

Enclothed cognition is the finding that clothes systematically influence our thoughts, feelings, and behaviors. What we wear activates specific mental schemas—the bundles of meaning we associate with a lab coat, a suit, or leggings. Wearing those garments can alter how we behave because clothing switches on the mental patterns we associate with it.

In one well-known study, participants who wore a white coat described as a doctor's coat showed better attention and performance on detail-oriented tasks than those who wore the same coat described as a painter's coat. The meaning doctor = careful and precise, combined with wearing it, boosted their focus.

Another set of studies found that people in more formal clothing showed more abstract, big-picture thinking and greater category inclusiveness than those in casual clothes. When we put on clothing with strong symbolic meaning, we do not just look different. We think and feel more like what that clothing represents. When we know our values, our vision, and our ethos words, we know what we want to have, do, and be. This cuts through so much social media noise about how we should dress. With our code, we can stay focused and use the principles of enclothed cognition to work toward our goals. If you want to be a successful writer, dress like one, whatever that looks like to you. If your dream life is a cottage in the Cotswolds, dress for it. If you want to be taken seriously, stop dressing like you are still figuring things out.

Color

Color works the same way. It is an emotional cue. Political strategists have understood this for decades. Heads of state choose the color of a tie, a scarf, or a suit based on the message they want to send that day. Red signals strength and urgency. Blue signals calm and trustworthiness. The choice is rarely accidental.

You can use the same logic in your selections. If you wear black all day, consider white, soft blush, lavender, peach, or another favorite pastel in the evening to help you shift gears. Color becomes a language between you and those closest to you. You may have a serious corporate career where you feel most confident in structured designs and deep neutrals, while your pale pink cashmere and silk loungewear is seen by no one but your husband. Both choices honor the principle.

72. THE PRINCIPLE OF READINESS

A lean wardrobe is not a wardrobe in denial. Life occasionally requires a costume, and there is no elegance in pretending otherwise.

Once you have a solid foundation to carry you through most days, it is reasonable to reserve a section of your closet for specialized pieces. The pieces that earn their place not through frequency but necessity. The principle is that you choose them deliberately, in advance, rather than scrambling at the last minute.

Consider the baby shower outfit. Unless you are attending three a week, you probably need exactly one. But if you choose it well, it will also cover a dressy garden tea, a spring wedding, and a daytime charity luncheon. When you find it, label it, slip a cloth garment cover over it, and hang it at the back. It requires no further thought until duty calls.

The same logic applies to a funeral outfit, which should be chosen and ready before you need it, because you will never need it at a convenient moment. Or the specialized sporting wardrobe: if you ride occasionally but not regularly, proper breeches and boots belong in the back of your closet, not improvised from whatever is clean. If your social circle includes black-tie events only twice a year, one excellent evening gown and the accessories to carry it will serve you better than three mediocre ones.

I learned this the hard way when I was invited to spectate at a high-level golf tournament. The event had its own unspoken dress code, not written but understood by everyone who attends regularly. I was there to be seen in the right context, not to play, which in some ways is the harder problem. What was called for was essentially a polished country-club day outfit: tailored, sporty, weather-appropriate, and comfortable enough to walk in all day. There were also bag restrictions I had not expected. Clear bags no larger than twelve by six by twelve inches, or small opaque clutches no larger than six by six inches. I pulled something together at the last minute, which is exactly the friction an elegance code exists to eliminate. One well-considered outfit for that world, set aside and ready, would have made the morning much easier.

Find out the rules, both specified and unspoken, for the events you are likely to be asked to attend, and put the pieces on your shopping list before you need them. The test is the same as for everything else in your closet: not a maybe, not something you will need to iron, alter, or talk yourself into on a pressured morning. When the occasion arises, and it will, you want to open that garment cover and feel relieved, not defeated.

Appropriateness Explained

Wearing clothes that are appropriate for an occasion are like having a great personal assistant—one who arrives before you do. She has already introduced you, smoothed the way, and signaled to the room who you are and why you are there. That is what well-chosen clothes do. They communicate before you speak. They earn you a moment of respect, a degree of welcome, and a decided advantage. Clothes that fight the room demand your attention. When your clothes are right for the occasion, you do not have to think about them, they just work for you, which means you are free to concentrate on the conversation, the connection, and the reason you came.

TECHNIQUES: HOW TO APPLY THE PRINCIPLES IN PRACTICE

What follows are techniques I have found useful for applying the principles above. If they suit you, use them. If not, find others that do. Be patient and stay loyal to the principles, and over time you will fall in love with everything in your wardrobe.

73. THE LEAN WARDROBE

Prioritize a lean team of high-performers over a crowded closet of mediocre fillers. We let our closets overflow because we buy pieces we do not love, hoping they will somehow help our underperforming pieces work better. I once bought a scarf I did not love, to wear through the belt loops of a skirt I did not like, thinking I would like both of them better together. It is obvious (now) why my nutty logic did not work.

Do you detest jeans? Do you feel weird in a dress? Could you live without ever owning another hat or tee shirt with words on it? Then do not buy them. You are building your personal elegance code, and you are allowed to stop wearing things you hate. Forever.

You never have to squeeze into another pencil skirt just because it is in fashion, wobble through an event with aching feet, or endure one more blouse that makes you uncomfortable. If rings make your fingers feel crowded, skip them. If you prefer bare ears and an unadorned neckline at a charity ball, those are valid choices. The only rule is this: pay attention to what you love and build your wardrobe around it. Imagine never being physically or mentally uncomfortable in your clothes again. If you take nothing else from this chapter, this is your new standard.

74. EASY DOES IT

Organizing gurus begin wardrobe updates with a full-closet purge. Most people don't do it because it is stressful and time-consuming. If the idea of emptying your entire closet onto the bed, fills you with dread, you are not alone. Try this instead.

The After-Wear Debrief

When you take off an item, pause for ten seconds and ask yourself: Did I feel great in this, or did it annoy me all day? Did it feel like me, or did it feel off? Is it worth laundering, mending, or tailoring? My strongest feelings about a garment usually surface right then. If it pinched, gaped, rode up, or felt blah, it is out. If you think it deserves another chance, fold it and put it in a box in another room, not back in active rotation. If one day you seek it out because you cannot wait to wear it again (you won't), it can return.

If the clothes you just took off did not work, think about what you wish you had worn instead. Did you feel frumpy? Did you long for something smartly tailored for that meeting with your boss? Would a warmer layer or a cooler fabric have been better? Be specific. One evening at the symphony, I realized I wanted an evening bag long enough to hold my phone, a key fob, lipstick and tissues, with an exterior pocket for the theater program so I didn't have to hold the program in my lap or continually open my bag to read it. I still do not have that bag, but it is on my list, and someday I will run across one. Would anyone else think this is important? Probably not, but this is what makes a closet—and a life—curated.

Keep a notepad in your dressing area and use these after-action reviews for a running wish list. Then, the next time you are shopping, you can buy only the items you have pre-identified that you need. This act alone can help you save money and raise the bar.

As a final litmus test, you could adopt my friend's humorous criterion for every outfit: *Would I feel confident if I were wearing this and ran into an old boyfriend?* If the answer is no, the garment goes. For you it might be *the love of my life*, *my celebrity crush*, or *the CEO of my dream company*. Choose whatever version encourages you to select clothes you love.

The Category-by-Quarter Edit

If you love the idea of reorganizing your closet by section but cannot manage it all at once, edit by category. This season, focus only on jeans. Try them all on, let go of the pairs that do not fit, tailor the ones worth keeping, and replace what you need. Next season, focus on skirts. The following season, try on all of your dresses. After that, move to blouses. In the fall, do knitwear. This approach spreads the cost of alterations and replacements over time and keeps the process from becoming a project you dread.

75. UNIFORM DRESSING

If too much variety drains you, you may become a committed uniform dresser. Does your dream outfit work in all four seasons and at most events with minimal tweaks? Do you want to be able to stay home, go out for coffee or dinner, or travel on short notice without changing your core formula?

For me, a low-decision-fatigue closet means a tight color palette: black, white, brown, and navy. I work from home and sit in front of a computer, so my base is almost always jeans or slim black ankle pants in fine three-season fabric with a bit of stretch. On top, I rotate crisp white shirts, fine merino V-necks, cashmere sweaters in flattering seasonal colors, and old-school classics like fisherman's sweaters and neutral twin sets. Then I change the shoes for the occasion and the weather: flat sandals in summer; loafers, ballet flats, or flat ankle boots when it is cooler. I don't wear much jewelry, but at night I may pull out the stops with some sparkle. Create your own formula that frees your attention.

A friend once threw down the imaginary gauntlet and told me she wanted a four-season uniform that would let her ride a horse, meet the queen, go to dinner somewhere tropical, sit on the floor and play with kids, and chase bad guys across a rooftop with only a change of footwear. We gave her a slim, three-button dark navy suit in fine stretch wool gabardine and a custom white shirt cut precisely for her body. Her wild and wildly active day could then be managed by removing the jacket, wearing the jacket by itself, untucking her shirt, rolling up her sleeves, adding or subtracting jewelry, or changing shoes.

It is a funny mental game to imagine your ultimate do-everything outfit. But there is something seriously appealing in it. What if you had such a streamlined wardrobe that a few outfits could handle everything? You would be mobile, need very little luggage, and require little closet space. You would not be bogged down by possessions, and you could afford to buy only the finest pieces. Perhaps you would have your garments custom-made in the exact fabrics and colors you desire. The fantasy is not just to dress better, but to dress better with less.

76. YOUR SIGNATURE

A signature is a shortcut to your code: a deliberate choice you make once, then keep returning to. It is a personal constant—a certain shade of lipstick, a go-to silhouette like the sleeveless shift dresses of Margaret Russell, former editor of Architectural Digest. It could be a style of shoe—cowboy boots?—a charm bracelet, or a stack of bangles.

A signature does three things for your elegance code.

It reduces decision fatigue. When you are tired, rushed, or overwhelmed, your signature tells you what to reach for. One swipe of your Chanel Pirate lipstick and you feel like yourself again. You can wake up in a blur, slick your hair into a neat chignon, and the day shifts. Your diamond studs, cowboy boots, your classic white menswear shirt from Charvet with a black blazer thrown over your shoulders, or your beige twinset and tweed skirt might give you the same coming-home feeling. Grab your uniform, and you are eighty percent there.

It anchors you to your interior. A signature does not come from a trend report; it comes from what you love. When you look in the mirror and think, *Yep, that is me*, your signature is a way of wearing your inner self on the outside, just enough that you feel aligned.

It travels well. In unfamiliar situations—presentations, travel days, social gatherings—your signature functions like a familiar friend in the room. You may know no one else, but your ever-present watch, your hummingbird pendant, or one of your artfully tied silk scarves says: *We have been here before. We know how to be ourselves.*

You do not have to choose the perfect signature on the first try. Play with it. Ask a trusted friend what she associates with you. Which elements show up in your favorite memories and photographs? That is your code sending up a flare: *This. Start here.*

SIGNATURES THAT BECAME LEGENDS

Grace Jones' sculptural tailoring. Often described as neo-cubist or architectural, her padded clothing creates abstract, non-human shapes. Her hoods are as iconic as her face.

Anna Wintour's bob and large sunglasses. You can draw just those two shapes and people know who you mean.

Diane Keaton's androgynous fusion. Menswear-inspired tailoring, vests, wide belts, and often a hat formed a consistent, playful uniform that rejected Hollywood trends.

Stevie Nicks' dark bohemian. Her kimonos, bell sleeves, layered lace, flowing shawls, and tall boots have a romantic, mystical edge. She often wears celestial, velvet, or crystal-embellished accessories that she has described as personal amulets.

Holly Golightly's little black dress. The updo and the oversized sunglasses are instantly recognizable and endlessly referenced.

Sade Adu's restrained minimalism. Sade embodies an unbothered, refined, confident persona, matching the smooth jazz-soul of her music.

Katharine Hepburn's independence. In an era of skirts, she championed masculine-inspired trousers, making wide-legged pants a symbol of female independence.

Nature Inspired

Choose what you love, then multiply. If you adore roses, consider using them everywhere: in your perfume, prints on your clothing, on your stationery, your bedroom wallpaper, and the name you give your cat. Give quart-size shrub roses as gifts. Amazon has sheets of colorful, waterproof floral paper that you could wrap around the grower's pot and tie with a ribbon; use rose wrapping paper. When someone sees a rose and thinks of you, your signature has transformed from a wardrobe choice to a personal emblem. You could do the same with daisies or hydrangeas if they are more your style. I met someone once who used an acorn and oak leaf as his signature. It was on his business card and carved into his Western saddle and his cufflinks.

Small but Consistent

A sleek chignon, glossy red nails, a Schott motorcycle jacket over everything from leggings to cocktail dresses, a particular color you always reach for. I read a novel years ago where the heroine always wore shades of blue: the palest ice blue to royal to iris, to gray-blue and blue-black. Which reminds me of a friend from many years ago who wore a giant London blue topaz ring, the exact color of her eyes. Your signature does not have to be dramatic; just dependable and meaningful to you. Do make it lifestyle-proof: it should function at school pickup, on a Zoom meeting, in an airport, and at dinner. If it collapses when you travel, work late, or chase a toddler, it will not reduce decision fatigue.

When elegance is not applied from outside but lived from within, your wardrobe stops being a source of daily frustration and becomes a daily confirmation of who you choose to be. That is the sovereign wardrobe. It does not have to be the largest or the most expensive, but you will be well-dressed and feel like you no matter your daily demands.

8

YOUR PERSONAL SAFE-HOUSE

We spend the first forty years of our lives accumulating possessions and the rest of our lives getting rid of them.
Elsa Maxwell

IN THE MOVIES, A safe-house for the hero might be a discreet townhouse, an apartment, or a house tucked away in the country. Inconspicuous from the outside, inside it has the charged stillness of a place built for survival. The door closes. The city noises recede. The world is held at bay for a moment. Here, our hero can regroup and plan what comes next.

The classic spy-thriller version is shadowy and spare, a place where someone arrives under an assumed name, checks the locks twice, and finally lets out a breath. The atmosphere is tense, but also soothing to those of us watching, because everything has been reduced to the essentials: a much-needed hot shower, clean clothes, a bed, a chair, a single glowing lamp, a map, a new passport, and a stack of cash. We unwind from the excitement of earlier scenes right along with our hero.

In other films, the safe-house is less severe and more seductive. We can see ourselves living there. It's a handsome apartment in Paris with high ceilings, elaborate Hausmann moldings and 1940's modern furniture, a Mayfair hideaway straight out of a Ralph Lauren ad, or Alexander Pearce's Venetian refuge in The Tourist, with tall windows, bookcases, and sculpture. These safe houses are orderly and luxe. They always seem to have pressed linen sheets, a well-stocked kitchen, a gorgeous bar, and a cleverly hidden safe.

Whether severe or sumptuous, a safe-house feels intentional. Nothing is random. Nothing is superfluous. Every object seems to say: you are safe here. Bathe, rest, rally your strength, and begin again.

And then there is the safe-house that matters most: yours. Not a hiding place, but a base. Not a bunker, but a refuge for you and those most dear. A space that shelters ordinary and extraordinary lives so that, just like movie heroes, those who seek solace can find respite and sustenance before heading back out into the world.

83. RAISE YOUR STANDARDS FOR HOME

When I think of my home as a safe-house, the first thing I consider is that it has to be on my side. Every room and surface, each piece of furniture, lamp, and decoration, exists for one reason only: to support me. This place holds the rhythm of my days and the quiet of my nights. It is my ally in what I do, what I dream, and who I become when the world falls away. Within these walls, I'm free to relax, breathe, and create without resistance.

Home is where we are most deeply resourced to be ourselves. Where else in the world do we have nearly complete command over our surroundings? That alone makes our living spaces worthy of full attention. We set the temperature, the lighting, the beauty, the scents, the spaciousness, the music, the privacy, the ease of movement, and the feeling of welcome. We shape the cleanliness, the comfort, the organization, and the overall mood. We choose what—and often who—we encounter when we walk in the door, and whether our homes add ease to our days or introduce friction.

84. A TWO-WAY STREET

Most of us pour vast amounts of time, money, and energy into our homes. We clean, maintain, and decorate them, dressing them up for holidays and fixing what breaks. Yet if we're not mindful of what we expect in return, the relationship becomes ridiculously one-sided: we do all the work; the house looks nicer, and one day we sell it, upgrades and all, to someone else who will begin the same cycle.

Your home is more than an expense; it's a partner in your elegance code. Each space should serve the life you're living now. Your bedroom, for instance, should fully support rest. Invest in a mattress that truly comforts you, smooth sheets, good pillows, and a soft quilt. We spend one-third of our lives in bed, so choose textures and colors that soothe you. Since sleep rituals differ, arrange the room to fit yours. Try dimmers on the lights to create an inviting mood as evening falls, and blackout linings in curtains if you work night shifts or love to sleep in on weekends.

Entertaining expert Colin Cowie suggests keeping bedside necessities, like a favorite book, hand cream, notepad, tissues, nail file, eye mask, earplugs, or similar essentials tucked away in a drawer or box to keep the space calm and uncluttered. Add chargers inside drawers so devices can be hidden at night; one friend found her sleep improved dramatically just by keeping her phone nearby but out of sight. A beautiful carafe or thermos of water prevents late-night wandering in the dark.

Your kitchen, too, should make it easier to nourish yourself, not harder. It doesn't need every gadget, only a few well-chosen pans, towels that dry, and dishes that make your meals look enticing. Keep only tableware that pleases you: colors you love, glasses that feel good in your hand. Think about how you really use the space. Do you share meals, play cards, work puzzles, help kids with homework, or make art? Design around those rhythms. A basket of games in the pantry or drawers installed under the table for placemats, tech chargers, or craft supplies can transform a room's functionality without clutter.

If your family loves to read, make sure your living room offers a comfortable chair for everyone, a place to set a drink, and proper lighting. Create intentional order where things pile up, like entryways, using hooks, lockers, baskets, or a converted armoire to corral everyday items or even conceal a small bar for cocktail parties. Every area of your home should welcome you to use it as you wish. A safe-house should never feel like a place our hero struggles. It can be streamlined, but it must be comfortable, pleasing, and genuinely useful.

The essential question for anyone living by an elegance code is: Do I feel the urge to escape my home, or does it support me so fully that I'm glad to return? As you set new expectations, the relationship changes. You no longer serve the house alone; the house serves you too. You'll still tidy, repair, and upgrade, but now every decision passes through one filter: Does this make my home more welcoming, beautiful, and useful, or less so?

Ralph Lauren on Home as a Canvas for Living

Ralph Lauren has always designed more than clothes or rooms; he designs ways of living. "What I do is about living," he says, "about living the best life you can and enjoying the fullness of the life around you—from what you wear, to the way you live, to the way you love." His family homes—from a Colorado ranch to a Fifth Avenue apartment and a Montauk beach house, are not showplaces but complete worlds, each one a unique expression of the life he imagines inside it.

For Mr. Lauren, home is a canvas. "Whether we live in the city, the country, at the beach, in a penthouse or a cabin, each is home and tells our story," he believes. His vision is to bring quality and good taste to the places we call home. He layers antiques, books, fabrics, and beloved objects to create what he calls "cozy luxury." As a result, his rooms feel cinematic and timeless, but are meant to be used. They have crackled leather, worn wood, and generous sofas that invite you to curl up and stay awhile. Your rooms are a narrative of who you are and what you value. Like Mr. Lauren, you build them over time, more collected than decorated. When you favor quality, character, and comfort over trends. Your home narrates an enduring story of a life well-lived.

85. ROOMS THAT GROW WITH US

Homes are far more adaptable than we imagine. Just because an architect once labeled a space *dining room* or *study* doesn't mean it must stay that way. A room's true name is whatever you choose to give it. Do you need space for impromptu dinners for twelve? Mornings of yoga or prayer? An art studio, gaming room, or dance floor in the kitchen? Would you rather use your hallway for putting practice or turn your dining room into a playroom, office, or music studio? Your spaces should evolve with your life, not the other way around.

Once you've identified your needs, walk through your house as an impartial designer might. Squint and see every space as raw potential. How could these rooms and corridors adapt to the life you're living now? Could the coat closet become a floor-to-ceiling storage area, with coats relocated elsewhere? Could bookcases line a hallway, as they do in English country houses? If your office work happens in the kitchen, could one lower cabinet be fitted with drawers and metal file racks instead of shelves? My great-grandmother, who could grow African violets like nobody's business, added glass shelves across her kitchen windows. They gave her both privacy and a perfect wash of light for her rows of thriving plants. The moment you give yourself permission to be inventive, you realize that a floor plan is only a suggestion.

Containers can also transform both space and style. In *The Roses of Ainsworth Manor*, Nell keeps mail on a large platter at the entry table, dog leashes in a sterling bowl, tennis balls in old trophies, and crossword puzzles in baskets around her office, formerly a ballroom. I can't remember the last time I made punch, so I use a carved crystal punch bowl on my desk to hold stacks of stationery for writing notes by hand. Pinterest teems with clever ways to repurpose ordinary objects into elegant solutions. If it's hard to see your home objectively—and it often is—consider hiring design help, even for a few hours. A fresh, impartial eye can reveal possibilities you might never have imagined.

86. RESTORATION, NOT PERFECTION

As I write this at my kitchen island, a bottle of water sits at my elbow beside stacks of notebooks filled with ideas for this book. A large, shaggy German Shepherd snores at my feet, his toys orbiting us like bright rubber satellites. There's drool on the windows at dog-eye level and scratches on the front door from his furious objections to the UPS man. My shoes lie akimbo under the coffee table where I kicked them off in conversation with a friend, while creamy Vendela roses lean in their vase, waiting to be trimmed and given a fresh drink of water. A warm spring breeze drifts through the open windows; a tuberose candle perfumes the air, and Dave Brubeck's jazz hums softly from the speakers. My house is very small: a little bohemian, a little elegant vagabond, but when I walk through the door after being away, it seems as glad to see me as I am to see it.

Even the most streamlined home carries joyful signs of daily life: a coffee cup near the sink, a book left open on a chair, the gentle mess of living. Existing in an ordered way is not the same as living with unrelenting severity. What matters is that your spaces are calm enough for you to relax and notice beauty. Visually noisy rooms do more than offend the eye; they raise tension and make it harder to think or rest. Studies show that cluttered environments reduce focus, increase mental fatigue, and are linked with emotional exhaustion and burnout. In contrast, even a modest reduction in clutter is associated with greater calm, control, and ease.

A well-known UCLA study on dual-income families found that women who described their homes as cluttered had cortisol levels that remained elevated throughout the day, compared with those who experienced their homes as restful and organized. In other words, living amid visual turbulence can keep your body in a constant low-grade stress response. Later research confirmed the pattern: people who see their homes as disheveled report more stress, more negative emotions, and lower life satisfaction. Part of this is simple psychology. Clutter makes it harder to experience a home as beautiful or truly "mine."

I learned this early. At sixteen, newly obsessed with fashion and design, I devoured magazines filled with exquisitely styled rooms, always punctuated by flowers. I wanted flowers in my bedroom too, but when I looked around, I realized a bouquet would vanish amid the piles of clothes, books, and makeup scattered everywhere. Beauty needs breathing room. That realization was the beginning of caring, really caring, about how my space is curated, and how I feel when I'm in it.

Barbara Barry on Living with Beauty

Designer Barbara Barry has spent a lifetime creating rooms that feel serene, sophisticated, and intimately luxurious. Underneath all she designs lies a simple belief that beauty is a positive force that supports life. It is not the sofa or the draperies themselves that make a life beautiful, but your awareness and appreciation of them.

Her rooms are built on the principles of simplicity, proportion, and harmony. She clears away what is not necessary so the eye can rest, chooses a few well-made objects over many mediocre ones, and pays close attention to how things feel: the hand of a fabric, the comfort of a chair, the way light effects the color of a painted wall throughout the day. Beauty, in her world, soothes the senses and makes daily rituals feel special.

This is the spirit of living your elegance code at home. The willingness to edit, choose slowly and thoughtfully, and honor the objects and arrangements that feel delightful to you.

87. GRATITUDE

I find that gratitude is a solution for nearly every worry, impatience, annoyance, or frustration. If I step back and look again, there is always, without exception, something to be grateful for. I rarely have to look far. Yes, I once caused a small microwave incident that left the whole house smelling like burnt broccoli for a week, but I caught it in time, and the house is still standing. I sometimes wish the garage were bigger, but my car fits fine, and if it were larger, I'd probably just fill it with more stuff. My garage things reliably expand to fill whatever space is available.

As we assess our living spaces, gratitude should come first. Having shelter and safety places us in rare company on this planet. Research consistently shows that practicing gratitude improves mental and physical well-being: lifting mood, lowering anxiety, and even improving sleep. We have so much to work with whether we have a little or a lot.

If you live in a small space with few belongings, you are in a wonderful position. A clean slate offers freedom. From there, you can choose carefully and mindfully what, if anything, to add. Many people would love to start over in exactly that kind of simplicity.

If you have a large home and feel overwhelmed by choices, be grateful for that too. You have the luxury of selection. Imagine yourself browsing your own private boutique, choosing only what still delights you. Keep what you truly adore and release the rest by donating, selling, or simply letting go, so your home can reflect your new elegance code back to you.

For now, it is enough to notice and make notes. In the next sections, you'll begin to patch any leaks you find, not all at once, but gradually, so your energy flows freely from your elegance code instead of seeping out through a hundred tiny cracks.

88. BLOOM WHERE YOU ARE PLANTED... OR NOT

Most of us will live in several places over a lifetime: dorm rooms, shared apartments, rented houses, starter homes, and everything in between. These spaces can feel temporary, like "not quite real life," so we put ourselves on hold while waiting for the next chapter. Once we move, we tell ourselves, then we'll decorate properly, invite friends over, plant flowers. In the meantime, we camp out in our own lives.

Experts say this happens because we classify things as "temporary" or "permanent." But in truth, everything is temporary. Even a so--called forever home may not be a final destination. When we treat a place as provisional, it becomes an excuse to withhold beauty, connection, and attention from the life happening right now.

The Middle Way

The Stoics offer a practical middle path: accept that external things are fleeting, yet live fully and well in the present, because this moment is the one we have. Houses, possessions, and locations lie partly beyond our control, but our attention, choices, and the way we inhabit them are ours entirely. A good life is present-indexed. It is not about how long an arrangement lasts, but how beautifully and intentionally we live today.

The most elegant way to live this philosophy is to connect with sensory pleasure wherever you are. Feel the support of the chair beneath you; notice how the afternoon light slants across a wood floor; listen to the kettle; inhale the scent of soap on your hands. When you pay attention to how your surroundings feel, you slip out of someday and back into the current moment. Your appetite shifts too: one perfect alabaster lamp transforms a corner more profoundly than five impulse purchases. A cleared surface polished with lemony beeswax feels infinitely better than a stack of random objects.

Savoring simple pleasures makes you more selective. You bring in fewer things, store less, and let go more easily of what isn't truly beautiful or useful. When you stop traveling through your life on the way to someplace better, you live in the only time you have. Make where you are now as gracious as you reasonably can—not because you expect to stay forever, but out of gratitude because you are alive and sheltered today.

The World As Your Home

There is also another path, equally elegant: to own little and decided to be at home wherever you are. Perhaps you are a wanderer, and the world itself is your home. That lightness can feel unencumbered and perpetually new.

89. THINGS THAT LEAK

Everything in life consumes time and energy to house it, store it, maintain it, insure it, dust it, display it, water it, or keep it in working order. Objects that aren't functioning properly demand the same attention in your home and in your mind. Their silent leak is easy to overlook but profoundly real. If the reason for keeping something is that you truly love it or genuinely need it, then make it a priority to repair, clean, or restore it so it can return to service. Care for it promptly and with intention.

Keep that list manageable, because when it grows unchecked, so do the elegance leaks. A house filled with broken, half-working, or unfinished tasks taxes your energy and focus. Plug those leaks early, and you'll feel your vitality and peace flow back.

90. YOUR HOME AS A FRIEND

Imagine coming home every day to a warm, delightful, welcoming friend. You walk in the door and she says, "Hi! I'm so glad you're here." She greets you with a chilled glass of Sancerre in a sparkling wine glass, or a hot cup of tea in a beautiful cup, and beckons you to sit and relax. There are shelves for your books, a comfortable chair with a table and a lamp nearby so you can read and place a drink. The bathroom is sparkling clean, and there is a fluffy white towel waiting when you step out of a warm bath or shower. The kitchen holds fresh, healthy food and a few simple tools for preparing and serving it. The bedroom feels spacious and soothing, even if it is small. The mattress is comfortable, the sheets are cool and smooth, and getting into bed at night holds the promise of blissful, restorative sleep.

Alexandra Stoddard on Happiness at Home

Alexandra Stoddard calls herself a philosopher of contemporary living. She treats beauty at home as a direct route to everyday happiness. In Living a Beautiful Life, she urges us to turn the ordinary into the extraordinary by choosing everyday objects that delight us. No detail is too small. Creating beautiful rituals feeds our senses and uplifts our spirits amid daily routines.

Mrs. Stoddard believes that feeling at home is really about self-attunement. In Feeling at Home, she walks readers through their rooms to uncover both practical needs and deeper yearnings, then suggests small, creative changes that make the home an "emotional center" where every object answers a need and lifts the spirit. Happiness, she says, lies in the passions we pursue and the pressures we decline, in the treasured objects we keep nearby and the ordinary moments we elevate into celebrations.

This is your elegance code: choosing, arranging, and editing so that your surroundings support the joyful, thoughtful life you mean to live.

91. REVISITING YOUR VALUES

Does your home reflect your values? Does it express how you want to live, the atmosphere you want to create, and the life you want to support?

If you value timelessness, does your home feel as though it will age gracefully with you? Timeless rooms do not shout. They rely on restrained colors, classic proportions, and objects chosen for endurance rather than novelty.

If you value nature, does your home bring the outside in? Natural materials, daylight, plants, stone, wood, and open views all remind you that you belong to a larger world. A home rooted in nature feels grounding, restorative, and alive.

If you value connection, does your house make room for people? A table that invites conversation, a sofa that encourages lingering, a kitchen that welcomes gathering, or a porch that draws people outside all support a life built around relationships. A connected home does not isolate; it welcomes.

If you value grace, does your home feel calm, thoughtful, and practical? Grace shows up in good flow, soft lighting, order, and spaces that make daily life easy. A graceful home feels composed but not stiff, beautiful but never precious.

Try this: pretend you are a stranger walking into your home for the first time. What values would you think live here? What story would the space tell about its owner? Would you see timelessness, nature, connection, grace, or something else entirely?

For an even clearer mirror, ask a close friend to do the same. Invite someone who knows you well to walk through and tell you what values they see reflected. You may be surprised by what they notice instantly, and by what you have stopped seeing because you live with it every day.

Carolyne Roehm on a Life Steeped in Beauty

Carolyne Roehm has spent decades weaving beauty through every corner of her life: fashion, gardens, interiors, tabletops, even gift wrap. A "passion for everything," as she calls it, is her constant thread: a love of color, nature, quality, and classicism that appears whether she is arranging flowers, laying a table, or renovating a house. For her, beauty is not a garnish added at the end; it is a way of paying serious attention to life.

Nature is her greatest teacher. She studies how the sun moves across her garden, how leaves pattern a glass roof, how a poppy's crinkled petal becomes a pleated silk dress in her mind. That close observation fuels everything else, from rooms to clothes to celebrations. If she falls in love with a flower, she wants to enjoy it in as many ways as possible: in the garden, on the table, in a sketchbook, on fabric. Beauty, for her, is something to be cultivated, not consumed once and discarded.

Her elegance at home is lavish but never passive. She believes a person's life is expressed in the little details, and she is tireless in learning, editing, and refining, not to impress others, but to heighten her own and her guests' experience of being alive.

This is another facet of your elegance code at home: treating your surroundings as a canvas for your passions and affections, using quality, color, and thoughtful detail to turn everyday living into an art form.

92. MAKING ADJUSTMENTS

Once you're clear on your values, you can start making small, concrete adjustments so your home supports them more clearly.

If freedom is one of your values, you might subtract clutter, over--furnishing, and anything that makes your rooms feel heavy or crowded. You might add open space, flexible furniture, and a sense that you can move through the room without obstacles.

If creativity is one of your values, consider subtracting perfectionism and too much matching. You could add a table for projects, a pinboard, art supplies within reach, books, intriguing objects, or an easel that invites experimentation.

If harmony is one of your values, try subtracting visual noise, harsh lighting, and too many competing patterns. You might add calm colors, balanced arrangements, and soft textiles.

If travel is one of your values, subtract what feels fixed, stale, or overly tied to the past. You could add souvenirs with meaning, books from places you love, adaptable pieces, and reminders of the wider world.

JOURNALING QUESTIONS

Before you begin, write your three to five core values words at the top of the page so they stay in view as you reflect.
What in my home feels most aligned with who I am?
What in my home feels out of step with my values?
What does my space support well right now?
What does my space make unnecessarily difficult?

What feels essential to the life I want to live?
What feels like excess or leftover obligation?
What would I keep if I wanted my home to feel more true to me?
What would I let go of if I wanted my home to feel lighter and more intentional?
Where does my space already express my values clearly?
Where could a change make my values more visible?
What values do I want more of in my home right now?

93. YOUR VISION

Your space should support your elegance code by helping you live your vision now and your vision for the future. A home is not only a reflection of who you are today; it is also a companion to who you are becoming. Personally designed rooms can help you experience more ease in your days now while also making space for the life you are building next.

If your vision is for a calmer life, your home can help by being easier to clean, simpler to reset, with fewer distractions, and more breathing room.

If your vision is for a more creative life, your space can make room for ideas, materials, books, and the occasional delightful mess. It can offer surfaces to work on, places to leave projects in progress, and corners that invite experimentation.

If your vision is for a more social life, your home can welcome people with comfortable seating, a place to gather, and enough order that you feel at ease opening the door. Hospitality becomes simpler when your rooms are arranged to hold conversation and company.

If your vision is for a more spacious life, your home can support that by letting go of excess, keeping surfaces open, and making movement feel easy. Space itself becomes one of your luxuries.

JOURNALING QUESTIONS

Looking at my vision statement, what do I most need my home to do for me?

What changes would bring my home into closer alignment with the life I am building?

How could my space help me live my vision with more ease, beauty, and consistency?

What would my home look and feel like if it were designed to support my future self?

94. THE SANCTUARY AUDIT

Now that you've looked at your home through the lenses of vision, values, and standards, you can sense how a space that supports your elegance code should feel: alive with meaning, beauty, and usefulness. Before new objects cross the threshold and take up residence in your life, let them pass a Sanctuary Audit. You can decide how many questions an item may fail. Again, the goal isn't a sterile showroom or an empty box; it's a home where what surrounds you enhances the way you live.

The Visual Noise Test: Does this object "yell" at me with loud branding or clashing colors? Visual noise is a steady leak of calm.

The Dignity of Use Test: Is this the best version of this tool I can reasonably afford? Choosing well once often saves frustration for years.

The Inherited Guilt Check: Am I keeping this only because someone gave it to me or I "should" like it? If it doesn't align with your vision, it leaks your agency.

The Multi-Step Friction Test: Does using this item require a workaround: a drawer that sticks, a lamp with a finicky switch, a gadget that only works on the third try? These are daily paper cuts to your grace.

The Surface Integrity Rule: Does this item have a true home, or will it just live on a counter "for now"? Surfaces are for your active use, not long-term limbo for undecided objects.

The Future-Thrift Question: If I saw this in a thrift store five years from now, would I buy it? If not, you may be storing tomorrow's donation in your living room today.

You don't have to apply the Sanctuary Audit to everything at once. Try using it as you go through items in one drawer, or on one shelf, or even just the next item you bring into the house. Over time, each mini-decision shifts your home toward a place that feels chosen and aligned with your elegance code.

9

Relationships and Conversations

In the end, we only regret the chances we didn't take, the relationships we were afraid to have, and the decisions we waited too long to make.

Lewis Carroll

Politeness is not distance from love, but one of love's most elegant forms.

For years, I did a circus act to keep everyone from being disappointed. I over-explained, over-apologized, and bent myself into agreeable shapes no one asked for. It was exhausting and, perhaps worse, ineffective.

As I matured, I resigned from the job of managing other people's feelings and took up a simpler post: to live my code, and live it well. I decided to begin with one assumption: that although I am nowhere near perfect, I am a good person and a good friend. I show up; and I try. I listen, I remember, I respect. That is enough.

What followed surprised me: when I stopped trying to control everything, relationships either deepened or dissolved, but always clarified. Connection requires faith; faith that consistency is more valuable than contortions. We honor others and ourselves when we stop auditioning for their approval and trust them to see our value for themselves. A little reserve and a little dignity give everyone the space and grace to make better decisions.

Respect Follows Courtesy

The decline of many relationships—whether romantic, familial, friendly, or even between nations—often begins with the loss of courtesy. With people we know well, it is not only that we stop saying "please" and "thank you." We also make assumptions about their motives, and those assumptions are often negative. As we become familiar with a friend or spouse, we develop a shorthand in how we speak and respond to each other that assumes we know what they are thinking and they know what we are thinking. If left unchecked, that shorthand can erode respect because it replaces clear communication with the impossible expectation that we can read each other's minds.

This is where living from an elegance code differs dramatically from common thinking. To the average person, courtesy can seem like something we do solely for the benefit of others, and therefore is at odds with our authenticity. In that light, the choice appears to be between being polite and being true to oneself. It is no wonder that many people default to "being themselves," or to behaving as everyone else does. But for the person who lives by an internal code, courtesy is not a shallow act. It is the outward expression of inward elegance. That poise is foundational because it creates peace for the one who lives it. The fact that it also puts others at ease and sustains relationships is an added benefit.

95. PRESERVING THE MYSTERY—BOTH OURS AND THEIRS

What draws us to others initially is fascination based on mystery:

their differences and unfamiliar rhythms. Over time, we mistake knowing someone's habits for knowing their soul. But people never stop unfolding; we only stop noticing. Every morning the people in our lives wake up slightly changed, carrying new thoughts, dreams, and joys. To live elegantly in a relationship is to continue to notice this, to meet the familiar as though it were new again and again. This may be a gift we give others, but it is primarily a gift to ourselves.

Relationships weaken when familiarity is mistaken for knowledge; they revive when respect and curiosity are allowed back in. Fortunately, love and joy are made of such powerful stuff that it is rarely too late to mend what we have left undone. Like light, they move swiftly and travel far. Nothing can hold them back for long.

96. AN ELEGANT PRACTICE

The next time you feel the urge to do a song and dance to keep someone happy, pause and ask, "What would a good friend do here, not a perfect one?" Then do only that. Say "no" when you need to, without a long defense. Let your actions match your code, and let other adults have their feelings about it, which they are entitled to do. Your friendships may grow greater, or fewer, but the ones that remain will be built on something real.

97. THE RELIEF OF HAVING A CODE

If you are in the habit of monitoring your friends' moods like a security camera, your elegance code may relieve you of that angst. If someone I love is hurt, they can tell me, and I will always take that seriously. But I don't try to read minds anymore. My job is to act in good faith and stay open to conversation, not to pre-correct my existence so no one ever feels any discomfort. That's an ethos in miniature: to offer clarity and openness, but to no longer sacrifice yourself to manage feelings you haven't been told about. When you catch yourself wondering, "Are they mad at me? Did I say the wrong thing?" perhaps pause and ask instead: "Have they told me there's a problem?" If not, return to living by your code until you hear further.

98. INNER CIRCLE AUDIT

Relying on others to validate your existence is unnecessary with an elegance code. You know who you are. You have decided what matters to you, what you believe in, and what you stand for. You move through the world, including your "close-in" world of relationships with confidence and grace.

Are you leaking energy on inner circle friends who act more like acquaintances? Do you trust everyone in your inner circle? Do some members re-center you, while others leave you feeling off balance? Does your circle gossip about those who aren't present? Is it likely they do the same about you when you're not present? Do you need to mask or downgrade your values when you are with them? What would happen to those relationships if you always lived by your code? Do you see yourself investing more in true friends and being politely unavailable to those who are not?

99. THE FREE EXPERTISE LEAK

Leaking expertise can sabotage your elegance code. It drains your energy, weakens your mystique, and, over time, can damage non-professional relationships. The people who genuinely want your help will ask for it. Everyone else may unconsciously resent being turned into your project, and they will often respond with indifference.

A striking illustration of this came in *Pearls Before Breakfast*, Gene Weingarten's Pulitzer Prize–winning 2007 feature in The Washington Post. He persuaded Joshua Bell, one of the world's greatest violinists, to play Bach in a Washington, D.C., Metro station during rush hour, dressed in jeans and a baseball cap. Three days earlier,

Mr. Bell had played the same music for a sold-out audience in Boston, where tickets averaged about $100. In the station, he played for 43 minutes while 1,097 people walked past. Only seven stopped to listen, and only briefly. He reportedly collected about $32 in his open violin case.

Same man, same genius, same priceless Stradivarius.

What people will dress up for, travel for, and pay dearly to hear, they may walk past without a glance when it is offered for free. It was not that the music had less beauty in the Metro station. It was that almost no one recognized what they were being offered. When expertise is given too casually, it can disappear into the background and be treated as ordinary.

Your advice works the same way: when you offer detailed, thoughtful guidance outside a professional setting, for free, and without knowing whether the other person is ready to receive it, you become Joshua Bell in the subway. The rare person who is capable of hearing you will sometimes stop and drink it in. Many will not. They are not bad people. They are simply rushing past, and what you're offering is not a priority.

From an elegance point of view, this matters for two reasons: On the outside, giving constant free advice makes you less mysterious and more expendable. You become the person people "pick the brain" of over coffee, and then forget to implement anything you said. On the inside, it leaks your energy. You spend your best ideas and deepest attention on people who have no stake in them and then feel flattened and invisible afterward.

In the Washington Post piece, Bell admits he felt nervous and unsettled as almost everyone rushed past without looking at him. He describes the strange experience of being "ignored" and how quickly his expectations shrank as he went from a world-class soloist who resents a single cough in a concert hall to a man who feels "oddly grateful" for a dollar in change or even a glance. Offering something exquisite into a void compresses your sense of scale, and of who you are allowed to be in the world, at least for a moment.

My own experiments with "free mastery" ended similarly. I once offered, unasked, to teach a free watercolor workshop to a local arts league. Many people signed up; only one person came. Years earlier, as a professional horse trainer, people paid me serious money to fix dangerous horses. Meanwhile, I watched friends suffer devastating accidents and never once ask for my help. When I tried to intervene out of concern, they brushed off my advice and hired mediocre trainers instead. Eventually, I understood: my generosity was not only wasted, it was eroding my dignity. I decided I would offer once, briefly, and after that, any advice would be paid or not given at all.

People who are masters are almost always the most generous with free advice because what took them years to learn now comes easily. If this is you, know that an elegance code does not mean you never help anyone. It means you stop scattering your mastery as if it is meaningless. You allow others to invest something in their own growth: their attention, effort, money, or at a minimum, a sincere follow-up.

This self-discipline is not cold; it is elegant. Consider Cindy Crawford, one of the most successful models in history. She has said that she does not give her grown children unsolicited advice; her daughter Kaia Gerber has echoed that her mother "doesn't give out advice unless you ask," but if you do ask, you get the unvarnished truth. Ms. Crawford loves her daughter and has every credential to instruct her, yet she withholds professional critique unless it is invited. That is what non-leaking looks like: You use your genius in ways that are most beneficial, rather than giving it away to people who do not want it.

Leaking almost always comes from generosity, but the long-term effect is brutal. You end up like Joshua Bell in the subway—playing your life's work to people who are not listening, then wondering why you lack the time or energy to do the work that matters most to you. Consider the discipline of silence, of letting other adults bear the consequences of their choices, and of reserving your best advice for the students, clients, and loved ones who have shown they are ready to receive it.

100. DON'T BE THAT PERSON YOURSELF

Most of us imagine "genius" as someone far removed from our lives: an expert on a podcast, a stranger on the internet, a name on a book cover. Meanwhile, we may live next door to a maestro-level professional, or even share a bed with one, without ever seriously asking what they know. We will chase strangers' advice online but never sit down with the master in our own kitchen.

Very few people have their ego under enough control to seek the expertise that exists within their own sphere. It feels safer to idolize someone distant than to admit, face-to-face with someone you've known for years, "You know things I don't. Will you teach me?"

If your life vision is large, this is where real acceleration lives. If you are surrounded by experts, at a minimum, stop ignoring them. Set your ego aside and ask the best, and often most unexpected, people in your life what they know. You may discover that the genius you've been searching for online has been living next door, or making coffee in your own house all along.

101. NEVER COMPLAIN, NEVER EXPLAIN

This is a maxim that Wallis, the Duchess of Windsor, had embroidered on a sofa pillow, and it is surprisingly brilliant for anyone living by an elegance code. To never complain is to refuse to make a spectacle of one's discomfort. To never explain is to avoid the exhausting habit of over-justifying oneself to people committed to misunderstanding. Together, the two phrases guide an elegance code with a genteel dignity that does not chase approval, defend every choice, or engage in unnecessary emotional labor.

102. WE CANNOT CRITICIZE LOVE INTO BEING

We each have the freedom to decide what we will accept and live with, and only we can know what that is. We are often reminded, though, that it is unlikely that we can criticize another adult into being different. Nagging and criticism do not reflect the life we want to live, and they do not work anyway. Any gain won through manipulation, threat, or criticism is temporary at best. It does not create the loving atmosphere we long for, and while it may force compliance for a moment, it does not produce closeness, trust, or willingness. An elegance code suggests a better approach: saying what we want in an inspiring way and encouraging behavior we love by noticing it when it appears.

103. THE "TALK"

You probably know what I'm referring to, because most of us have either given "the talk" or been the recipient. That it is so often treated as a comedic device in books and movies gives us a pretty good idea that it rarely goes the way well-meaning relationship advice promises it will. I am by no means a relationship expert, but I suspect this may be because sometimes "the talk" is just another way of trying to control, disguised as being "open" and "honest." In effect, we ask another person to sit there while we plead, complain, nag, or argue our point, as if enough intensity might produce agreement. But a conversation that exists to wear someone down is not really communication. It is pressure.

104. WHEN TALKING LESS HELPS MORE

Your elegance code contains in its values and vision a gentler way forward in relationships. We accept we are the center of our own balance, and we care for ourselves very well, so we do not have to be disappointed in others so readily. Others may disappoint themselves through their actions, but when our sense of self is no longer tethered to their behavior, it becomes harder to lose our footing.

This restores dignity and gives us breathing room. It allows us to ease up on the endless interpretation and judgment of one another and return to the more beautiful work of appreciating each other, respecting each other, and enjoying each other's company. We are relieved of the monstrous job of managing the behavior of the adults in our lives. Sometimes the highest wisdom is that when we stop managing our relationships, we remember why we value them.

105. POSITIVE PROJECTIONS

I first encountered the idea of a "Spouse Fulfilling Prophecy" in Laura Doyle's book *The Empowered Wife*, where she describes the power of focusing on what we want more of in our partner. Inspired by how broadly this principle applies, I generalized it into what I call a Grace-Fulfilling Prophecy. The essence is simple: we all long to be seen and appreciated, and when we sincerely notice and name the grace we see in others, we see more of it. What I found remarkable about Laura's approach is the deep positivity and optimism behind it. You may begin by using these techniques to improve a relationship, but you eventually discover that it was never about the other person; it is about becoming the person you most aspire to be. We naturally want to influence others, but we want to do it in a way that feels uplifting and kind.

Practicing a grace-fulfilling prophecy is wonderfully simple, but it requires an inner shift. Instead of complaining about what is missing or criticizing what was done "wrong," you intentionally look for something—anything—in the action to appreciate and name out loud. Not praise followed by a "but" and a critique. Just praise, and you let it go. Then you watch for the next right thing, however small, and you acknowledge that as well. That is the whole method. Natural Horsemanship trainers teach a version of this when they say to look for what the horse is doing right and "reward the slightest try."

This same principle shows up in other intelligent species as well. Early marine-animal trainers like Karen Pryor, discovered dolphins learned complex behaviors fastest when they ignored mistakes and instead consistently rewarded even the smallest movement in the right direction. Over time, the dolphins naturally offered more of what was noticed and rewarded. People are no different. We move toward what feels good.

106. POSITIVE SELF-COACHING

The same principles that Karen Pryor uses with dolphins and dogs, and that Laura Doyle uses in marriages, can be turned inward as a form of elegant self-coaching. Instead of finding fault and scolding ourselves for every misstep and replaying our failures on a loop, we can experiment with ignoring the behaviors we want less of and rewarding even our smallest moves in the right direction. Criticism keeps our attention locked on what we do not want; appreciation draws our focus toward what we are becoming. When we notice and "mark" even the slightest effort toward our vision—a kinder response, a better boundary, a five-minute walk—and pair it with a reward, we teach ourselves, over time, to move toward that future with more ease and less shame. The reward could be as quick and uplifting as a "Way to go," or "Good job," or "I'm so proud of me." It could be a five-minute break to play a game on your phone. The most important thing is that when we do something well, we celebrate it, instead of immediately moving the goalposts.

The same approach works when you are learning something new.

Picture a woman teaching herself to play the piano as an adult. The usual inner voice says, *This sounds terrible. I am too old. I will never be any good.* Every mistake becomes proof that she should quit. Now imagine she applies Karen Pryor's and Laura Doyle's logic to herself. She decides not to comment on wrong notes at all. Instead, she pays attention to the moments that match her intention: the one bar she plays smoothly, the day she sits down to practice even when she is tired, the tiny improvement in her left hand from last week to this week. She "marks" each of these efforts with a brief, specific acknowledgment: *That was smoother. Way to go, I showed up again. My timing is improving.* Over time, she begins to associate practice with good feelings rather than humiliation. That is how she inches closer to the sound she wants.

LIVE WELL

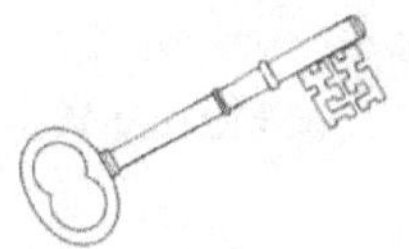

10

MANNERS

He that respects himself is safe from others; he wears a coat of mail that none can pierce.

Henry Wadsworth Longfellow

IT'S A VAST, UNSTABLE world. You may be absorbed in the orbit of your own life, but beyond it eight billion people are acting and reacting across the globe, every hour of every day. Sometimes they behave with reason; sometimes their intentions are good but their judgment is poor; sometimes they act from sheer thoughtlessness or naked aggression. The moment you step outside your door, you enter the blast radius of other people's impulses, and you will pay for their mistakes if you do not know how to live among them.

Manners create a buffer: they buy you space, time, and a higher vantage point from which to watch, think, and choose, instead of being pulled, pushed, or tripped by events. Used this way, manners prevent you from knotting yourself up in emotion or drifting off course every time the wind blows. They keep you aligned with your vision, so that in everyday turbulence you move with deliberation rather than disturbance.

107. SELF-MASTERY

For most of history, to be "civilized" did not mean to be soft; it meant to be self-governed. A person who could master their impulses, measure their words, and restrain their temper marked themselves as safer to be near, and higher-status. Royal courts and salons, military commands, and financial trading floors all understood this instinctively: those who could not control themselves could not be trusted with lives, information, money, or power. What we now call "good manners" began as a visible code of self-regulation—a shared language that allowed ambitious people to signal, without speaking, that they were fit for serious roles.

Over the last century, manners came to be seen as fake, merely decorative, and a relic of hierarchies people wanted to escape. Being "real" was elevated above restraint; personal expression above discretion. The result is a culture where outbursts, oversharing, and public displays of "authenticity" are common, even rewarded. Where manners once softened the more base aspects of human nature, today those raw impulses are amplified and encouraged in everything from reality shows to politics. An anonymous 1867 manual, How to Shine in Society; or, The Art of Conversation, advises civilized men and women, when they must disagree, to begin by stating the extent to which they agree with the speaker, then by clarifying that they take no pleasure in differing; the disagreement is with the idea, not an attack on the speaker's character.

108. ON EDGE

In personality research, emotional instability—what psychologists call neuroticism or negative emotionality—is one of the strongest predictors of anxiety, depression, and lower well-being. It describes a disposition toward frequent, intense negative states such as anger, anxiety, and irritability, and it greatly increases vulnerability to stress-related disorders. People high in this trait react more intensely to small stressors and recover more slowly, leaving their stress system "switched on" for longer and eroding their health, relationships, and life satisfaction over time.

Now place that temperament in an environment that rewards constant emotional display—especially social media, where heavier, more compulsive use is consistently linked with higher depression, anxiety, stress, and loneliness. A culture that normalizes and amplifies emotional reactivity does not merely reflect people's inner turmoil; it manufactures chronic stress and dissatisfaction by keeping everyone's nerves permanently on edge.

Every excess produces its counter-movement. As people grow weary of escalating conflict and lack of forward progress, the person who governs their impulses, conceals their reactions, and moves with deliberate grace will stand out. The return of manners will probably be one of the most significant status shifts of this century: toward those who can control themselves while others cannot.

109. THE ALTERNATIVE

When you operate with an elegance code, you do not need to respond to every meaningless slight because you have your values and vision to ground you, and your time is valuable. As a secret agent of elegance, unless the rudeness breaches your physical perimeter or compromises your mission, you treat it as junk data.

If you have erred, apologize immediately and move on. If you are not mistaken, stay cool. Stay relaxed. Stay in your space. The moment you get visibly upset, you have blown your cover.

Most etiquette books treat manners as a favor you do for others at a cost to yourself. The elegance code treats manners as self-protection. Manners are a buffer zone—a force field that creates both literal and psychological distance between you and an aggressor, or between you and the hurly-burly of an ordinary day at the office.

In my novel *The Gilded Talisman*, Alexander Girard uses manners as a buffer and a tactic. By being exquisitely formal, he signals that the theater of operations is governed by his rules. If someone is rude to him and he responds with flawless politeness, he has not "lost"; he has refused to enter their mud pit. This is how he protects his balance and accomplishes so much.

Manners are a method by which we maintain our self-sovereignty.

110. THE MORAL HIGH GROUND

Losing your temper is a major leak and a security breach. Bond rarely shouts. Why? Because shouting is a leak; it reveals exactly what hurts you. Maintaining your manners during a conflict isn't about being the "better person" in a sentimental sense; it's about being the person who cannot be rattled. When you remain polite while someone else escalates, you are the one holding the power. You are the one who is "unhackable."

Never Make an Enemy by Accident

A core principle of intelligence work is never burn a bridge you may need to cross later. A casual insult or thoughtless lapse in manners can turn a neutral party into a permanent enemy, and enemies do not simply disappear because you forget about them. They wait, they watch, and they look for an opening to repay the slight.

There is such a thing as an enemy in life. Even Judith Martin ("Miss Manners") writes about genuine antagonists and the need to maintain your dignity. Elegance dictates that if you must create—or defeat—an enemy, you do it intentionally, after calculating the probable cost, not carelessly because you were tired or irritable. Most people collect enemies by accident: a sharp remark here, a public humiliation there, a moment of contempt they never even register. Years later, they are blindsided by resistance they cannot trace. The elegant operator assumes that every unnecessary hostility will return against them in some form, and so treats restraint as a form of long-range self-defense.

111. NO TRACE

When my dog follows a scent, he lowers his nose and reads the air and the ground. Invisible to us, every creature sheds a trail of particles as it moves: skin cells, hair, sweat, signals that announce, "Something passed this way." He can track a stranger long after they have vanished from sight by the residue they leave behind without realizing it.

Human beings are no different. We leave a trail of comments, glances, tones of voice, forgotten slights, and small humiliations in our wake. Many people move through the world leaking irritation and contempt, then feel surprised when resistance and resentment seem to meet them everywhere. While you cannot control every impression you make, you can control your manners.

When you are consistently courteous to everyone, from the waiter to the rival, you leave almost no trail. You pass through rooms and situations without creating unnecessary friction. Formal manners act as a containment field for your emotions so that what you leak is minimal and deliberate, rather than turbulent and damaging.

No-Trace Interactions

Imagine a tense staff meeting where a deadline has been missed, and everyone is bracing for blame. One person responds with sarcasm, another with defensiveness, and the mood in the room turns sour. You feel the same frustration they do, but you let your manners do the speaking. You listen without interrupting. You answer questions in a calm, neutral tone. You acknowledge other people's efforts and stick to the facts instead of assigning blame. When the meeting ends, no one feels humiliated by you, even if they disagreed with you. You have made your presentation; you have protected your integrity, and you have left almost no trace of resentment behind.

Imagine you are at a family dinner and your mother-in-law makes a remark about your parenting or your appearance. Around the table, you can feel everyone tense, waiting to see what you will do. You have options. You could snap back, go silent and seethe, or make a scene. Instead, you choose no trace. You keep your tone even, your face relaxed, and you answer with courtesy: "Thank you for your concern," or "I hear you. I see it differently, and that is all right," then you shift the conversation to a neutral topic. You do not pretend it felt good, but you also do not leak your anger into the room. Hours later, people may remember what she said, but they will also remember that you stayed courteous and respectful. You protected your dignity and left as little resentment behind you as possible.

Choosing not to react in kind is not just a strategy; it is an expression of who you have decided to be. This is where the rubber meets the road, because your elegance code is about you, not about correcting other people. You do not control your mother-in-law, or anyone else. You control yourself. Responding to criticism with criticism will never produce the repair or recognition you want; it can only escalate the tension. Manners are freedom. You are free to decide that your standard is higher than any pettiness, and to let your code determine your manners when your feelings are inflamed.

112. MANNERS ARE NOT AGREEMENT

Do not mistake manners for compliance. You lose nothing by being polite, and you have everything to gain. When someone tries to provoke you, they are probing for your internal cipher. If you react with anger, you hand them the key. If you respond with cool, scrupulous courtesy, you bar the door and keep your system closed.

We maintain the moral high ground not for "niceness," but for security. If you decide you must go to war with someone, you do it after you have thought it through and by design, not because you lost your poise at a dinner party or in a moment of wounded pride.

113. MANNERS AS SPACE

Here is a practice exercise. Try it for a week in situations you feel are appropriate, and see if it helps you remain self-contained. When someone is rude or short-tempered, resist the urge to ignore it completely or to be snarky in return. Instead, create a buffer.

In your response, consciously:

- Use their formal title (Mr., Mrs., Ms., Dr., etc.)
- Use full sentences
- Avoid slang
- Respond with a calm, relevant question

Notice what happens. The sudden formality creates space without escalating the tension. Most people instinctively step back into their own lane; the distance gives them a moment to hear themselves, and you have neither escalated nor stooped to their level.

Afterward, ask yourself: Was it easier to stay connected if the person was someone you love? Did the formality help you stay in your own frame? How did you feel about yourself afterward: more scattered, or more in command?

114. WHY MANNERS FEEL DIFFERENT NOW

Exquisite manners stand out because almost everything else has blurred into sameness. Dress codes, greetings, and public behavior are all looser. "Polite enough" has become the ceiling, not the floor. In a culture of constant low-grade rudeness and distraction, courtesy is refreshing.

Status, in every era, is a moving target. When a particular look floods the landscape, its power as a signal dies. The moment "old money" style becomes a TikTok filter, it no longer separates anyone from the crowd.

Humans, however, do not stop ranking one another just because the clothes stop helping. We are tribal by instinct, always sorting, always pigeonholing, always asking, "What are you? Where do you belong?"

In that world, you are measured less by what you can buy and more by what you embody. How you speak when there is nothing to gain. How you listen when you are bored. Whether you follow through when it is not convenient. How you treat those who cannot help you. These actions become the new emblems of rank. They are harder to fake, slower to acquire, and far more revealing of one's intelligence and self-command.

Once status moves from the surface to the core, manners are no longer decorative; they are diagnostic. They expose your character and your emotional stability in a way money cannot. In a culture drunk on display, genuine consideration becomes subversive. Courtesy turns into a new form of power, an aristocracy built not on inheritance, but on discernment and self-mastery.

115. MASTERING THE PAUSE

One way to incorporate more elevated conduct into your elegance code is to master The Pause.

The Pause moves you from reactive to intentional. A three-second pause will feel like an eternity in the moment, but it brings your reasoning brain online instead of your reflexive one. It signals to the other person that you are choosing your words rather than firing them. That signal alone changes the dynamics of most conversations.

The mechanics are straightforward. After someone speaks, take a breath and wait three full seconds before responding. When you feel the rising heat of being challenged or criticized, acknowledge it internally "I'm being triggered," and mentally say: pause. Put both feet flat on the floor. It grounds your body and steadies your tone in a way that is almost immediate. Then use your hands to gesture, lean slightly forward, and ask a question. "Can you say more about that?" or, "Can you repeat that?" works perfectly. If the person has said something rude or intrusive, they will probably rephrase or demur entirely.

Asking a question does something specific in the brain of the person you are speaking with. Research in cognitive neuroscience shows that curiosity activates the brain's dopamine system, the same system involved in motivation and reward. When you ask someone a question, you do not just buy yourself time. You trigger a neurological state in them that is associated with engagement, openness, and the desire to respond. You pull them toward connection rather than combat. A tense conversation does not escalate when one person asks a sincere question; it redirects.

Then pause again when they answer. Let them finish completely. End your response with one more question. You find that the conversation has moved, almost without effort, from confrontation to exchange, and that you have maintained your composure throughout.

116. CORRECTION OR COMMOTION

When you encounter criticism, ask yourself one question: "Is this a valid critique of my conduct?" If yes, correct it immediately. Do not be too proud to apologize. Self-correction is not weakness; it is an essential part of your code. If the criticism is not valid, you do not need to engage with it, defend against it, or explain yourself. Other people's opinions of you—good and bad—are data.

You decide which data is worth acting on.

Never match the frequency of a chaotic person. If they are at a ten in volume and anger, you stay at a three in volume and a ten in composure. Escalation is a major leak of energy, dignity, and strategic position. This is not passivity. It is command. You are not suppressing yourself; you are choosing the terms of your response so your words come from clarity, not an adrenaline spike. Delaying your response does not weaken your position. It gives you time to answer, should you choose to, with considered language and in alignment with who you have decided to be.

117. MANNERS BUILD A REPUTATION FOR CONSISTENCY

Fashion designer, director, and entrepreneur Tom Ford once remarked that "dressing well is a form of good manners," a line that has followed him through countless profiles and interviews. His public image is a study in immaculate tailoring and measured speech. Whether directing a film, boarding a plane, or meeting a friend to see a movie, he invariably shows up in his signature look: a dark suit and an open-collared white shirt, no tie. His overall presentation is one of deliberate, relaxed authority. He dresses according to his own code. He is also well known for personal conduct that money cannot manufacture: attentiveness, consideration, and the rare discipline of making people feel that their company matters to him. His clothes are impeccable, but the message underneath them is singular: you are worth the effort I have made.

Tom Ford's early years looked nothing like his later reputation. He dropped out of NYU, spent his nights at Studio 54, moved to Los Angeles to try acting, and eventually landed at Parsons studying architecture. The man who would later become synonymous with precision, control, and bringing the Gucci brand back from the dead was, by most accounts, a work in progress for a long time. At some point, he decided who he intended to be, then built his style, his manners, and his business acumen to match that vision. You can do the same thing as you build your own code.

The Mechanics of Exceptional Conduct

Most people know how to behave well. The difference is not knowledge; it is execution. People with exceptional reputations have decided that certain choices are not negotiable, and then they hold that line regardless of mood, circumstance, or audience.

They make eye contact when someone speaks to them. They do not glance at their phones. They use people's names because using a name tells someone directly: I see you, specifically. When they commit to something, they follow through every time, because a single broken commitment costs more than the inconvenience it saved. When they are wrong, they say so plainly and move on: no qualifications, no deflection, no "I'm sorry you felt that way." They arrive on time, because chronic lateness is not a personality quirk. It is a choice, and it tells the people waiting exactly where they rank in your priorities.

The discipline that makes them most rare is that they do not make people feel like an interruption. When they are with you, they are with you. Their attention does not drift to the next conversation, the next table, or the next thing on their schedule, although their days are as full as anyone else's. In an age built on distraction, that kind of presence is rare currency. It is remembered long after the conversation ends.

None of it is complicated. All of it is demanding. The gap between knowing these things and executing them—in every encounter, under every condition, without exception—is where reputation is built or destroyed.

118. MANNERS AS A FILTER

Most people move through life in low resolution: loud, hurried, reactive. When such a person meets someone with disciplined manners, they collide with a wall they cannot see. Politeness becomes a soft refusal, a formality that never breaks form yet never yields ground. The low-resolution personality experiences this as boredom, stiffness, or an invisible pressure and soon looks elsewhere for stimulation. The filter has done its work: no scene, no quarrel, just separation.

Research suggests why this works so efficiently: formal language and courteous behavior do not only reflect distance; they create it. In experiments, people chose more polite phrasing when they wanted to increase social distance, instinctively using manners as a regulator, not just a signal. Elegance, then, is not merely an aesthetic; it is a tool for managing proximity.

Testing for Attentional Intelligence

To move past this shield, a person must slow down and pay attention. They need to notice the pace of an interaction, the pauses, and the care taken with words. Elegant people are not testing how charming you can be; they are watching to see whether you are present enough to read subtext. Manners filter out those who only exist on the surface. The impatient, the impulsive, and the self involved often lose interest when they cannot control the interaction with brusqueness.

The Court Lesson

Louis XIV understood that form could rule where force could not. His court at Versailles was not just a palace; it was a machine built out of ritual. Courtiers were bound by rules for how to stand, how to address him, even how to approach his gardens. Those who failed to read these signals excluded themselves; they revealed their lack of refinement and lost access to power.

From these early "étiquettes," printed cards instructing nobles where to stand and what to do, modern etiquette emerged. The king did not need to shout or threaten. The code filtered for him. Only those who could navigate the choreography of manners were allowed near the center. The rest eliminated themselves.

The Executive's Shield

Manners are effective because they make open conflict unnecessary. Aggression invites resistance; composure redirects it. When your bearing is impeccable, people do not charge you. They hesitate, reconsider, or step aside.

At Versailles, status was measured in access. To stand near the king during the lever or to hand him a shirt was worth more than gold. Those who did not understand the code tried to force intimacy. They spoke too freely, approached too fast, laughed too loudly. They mistook the king's courteous phrases for encouragement.

The response was never open humiliation. The king and his ministers simply followed the rules with icy precision: formal address, measured speech, strict adherence to protocol. The overeager courtier was kept at the outer edge of the circle, acknowledged but never advanced. The message was unmistakable to those who could read it: you have not earned proximity. Etiquette did what cruelty would have done, but without a single raised voice.

In modern business, the same principle operates in a different form. Busy executives recreate Versailles with calendars and assistants instead of royal chambers and guards. A skilled assistant acts as a gatekeeper of their time, using courteous questions and formal processes to decide who gains access and who does not. The assistant asks about the purpose of the meeting, the expected outcome, and who will attend. Those who are vague, pushy, or entitled are redirected to forms, links, or junior staff. Those who are precise, respectful, and prepared are moved forward. The executive never has to say "no." The system of manners, the emails, protocols, and polished replies, filters out the unserious and the intrusive.

Psychologists describe politeness as a way of regulating social distance, a means of deciding who comes closer and who stays on the far side of the line. The door may be closed, but the lock is often hidden inside a gesture of respect. Those who live by an elegance code find a profound sense of social safety. People who thrive on conflict or emotional "leaking" find no purchase on a smooth, elegant surface. They slide right off.

Eventually, without effort, your social circle becomes a collection of those who match your frequency. In *The Gilded Talisman*, Madame Girard says to Maren, "He will not chase you, and he will not fight with you."

This isn't a lack of passion; it is the ultimate filter. It says: *"I have built a world of order and beauty. If you wish to be in it, you must be capable of matching its peace."*

11

STACK THE DECK

To improve the golden moment of opportunity and catch the good that is within our reach is the great art of life.

Samuel Johnson

MOST OF US LIVE as though the cards have been dealt and our only job is to play the hand. We accept the education we were offered, the social circles we landed in, the habits we inherited, and the environments that surround us as though all of it were fixed. As though we are passengers, not architects. What almost no one tells you is that there is another way.

I call it stacking the deck, and first wrote about the concept in my romantic suspense novel, *The Gilded Talisman*. This is how those who routinely achieve and exceed their goals operate. It is a moral and ethical method of engineering an environment where success becomes the path of least resistance. Elite athletes, top leaders, and the most accomplished figures in business and the arts understand that willpower is a finite resource. Rather than relying on it, they design systems and situations that remove friction, protect their energy, and eliminate the circumstances most likely to derail them.

In *The Gilded Talisman*, Alexander Girard understood this at a remarkably young age. While still a university student, he recognized that no institution was going to hand him the complete set of tools he needed to build the life he envisioned. So he built his own syllabus. In his words: *"I made a list: languages I wanted to speak, books I wanted to read; history, philosophy, astronomy, art, music, even some basics of mapmaking and cryptography. Then I found ways to learn them."* He notes that the most prestigious colleges in the world have lectures and courses online that are free, including Harvard, Yale, and M.I.T.

Alexander did not do this because someone told him to. He did it because he grasped that preparation is not passive. It is the most elegant form of ambition there is. He continued to apply the same logic to the rest of his life: his tight, handpicked inner circle, how he spent his time, and the work he chose. He arranged his own life to give himself the greatest possible chance of succeeding. What Alexander did, with extraordinary intention and almost no fanfare, was stack the deck in his favor. That is precisely what this chapter invites you to do.

119. CREATE YOUR OWN SYLLABUS

Somewhere along the way, most of us absorbed the false assumption that formal education is the only legitimate container for learning, and that once it ends, the syllabus closes with it. It does not. Your education is never finished. It is unsupervised now, which means, for the first time, it is fully yours.

Begin with a blank page and a single question: What have I always wanted to know? Do not edit yourself. Do not stop to ask how you will learn it, how long it will take, or whether it is practical. That conversation comes later. For now, the only rule is honesty.

Take out a piece of paper or your notebook. Write down everything. The French you have always wanted to speak. The history of Europe you never studied the way you wished. Ballroom dancing.

Watercolor. How to serve a volleyball. How to groom a poodle. The wines of Burgundy. The architecture of Rome. South Africa. Sanskrit. Sourdough. Mathematics for the sheer beauty of it. Write until the page is full and then keep going, because what you are doing in this moment is not making a list. You are drawing the outline of your own mind: the full shape of your curiosity, your values, and your vision for the person you are still becoming. Nothing on this page is too small, too impractical, or too late. Alexander did not ask permission to want what he wanted. Neither should you.

120. SIX DEGREES OF SEPARATION

Now go back down your syllabus and beside each item, casually jot a few ideas for how you might learn it. This is not a commitment. You are not signing a contract or booking a flight. It is brainstorming, a playful exercise in possibility, and the only rule is that you are not allowed to write, "I don't know anyone who could help with that." Because here is what the research says: you do.

In the 1960s, social psychologist Stanley Milgram of Harvard University conducted a now-famous experiment in which he asked ordinary people to forward a letter to a complete stranger in another city, using only personal acquaintances as the chain of delivery. What he discovered stunned the scientific community. On average, it took six steps. Not six hundred. Not sixty. Six. His findings have since been replicated across email networks, Facebook's billions of users, Microsoft Messenger data, and actor networks, and six degrees keeps appearing as the natural, recurring architecture of human connection. In 2023, mathematicians at Bar-Ilan University proved it is not a coincidence. It is the inevitable result of the way human beings independently build their social networks.

What this means for your syllabus is extraordinary. You want to learn to speak French? You are, at most, six people away from a fluent speaker willing to meet you for coffee. You want to ride horses, learn to watercolor, understand the history of the Ottoman Empire, or find someone who has traveled extensively through South Africa? Six people. The knowledge you want is not behind a locked door. It is inside someone's head, and that someone is closer to you than you think.

Here is how to test it. Pick one item from your list, just one. Ask yourself: Who do I know who might know someone connected to this? Send a message: "I've been wanting to learn more about [subject]. Do you happen to know anyone I could talk to?" Then let the chain do what it was built to do. You will be surprised how fast six degrees collapses into two or three. Most people are delighted to be asked. Most people are even more delighted to connect two curious individuals who share an interest. You are not imposing. You are taking part in the oldest and most natural form of human learning there is: one conversation at a time.

121. YOU ARE ALLOWED TO ENJOY YOUR LIFE

It sounds absurd, but we can easily get channeled into a life built entirely on obligation and forget to ask whether any of it is something we want. Years ago, I found myself in exactly that position: my days packed edge to edge with commitments I had freely agreed to. No one had twisted my arm. I had said yes until there was no space left to breathe. Eventually, I had to stop and take a hard look at where my time was going and whether it matched where I wanted to be heading.

There are 1,440 minutes in a day and about 720 hours in a month. That is an empire of time, and yet we talk about it as though we live under occupation. We insist we "don't have time," as if some hostile force is confiscating our hours at the border. The truth is, we do have time; we just forget to design it. We treat our calendar like a dumping ground for tasks and errands instead of a tool to organize and protect what is precious. Yes, there will always be non-negotiables: caring for the people and creatures we love, eating, sleeping, working, tending to ourselves. But beyond that, most of us have more open hours than we will admit, because acknowledging those hours means accepting responsibility for how they are spent. The question is not whether you are busy. The question is: how much of that busyness constitutes a life you enjoy, and how much is merely existing?

Enjoyment is not frivolity. It tells you what you prefer, what gives you energy, and what brings you to attention. When you enjoy something, you feel awake. Time seems to pass in minutes but leaves you fuller rather than emptier. People who consistently stack the deck in their favor do something radical: they take their "enjoyment data" seriously. They understand that a life built only on duty may earn admiration from the outside world, but it seldom produces a morning you are eager to wake up to.

I have known no one as happy to be alive as my dad. He squeezed every drop of enjoyment out of the years he was here. He worked hard, and I am sure his work was not always pleasant, but he shaped it into something he wanted. I suspect he achieved so much because he woke up every day with enthusiasm. He was charming and energetic, and always had a project to look forward to. Even in retirement, he was not one of those grandparents who lives vicariously through their children or grandchildren. He was thrilled to see the family (I think) and curious about what everyone was up to, but he had his own interests. I doubt he was bored a day in his life. Pleasure is not the enemy of ambition. It is often its most reliable accomplice.

If you were to examine your current month as a strategist rather than a defendant, with no explanations, only evidence: how much of it would you say you have designed to be enjoyed? What is one pleasurable thing you could add to your day? A walk, a book in the bath, fifteen minutes with a guitar, a cup of coffee in silence? What are a few hours you could clear for yourself each week if you treated your own happiness as a legitimate appointment? What blocks of time could you guard?

If anyone gets access to me before noon by any method, I must like them enormously, or something is on fire, because that is my non-negotiable writing time and I guard it like a dragon guards treasure. That block is not up for casual sacrifice; everything else arranges itself around it. What blocks of time could you guard for work you love, a new career search, learning a skill from your syllabus, or private time to do what matters to you?

If you opened your calendar right now and circled at least three small pockets a week as "for me," where would they go?

122. THE SIGNAL YOU SEND IS THE SIGNAL THEY RECEIVE

In 1992, neuroscientist Giacomo Rizzolatti and his team at the University of Parma made an accidental discovery that reshaped our understanding of human interaction. While studying motor neurons in macaque monkeys, the researchers noticed certain neurons fired not only when a monkey performed an action, but also when it observed another individual performing the same action. These became known as mirror neurons. Later research confirmed that human beings have equivalent systems, and that they extend beyond physical actions into the realm of emotion.

The practical implications are direct. When you walk into a room carrying tension, people feel it. When you are calm, people around you settle. When you are hostile, people brace. When you are at ease, others relax. This is not intuition or social sensitivity. It is neurobiology. Other people's brains are, below the threshold of conscious thought, reading and mirroring the emotional signals you broadcast.

This has an immediate consequence for anyone who wants to communicate more effectively. You cannot control how other people behave in a conversation. You can control the signal you send into it. If you want a conversation to be productive, you must arrive in a productive state. If you want someone to hear you, you must speak from a place that does not trigger their defenses. If you want to de-escalate a conflict, you have to lead the way. The other person's brain will follow.

123. SET YOURSELF UP TO WIN

You are your own best advocate. Allow yourself to win at everything you attempt. I can hear your skepticism: Everything? Yes. With a few reasonable caveats: that your goals are good for you, within your ability, and, critically, within your control.

Break tasks into micro-steps so small they feel ridiculous, therefore entirely doable. Five minutes or less. If you break down a task and it is still too hard, break it down again. Will it take longer to get to a goal using micro-steps? Maybe. But compared to never, micro-steps are a lot faster, because never is what happens when a project feels too overwhelming to start.

Micro-steps work because they are easy, and each session is a win. Winning is fun. Think about it. You could string win after win together all the way to the finish line. You can tackle a junk drawer, get in shape, or write a novel. One micro-session at a time.

124. REST, ORDER, AND BEAUTY

Rest, order, and beauty are not luxuries or rewards. They are responsibilities. Let us stop reserving them for odd weekends and the mythical day when everything is finished. When we are rested, our minds are clearer, our bodies are happier, and our tempers are rational. When our surroundings have some order, we can find what we need when we need it, leak less energy, and think more expansively. When we take a moment to notice beauty, we remember that life is more than work.

If the world is in charge, it will produce one more message, one more request, one more chore. Your elegance code reverses that. It puts you in charge and treats rest, order, and beauty as part of your essential infrastructure.

Caring for ourselves is not self-indulgence. It is maintenance. This means we build rest, order, and beauty into the structure of every day. We go to bed on time because tomorrow's version of us needs a working brain. We put things back where they belong because we respect our time and attention. We decorate, cultivate a garden, and arrange flowers, not to impress visitors, but because we deserve spaces that are both lovely and functional. This, too, is stacking the deck.

125. BE EXCLUSIVE

We are valued at the level we allow. Your time and energy may be important to others, but if you treat them as important to yourself first, you change the terms of every relationship through elevation. This is one of the most effective ways to stack the deck, because it does not require you to chase, convert, or control anything outside your elegance code. Scarcity clarifies. When your presence cannot be assumed, people who value it will say so, and those who do not confirm that as well. It raises the frequency at which you operate and attracts those who want to meet you at a higher level.

The Mass Invite

Consider the modern habit of the mass invitation: the group blast, the @all, the bulletin board event, the reply-all summons addressed to everyone and therefore, in the truest sense, to no one. These are not invitations. An invitation is a personal act. It says: I thought of you specifically. I would love to see you.

A blast says something rather different: I need an audience, and I am casting a wide net. A friend of mine decided some time ago that she no longer responds to invitations posted on bulletin boards or addressed to a collective. Her reasoning was elegant: if her presence is not worth the effort of a personal invitation, then her time is not worth the effort of a personal response. What the sender wants, she observed, is not so much her company as another body in the room, and she has better things to do with an evening than fill a quota. She is not unkind about it, she simply does not go.

This is not snobbery. It is discernment, and there is a significant difference between the two. Snobbery excludes people to feel superior. Discernment protects your energy so that when you do show up, you show up fully, with attention, charm, and presence. The people who receive your time as a rare thing will treat it accordingly. The people who have grown accustomed to your automatic yes will barely notice you were missing.

The Invitational Mindset

Instead of asking, "Why should I say no?" consider asking, "Why does this deserve a yes?" Steve Jobs famously said that focus means saying no to a hundred good ideas to ensure you have room for the great one. Your social and professional calendars operate by the same logic. Every automatic yes is a no to something you might have loved, created, or rested into instead. The person who says yes to everything is available to everyone and essential to no one. The person who says yes with intention becomes someone worth inviting.

The Corollary: Earn Your Seat

There is, of course, a corollary. When you do say yes, you owe the room your full presence. You arrive appropriately dressed, switched on, and prepared to engage. You are not a spectator. You are a participant, and participation has a standard.

You have almost certainly shared an evening with that one person who contributes nothing. He sits in the corner of the conversation like a drain rather than a current, pulling energy out of the room rather than adding to it. His presence makes the evening slightly heavier for everyone. Do not be that person. If you are going to take up a seat at the table, earn it.

This does not mean you must perform. Not everyone's natural role is the sparkle: the wit, the raconteur, the one holding the room. Some people's greatest gift in a social setting is the quality of their listening, and a good listener is rarer and more valued than most people realize. Good listening is not, as my Aunt Lee used to say, "being a bump on a log." It is eye contact, a well-timed nod, a follow-up question that tells the speaker you were paying attention, a contribution that moves the conversation forward rather than stalling it. It is an active thing, and a form of generosity. The rule is simple: if you are reluctant to be a good guest, do not go. Your exclusivity only means something if your presence, when given, is worth having.

126. LOVE YOUR WORK

If you can do what you prefer, wonderful. But if this season of life does not allow for that, do not abandon the idea of enjoying your work altogether. Use your creative intelligence to shape the job you have into a job that interests you.

Even the most ordinary task has room for artistry. Martha Stewart built an empire on exactly that premise, showing an entire generation of homemakers how to turn drudgery into a domain of expertise and beauty. We are all responsible for shaping our atmosphere by bringing quality and flair to our work.

I often think of the woman who helps care for my home. Many

people would assume that cleaning someone else's house could not possibly be a satisfying job, but she seems to take pleasure in what she does. She moves through the space with care, unhurried, adding extra flourishes as she goes. She folds towels just so and leaves whimsical shapes in the toilet paper and paper towels: details that make a house feel loved.

I cleaned houses during my college breaks, and I am sorry to report that I brought nowhere near this level of attention to the work. Watching her now reminds me that joy lives in the attitude, intention, and playfulness we bring to the work right in front of us. This, too, is living from your code.

127. CRAFT A GENTEEL OPERATING SYSTEM

Watch footage of Queen Elizabeth in a crowd and you will notice something difficult to name at first. She was a small woman, often dwarfed by those surrounding her, and yet she was the fixed point in every room. It was not just the hat or the bright colors she wore, though those helped. It was what she was not doing. She was not scanning the room. She was not fidgeting, leaning, checking, adjusting, touching her hair, or self-consciously aware of being watched. She was still. Completely, deliberately, almost unnervingly so, and that stillness created a gravitational field that the movement of everyone around her only amplified. She had, without apparent effort, separated herself from the crowd by the discipline of not joining its clamor.

This is what a genteel operating system looks like from the outside. It is not softness. It is not niceness. It is a quality of self-possession so complete that it reads, in a world of constant reactivity, as almost otherworldly. The noble person (and the nobility I am characterizing has nothing to do with birth or title) exists on a different frequency. Where others are pulled into drama, they remain unruffled. Where others fill the silence, they are comfortable with it. Where others telegraph every emotion as it crosses their face, they have learned the extraordinary power of the unreadable pause.

The average person operates on reflex. They are provoked and they respond immediately, automatically, at full volume. The genteel person operates on a slight delay, and that delay is everything. In it lives the choice of how to respond, what to say, and whether to engage at all. Those three seconds, as we discussed earlier, are where character becomes visible.

This does not mean coldness. Quite the opposite. Because they are not wasting their energy on reactivity, the genteel person can offer something far rarer: attention. They listen without preparing their rebuttal. They look at you when you speak. They disagree without needing to wound. In close relationships (marriage, family, deep friendship), this quality builds trust. People know they can bring their mess, their fears, and their failures, and they will not be met with judgment or theatrics. That trust is not easily earned and not easily replaced.

At work and in public life, the effect is equally distinct. A genteel person who handles pressure without visible strain, who does not gossip or escalate, who treats the intern with the same courtesy as the executive: that person accumulates an authority that loudness and aggression cannot match.

In a world that rewards uproar, choosing not to react is not passivity. It is, in the most precise sense of the word, resistance. It says: the commotion outside does not set my temperature inside. I will move through my life at my frequency, by my code. That, in the end, is what Queen Elizabeth was communicating without saying a word, and it is available to anyone willing to practice it. King Charles has the same quality, which tells you something important: this is not a personality type. It is a discipline. It can be learned.

128. LEARN TO COMMUNICATE YOUR IDEAS

Professor Patrick Henry Winston spent decades at MIT directing the Artificial Intelligence Laboratory, and for more than forty years he gave the same January lecture to overflow crowds. It was called *How to Speak.* Its premise was that your success in life is not determined by the brilliance of your ideas. It is determined by your ability to communicate them. What you know is only part of the equation. The larger part is whether you can get other people to understand it, believe it, and act on it. An extraordinary idea that cannot be communicated is an idea that does not exist in the world.

This is another way of stacking the deck. Most people invest enormous energy in becoming competent and almost none in learning to express that competence. They assume the work will speak for itself. It rarely does. Learning to articulate your ideas with clarity, force, and memorability is one of the highest-leverage skills you can add to your syllabus, because it multiplies every other skill you possess. A doctor who can explain a diagnosis, a designer who can defend a concept, a manager who can rally a team: these are not merely competent people. They are people whose competence lands.

> Dr. Winston's talk, *How to Speak*, has been an MIT tradition for over forty years and is available free on MIT OpenCourseWare. In Further Reading at the end of this book, I cite the talk and how to find it. It is very much worth watching.

129. BE A CELEBRITY

In that same lecture, Dr. Winston shared an anecdote that has stayed with me. He found himself at a dinner seated next to Julia Child and asked her, as the evening wore on, how it felt to be famous. She considered the question for a moment, then said: "You get used to it." Dr. Winston said the remark struck him like a thunderclap, not because of what she said, but because of what it implied. You may get used to being famous. You never get used to being ignored.

What Dr. Winston was describing was not vanity. He was describing strategic visibility: the idea that recognition is a tool, and people whose ideas are heard widely have cultivated a level of prominence that makes the hearing possible. You do not have to be a household name. You do not need a television show or a million followers. Within your field, your community, your industry, or your neighborhood, become known for a wise perspective, a skill, or a standard of excellence. It is one of the most powerful things you can do for your ideas. Celebrity at any scale means your contributions get a seat at the table. That is not relying on luck. It is stacking the deck.

130. BUILD YOUR VISIBILITY

Visibility does not require a publicist or a podcast. It requires something far more accessible: consistency and a point of view. Begin where you are. If you have professional expertise, start sharing it in writing, in conversation, in the rooms you occupy. The person who regularly says the intelligent thing, who sends the thoughtful note, who shows up prepared when others have not, is building a reputation. Reputation, accumulated over time, is visibility.

Dr. Winston's lecture is itself a masterclass in this principle. He had something worth saying and continued to say it with discipline and craft. You do not need forty years. You need a point of view that you express articulately. Write the article. Give the talk. Raise your hand in the meeting. Host the dinner. Teach the workshop. Each of these compounds your visibility so that people associate your name with intelligence, expertise, taste, or reliability. That credential helps get more of your ideas heard and implemented.

131. CURATE YOUR INNER CIRCLE

Jim Rohn's oft-quoted observation that you are the average of the five people you spend the most time with sounds like a motivational poster until you sit with it. Then it becomes slightly alarming. Look at the five people who have the most access to your time and energy right now. Are they smart and curious? Do they challenge you? Do they make you want to be better, think bigger, or work harder? Or do they keep you comfortable, make you feel small, or convince you that the world is a difficult and limited place?

The Environment You Choose

The people in your inner circle are not just your social life. They are one of the most powerful strategic advantages available to you in stacking the deck. Most people leave this advantage to chance or neglect it completely.

Every serious student of achievement, from athletes to artists to founders, understands that environment shapes performance. You can think bigger than the room you are standing in, but it takes Herculean effort. You can sustain ambition that no one around you recognizes or reflects back, but the energy required is enormous. The five people you allow closest to you form the habitat inside which your work, your confidence, and your vision of what is possible either expand or contract. This is not just metaphor. It is mechanics.

The Gilded Talisman's billionaire Alexander Girard understands this. He does not wait for the right people to find him. He is intentional about who he learns from, who he collaborates with, and who he allows into the milieu where his thinking happens. A gardener who never thins the beds does not end up with more flowers; she ends up with a tangle where nothing exceptional can grow. Your inner circle works the same way. The people you choose to keep close to you either expand your sense of what is possible or confirm your limitations, often without either of you noticing.

The Energy Misallocation

Most people do not deliberately choose who belongs in their inner circle. Think about the five people who occupy your innermost circle. Are they there by default, by relation, by habit, or by your own sheer insistence?

Be honest. Do these five people encourage you or discourage you? Are there family members in your inner circle who greet your openly shared plans and ideas with amusement, disdain, or reasons you will never succeed? If so, this is an elegance leak and a profound misallocation of strategic resources. Is there an old friend in your inner circle who was comfortable with the previous version of you and finds the current one unsettling? Do those in your inner circle truly want to be there, or have you spent years chasing closeness with people you wish would reciprocate, but who are really not interested?

Not everyone you love, or who loves you, belongs in your inner circle. Love and influence are not the same thing. Proximity does not equal alignment. Does this mean you have to abandon the people you love? Of course not. You can love someone deeply, honor the relationship sincerely, and still recognize that their fears, limitations, or worldview should not be the weather system inside which you make your most important decisions. This is not about withholding information or distancing yourself. It is about sequencing. Share the outcome once you are confident in it. The people who would have talked you out of it in the planning stage will often be the first to celebrate with you upon completion.

The Garden You Are Neglecting

If you are pouring yourself into inner circle relationships that resist you, you are likely overlooking high-quality relationships within reach. You may have a colleague, a peripheral friend, or someone you admire who is smart, generous, and always in your corner. Who do you call when you need a pep talk or a wise listener? When you are discouraged and need to think accurately? Who inspires you and helps you feel like the most competent version of yourself? Who tells you the truth? That is a gold-standard relationship. What are you investing in it in return?

It often happens that the relationships that feel obligatory absorb the lion's share of your attention. This is one of the more invisible ways people hold themselves back: the habitual misallocation of attention. They water the concrete and neglect the garden.

Which brings us back, more pointedly than Rohn perhaps intended, to his observation. If you are not growing, if your outcomes feel smaller than your capabilities, do not look only at who discourages you. Look also at the high-quality people within your reach whom you have neglected. Ask yourself what might still be possible if you re-evaluate your circle and put effort into those relationships.

Acquaintances are people you like and enjoy: colleagues, neighbors, familiar faces in a shared context. The connection is sincere but circumstantial; if the context disappears, so usually does the bond. Treat them warmly. Share nothing of consequence.

Friends are people you have chosen, and who have chosen you back, outside of circumstance. You share history, affection, and goodwill. They see the finished chapters of your life, not the rough drafts, and not the strategy.

Family are people to whom you are bound by blood, marriage, or long shared history. You may love them deeply, and they may love you, but that love does not automatically qualify them for inner circle access. Some family members are indeed also trusted inner circle members. Others are best placed in an outer ring, where you can love and honor the relationship without including their fears and opinions in your choices. You are not demoting them; you are right-sizing their influence so that it matches how you experience them in your life.

Your inner circle is the smallest ring, the hardest to enter, and where you place your most deliberate relational effort. These are the people you might call before a decision, not after. They have earned the right to your doubts, your half-formed ambitions, and your private fears, because they have shown, repeatedly, that they hold those confidences with care. They tell you the truth with tact. They are invested in your growth, not merely entertained by your company. You leave an hour with them feeling more alive, more capable, and clearer than when you arrived. Your inner circle will probably number five people or fewer. If you can find three who meet your standards, you are richer and better positioned than most.

These distinctions are private, internal calibrations: not grievances to air and not verdicts to announce. You are mentally assigning the proper level of access to the various people in your sphere and directing your deepest relational investments accordingly.

132. FRENEMIES

This category should be wrapped in caution tape. Pay particular attention to people who call themselves your friends but greet your good news without warmth or celebration. A promotion, a finished project, or a personal victory lands with them in a cloud of silence, a quick subject change, or a faintly backhanded comment.

These are frenemies: people whose affection appears sincere on the surface, but whose resentment runs just beneath it. Robert Greene devoted an entire chapter of *The 48 Laws of Power* to this figure, and the warning he issued there is worth taking seriously: the frenemy is more dangerous than an open enemy, because you have already let them inside your perimeter. They minimize your work or do not acknowledge it at all. They are not rooting for you. They will not help you, and they may subtly undermine you — not always from malice, but from the drag of their jealousy or doubt.

One of the most frustrating elegance leaks is trying to convert a frenemy into a friend or ally. You pour energy into proving yourself to someone who has no intention of seeing you or connecting with you. Distance yourself from them, not dramatically, but deliberately. Be cordial. Keep interactions light. Share nothing of your private ambitions or your interior life with them. They have not earned that access.

Compassion and Clarity

An elegance code allows you to see your circles with compassion and clarity. It frees you from trying to convert the unconvertible. It lets you inwardly place people at the level where they belong, care for them there without resentment, and direct your energy toward the relationships that can bear the weight of your vision.

12

THE SECRET FLIP

The great enemy of the truth is very often not the lie... but the myth, persistent, persuasive, and unrealistic. Belief in myths allows the comfort of opinion without the discomfort of thought.

John F. Kennedy

MOST PEOPLE TRY TO change their lives by changing their circumstances: the job, the city, the relationship, the wardrobe. They swap scenery and cast members but keep running the same internal script, then feel betrayed when everything starts to feel the same again.

The Secret Flip is a revolutionary way to think differently about yourself and your place in the world. When you operate by your own elegance code and direct observation instead of the myths and stories society promotes—what passes for "normal" or "what people should do"—the signals you have spent your life obeying lose their power.

The facts of your life may not change overnight. Your interpretation of those facts can, and that shift in meaning determines whether you move through your days like a supplicant or like someone with private internal standards. This chapter is an invitation to flip the script.

People who exist at a certain level do not live in a different world. They run a different operating system. The same cues come in: the irritated colleague, the impersonal red tape, the do this or else letter, the social expectations. Most of us were trained to interpret those cues the way society tells us we must.

People operating from a code receive those exact same cues and flip the meaning 180 degrees. Friction means their code is working. An irritated person means their boundary is holding. The bureaucracy is just doing its job. Same information. Opposite interpretation. Over time, that flip compounds into a completely different life.

133. FRICTION AND IRRITATION

For most people, the rule is simple: if someone is annoyed with me, I must have done something wrong. The status flip is the opposite: if I have acted according to my code and someone is put out about it, that is proof that my boundary is effective. You do not have to enjoy upsetting people, but you can stop treating mild displeasure as anything other than information: my center is distinct from theirs, and that is fine.

> A powerful reflection question here is, "Is this discomfort because I have betrayed myself, or because I have finally stopped betraying myself?" If it is the second, the friction is not a problem to fix; it is proof that you are solidly in your own lane.

134. TIME AND AVAILABILITY

In the average script, other people's requests define your schedule, and being constantly reachable feels synonymous with being responsible. The status flip treats time differently: my schedule is primary; other people's requests fit around it, not through it.

Historically, high-status people treated their hours as scarce and important: limited calling hours, audiences only at set times, long delays before responses.

In modern life, the pattern continues in a subtler form. People with higher perceived status feel more control over their time and environment and adjust others to fit them rather than the other way around. So where you might think, "They've called three times; I'm being rude," the higher-status inner script is closer to, "They've called three times. I'll respond when it suits my priorities." The persistence of a system is not proof of your obligation. It may be proof of theirs.

135. OBLIGATIONS AND "SHOULDS"

Most people live by an unspoken rule: if someone wants something from me and they are exasperated, I am probably obligated and I have failed. A person of status lives by a different rule: I am obligated only by my code, my explicit commitments, and my conscience, not by other people's expectations or disappointment.

We all answer to someone. Even CEOs answer to boards, and boards answer to shareholders; no one is completely free. The difference lies in what we recognize as binding. People who grow up with entrenched privilege treat external "shoulds" as suggestions to be weighed against their own standards and rank, rather than commands to be obeyed by default. Applied to something as mundane as repeated calls from a dentist's office, the old internal script says, "They keep insisting; I am neglecting my responsibility to make an appointment." The flipped script says, "They are running their system; I am running mine. Health is part of my code; I will act when it aligns. Their automated urgency is not my moral emergency."

136. THE CORE DIAGNOSTIC

At the center of this chapter is one diagnostic question: "Is this friction happening because I violated my code, or because I honored it?" If you violated your code, you adjust yourself. If you honored it, you allow the friction to belong to the other person or to the situation.

That is a very different rubric from "No one is upset, therefore I am okay." It moves you from chasing universal approval to guarding your internal alignment.

137. ONE PERCENT RULES FOR NORMAL PEOPLE

The point of the Secret Flip is not to imitate the worst parts of entitlement. It is to borrow the parts that protect soundness and dignity. When someone is mildly bothered because you honored your values, treat that as a green light, not a red flag. When systems nag you—appointments, platforms, subscriptions—remember that their effort is not evidence of your duty, only of their priorities. This is as it should be.

When you feel tired or over-demanded, ask whether this is a cue to take action or a cue to protect your system. When rules appear, remember that some are universal but many are just defaults; your elegance code decides which are binding in your life, based on your values, vision, and center of balance. Once you have named your code, you can use small frictions as feedback that you are living by that code, instead of forever trying to earn a gold star in other people's systems.

If you adopted this flipped interpretation even ten percent more often, where would you notice the difference first: in your calendar, in your guilt level, or in your relationships?

138. IT'S ALL NEGOTIABLE

Most people meet a system of forms, deadlines, policies, and "this is how we do things here," and assume it is fixed. Their job is to comply, quickly if possible. People who occupy a different tier read the same systems as negotiable. Rules are the default, not decrees. Processes are first drafts, not holy writs.

They ask for exceptions, request alternatives, or simply proceed as though their case might reasonably be handled differently. This does not always make them admirable, but it does make them powerful. You do not have to become a scofflaw to borrow the flip. You can begin by asking yourself whenever you meet a rigid system: "Is this truly non-negotiable, or is this just the easiest way for the system to manage the masses?"

COUNTERWEIGHT

The Secret Flip is a dangerous tool in the wrong hands. Interpreting every irritation as proof of your superiority is not elegance; it is delusion. If you invoke your code to excuse cruelty, laziness, or broken promises, you have not flipped the script; you have armored your worst impulses.

There will be times when friction appears because you were careless, unkind, or blind to firm constraints. In those moments, the honest answer to the diagnostic question—"Did I violate my code?"—is yes. Then the flip does not apply. You adjust, you repair, you apologize.

The power of this chapter lies in precision. Use the flip only when you are genuinely aligned with your values and have done the work to define them. Without that inner rigor, your code is a hollow excuse for entitlement. With it, you can endure other people's displeasure without collapsing, and remain corrigible where you are truly at fault.

139. TIME AND ACCESS

For most people, time is something other people take. The phone rings, they run to answer; the email lands, or someone "just has a quick question," and the day rearranges itself around whoever is loudest or closest. Availability feels synonymous with responsibility. Higher-status people invert that. Their schedule is their fundamental structure; other people's requests slot in around it, if at all.

Historically, this looked like calling hours, appointment-only access, and long, unapologetic gaps between responses. In modern form, it is the person who guards their mornings, controls when and how they are reachable, and treats their own priorities as the spine of the day rather than the leftover margins. The flip here is easy to say but difficult to practice: "My time is the default. Other people's access is the exception." Once you adopt it, even partially, your calendar looks a little more like it belongs to you.

The Recognition Flip

The default assumption in modern life is that to be seen is to matter: followers, mentions, VIP status, and public recognition. The system trains us from childhood to believe visibility is a value, and the reward circuits that fire when we are noticed and admired feel indistinguishable from being loved.

This was not always so, and it is worth understanding why it is so now. For most of human history, anonymity was the default for most people. Peasants, laborers, servants, and women lived obscure lives. The few visible people—royalty, nobility, clergy, some successful merchants—were visible because their roles required them to be. They paid for that visibility in the loss of privacy that always accompanies it. To be seen was to be watched, judged, and constrained. An interior life belonged to those who were left alone.

The democratic revolutions of the eighteenth and nineteenth centuries promised anyone could become visible. *You too can be famous, recognized,* and important. This was offered as liberation from the old hierarchies. In many ways, it was. But it had an unintended consequence. Visibility, once a burden borne by the few, became repackaged as a life goal for the many. Alexis de Tocqueville, traveling in America in the 1830s, wrote about this in *Democracy in America*. He observed that in democratic societies the threat to freedom was no longer the king but the neighbors. The insistent pressure of public opinion whispered: *You are no one if no one knows you.*

By the time mass visibility was democratized, the powerful had moved on. The aristocratic classes, having had visibility for centuries when it was useful, had developed the inverse skill: the deliberate cultivation of privacy as an indication of higher standing. The hidden country house, the discreet membership, the unphotographed wedding. You can drive past the residue of this in any wealthy neighborhood today: large windows facing the road, the architecture displaying itself for admiration; at the next level, the house disappears behind hedges, walls, trees, gates, long drives. What the road sees is foliage. The flip from *display* to *retreat* is a tell of status.

Then two industrial systems arrived to entrench the quest for visibility into a nearly inescapable obsession.

The first was modern advertising. Edward Bernays, working in the 1920s, made the infamous decision to change advertising from product features to identity signaling. The car was no longer a way to get places; it was the woman you became by driving it. A cigarette was no longer a smoke; it was independence, sex appeal, and sophistication. Every purchase became a way to construct a public self.

The woman anxious about visibility responds as expected. The woman with an elegance code is not for sale to that pitch. A century of surreptitious advertising has produced a culture in which the language of identity and the language of consumption are now nearly indistinguishable. You cannot escape the lure of advertising by knowing its effects. You elude it by owning something more valuable than what advertising sells—your code.

The second system to arrive was social media. A platform that monetizes attention requires that you perform for an audience, because the performance generates engagement, which generates data, which generates revenue. The platform's incentives are perfectly aligned with training you to believe that being seen is proof that you matter. A woman who logs off and lives privately produces no revenue. She is therefore useless to the system.

So the system trains for visibility. None of this requires a conspiracy. It requires only that the structures select for compliance.

This is where your code interrupts everything. An elegance code is not a slightly nicer way of being seen. It is a whole different operating system. Once you have located your values, your vision for your life, and your center of balance, the visibility apparatus loses its grip. You do not need the dopamine hit of being noticed because you are already aligned. You do not need the affirmation of strangers because you affirm yourself. You are not purchasable through identity-signaling because your identity is established on your own ground. You are no longer steerable through approval because approval is not a currency you accept.

What this looks like in practice: you appear in public without posturing. You dress for yourself rather than for a phantom audience. You can decline to share your accomplishments on social media without feeling you have failed to capitalize. You change your mind in private. You can attend an event without documenting it. You can turn down the opportunity for praise without feeling empty. Your inner life is yours.

This flip is not from visibility to invisibility. You may choose to be seen as much as you like. The flip is from visibility as a value to visibility as an occasional circumstance.

140. THE PRICE OF ADMISSION

The average script views a bill as an imposition: enjoying the hot shower but resenting the water bill, or enjoying the warm house but resenting the gas bill. The flip sees a bill as the price of admission.

The same logic operates beyond personal bills. Owning a private jet would cost millions; flying out of an airport costs the price of a ticket. A 30,000-acre wilderness preserve would cost a fortune to acquire and maintain; an annual national parks pass costs eighty dollars. A private fire department, a private road network, or private bridges would bankrupt almost anyone. The collective cost of public infrastructure is a fraction of what self-administering the same services would cost an individual. The flip is to recognize the bargain of civilization and stop leaking energy into resenting the benefits it provides.

141. STUFF HAPPENS

Most people are trained from an early age to see life as something that happens to them. The job market collapses, the boss is unreasonable; the family is demanding; the economy is unfair. They adapt, endure, and explain. The flip is a different reflex assumption: "I shape what happens here." When something goes wrong, it is just as annoying, but the internal question is different. It is not, "Why is this happening to me?" but, "In what ways am I responsible? What can I change? What lever can I pull? Who can I call?"

The same setbacks happen to everyone, but an average mindset resigns itself to, *I guess this is just how it is for people like me.* The flip sees the situation as a design problem. It is important that this mindset does not curdle into entitlement or unethical behavior, as it can in its worst forms. If you remain ethical and positive, the underlying cognitive habit is worth noticing: a woman with a code assumes she has agency. Your elegance code lets you borrow the best of that assumption without its arrogance. Instead of deciding a situation is fixed because it is unpleasant, you ask, *Where, exactly, is my area of influence here?* That one question moves you, inch by inch, from background character to author.

142. THE BEAUTY FLIP

Average thinking treats one's face and body as a problem to be fixed, and beauty as something applied with makeup and processing. The flip starts with a different premise: I am fine as I am. Aerin Lauder sits at the helm of a cosmetics empire, yet she wears minimal makeup. The signal is not indifference; it is the confidence that there is nothing to compensate for.

In my novel *The Roses of Ainsworth Manor*, Nell Ainsworth remarks on the gap between how social media packages "old money" and how it looks in person. Old money often resembles an age-progressed version of its childhood photographs. The haircut, color, and overall impression change very little because frequent dramatic reinvention reads as instability or striving.

Nell describes her friend Deirdre this way:

> ...her brunette hair has never been coloured, so it's thick and healthy. She buys Mane & Tail shampoo and conditioner at the tack shop, figuring if it works for her horse, it will work for her. Skincare comes from the chemist: Ivory soap, Pond's cold cream, and a moisturiser like Oil of Olay. She is scrubbed fresh and wears not a spot of makeup, unless it's a tinted lip balm and

> a swipe of bronzer brushed where the sun hits naturally; she has no interest in what is popularly known as "sculpting." She wears hand-me-down cashmere from N. Peal, Johnstons of Elgin, or Pringle. If she's feeling modern, it's Loro Piana. If she wears a watch—and Deirdre does—it's a Reverso or the smallest, most feminine Cartier Tank: no oversized men's pieces, nothing that would call attention to her. She sports a plain gold wedding band on her left hand and a battered signet ring on her right, the only daytime jewellery other than the pearls her great-grandmother gave her. No diamonds before six. She wouldn't dream of using fillers or extensions to change her natural features. Her look isn't about showing off, looking young, or looking "hot." It's built on a foundation of certainty that she is enough, and she always will be.

A similar logic governs branding. With high-status individuals, you will almost never see an obvious designer logo. Their thinking might as well be: Why on earth would I walk around with someone else's name on my body? Carolyn Bessette-Kennedy was said to have external labels removed from clothes and accessories before she would wear them. Operating from an elegance code, the cut, fabric, and line of the garment serve the wearer; the wearer is not a walking clothes hanger for the brand.

143. THE CONFIDENCE FLIP: CERTAINTY BEFORE ACCURACY

Average thinking says, "I should not speak until I am absolutely sure I am correct." High-status individuals flip that. Their unspoken rule is closer to: if I speak as though I am certain, people will assume I am right enough. I can adjust later if necessary. The content of the idea matters, but the manner of delivery does a disproportionate amount of the work.

In one series of studies published in the Journal of Personality and Social Psychology, psychologist Peter Belmi and his colleagues found that people who saw themselves as higher social class spoke and rated themselves more confidently, even when they were no more accurate than others. They had been raised to expect that their opinions carry weight and their perspectives deserve airtime. Other individuals, by contrast, are trained in the virtues of humility, deference, and "not getting above yourself," so they self-edit before they speak; they double-check, soften, and hedge. Observers consistently mistook confidence for greater competence. The result is that the least self-doubting voice in the room is often the one people follow, not the person who is most intelligent and informed.

This does not mean you should bluff, posture, or pounce on every half-second of silence. In conversation, most people rush to fill any gap. Those who can tolerate a few beats of pause without scrambling to talk are read as more composed. Research on "powerful" versus "powerless" speech suggests that it is not deliberate pauses, but hedges and hesitations—*I might be wrong, but..., um, kind of*—that erode credibility. The takeaway is to speak up when it is your turn, without the nervous scaffolding.

The Compliment Flip

When complimented, many people deflect, minimize, or return the compliment with one of their own. *Oh, this old thing* is a classic deflection. The flipped response is *Thank you*. Full stop. Diminishing a compliment is an elegance leak. So is explaining where the item came from or mentioning how cheap it was. There is also no requirement to return a compliment.

The reason this is a flip: deflecting compliments looks modest but is a leaky way of seeking reassurance, and it places the complimenter in the awkward position of having to defend their compliment. Whether or not you trust the giver's taste, it is more efficient to accept a compliment and change the subject. When I get too precious about accepting compliments, Golda Meir's alleged comment to a self-deprecating diplomat always makes me laugh: "Don't be so humble, you're not that great."

144. QUESTIONS AND CURIOSITY

Have you noticed how few questions people ask? For most, not knowing is something to hide. Elegant people flip that because they do not equate ignorance with shame. Their assumption is: the world is vast and I have priorities, so of course there are things I do not know. When they want to know something, they ask. Not apologetically, not with a softening preamble like *Sorry, I'm not sure if this is obvious, but...* or *You probably know more about this than I do...*, just a straightforward question, delivered with curiosity and the expectation of an answer.

Curiosity is a consistent quality of elegance. Princess Diana was famous for her warmth and her way of making strangers feel seen. If you watch footage of her interacting with a crowd, you see the same pattern again and again: she does not hurry; she asks questions, then listens carefully to the answers. She does not pretend to know everything, and she appears more charismatic as a result.

Your elegance code encourages you to be direct: *How does that work?* or *Walk me through that.* You are busy but interested, and you have a right to have your questions answered. The diagnostic for this flip is: Am I asking enough questions? If not, is that because I don't want the answer, or because I don't want to appear ignorant? If it is the second, this is a place where your code can reclaim territory from social anxiety.

The Question Flip

There are questions, on the other hand, that polite society agrees one must never ask: *How much did that cost? How old are you? What does that pay? How much did the house go for?* One learns by adolescence that certain questions are nosy or vulgar, and spends one's adulthood carefully not asking them.

Here is the surprising part. High-status people do not ask these questions either, but not for the same reasons everyone else avoids them. The flip is not about manners. It is about disinterest.

Most people believe a status woman refrains from these questions out of squeamishness or breeding. The reality is plainer: she does not ask because the answers are of no interest. Her own choices are not contingent on what other people pay, earn, or buy. She is not gathering comparative data because she is not living comparatively. The price of someone else's house is not relevant to her—but if it ever becomes relevant, if she needs the information, you can be sure she will ask directly. She does not ask the age of the woman across the table because she does not evaluate herself with those comparisons. The salary of an acquaintance is not relevant to whether her own work feels meaningful. If there is no useful information in those answers for her personally, the questions never form.

The second half of the flip is also thought-provoking. When she is asked these same questions, she does not flinch. The Duchess, when asked her age, says it without ceremony. The man asked what he paid for the painting names the figure. The woman asked her income answers if she chooses to, and declines if she does not, but does so without apology. Her inner balance is stable, so the question itself threatens nothing.

The logic is subtle but fascinating: the average person experiences personal questions as intrusive because the answers would reveal her place in the comparison. A person with an elegance code experiences them as merely unimportant or unnecessary. When you operate with your elegance code, you need not defend your position. The questions slide off because there is nothing for them to attach to. The magic of operating from your code is not that it raises you a rung on the ladder, but that it allows you to step off the ladder altogether.

You can borrow the Question Flip without becoming rude or evasive. Notice the next time you feel the urge to ask a comparative question: *How much did you pay? What does she make? How old is she?* Ask yourself what you would do with the answer. How would it affect your values, vision, and center of balance? If the answer is *adjust how I feel about my own situation*, that is a leak to plug, because with a code it is information you do not need.

The next time you are asked a question like this, notice your reaction. Is there a threat in the question itself, or in your sense that your answer would somehow diminish you? If you can answer plainly, or decline plainly, without feeling either disclosed or exposed, your code is working.

13

CREATE YOUR AESTHETIC

Permission to Nell is irrelevant. She knows with absolute confidence that she belongs anywhere she wants to be. She's disarming, sometimes exasperating, but impossible to look away from. Nell makes life feel as though everything is possible.

The Roses of Ainsworth Manor by Nina Gates

RETAILERS AND INFLUENCERS PERPETUATE the myth that to be stylish, elegant, and unforgettable, you must wear certain clothing and accessories. This is a nice idea, and it would be so much easier to be beautifully dressed if it were true. Clothing does communicate through its unique sartorial language, and for this reason it's a mistake to ignore it entirely. A new outfit can make you feel extraordinary in the moment; however, it cannot create style, and it will not make you elegant. Audrey Hepburn was stylish in Roman Holiday wearing Gregory Peck's pajamas. It was not her clothes, but her inner sparkle that made her unforgettable. Her partnership with Hubert de Givenchy was one of fashion's great love stories, but his creations only framed what was already there. Clothing can signal our affiliations, priorities, and worldview, but it cannot supply character or substance. And while an outfit could conceivably make you unforgettable, it's worth asking whether that's the kind of unforgettable you want.

Don't get me wrong; I love clothes. I am passionate about the art and science of fashion and studied it in college. Pouring a tall glass of iced tea and flipping through the latest Vogue is one of my favorite ways to spend a rainy afternoon. Seeing what talented designers offer each season never gets old. I love to duck into interesting shops when I travel and take in beautifully styled shelves and windows, the way an art lover walks a gallery just to enjoy what human beings are capable of making. However, if one could pull out a credit card and buy elegance, the world would look very different than it does. Most of us have tried exactly that—bought the dress, the bag, the shoes that were supposed to transform us, only to discover by the third wear that we felt exactly like ourselves again, only with less money and more dry-cleaning.

The hard but hopeful truth is this: clothes cannot make you elegant, but they can help you express yourself. The way you dress, decorate, entertain, and travel can support your sense of identity, reinforce your values, and give form to your vision. Elegance is free. It lives inside you, not in what hangs in your closet. That means it's available to anyone willing to do the patient work of determining their own through-line: their values, their vision, and their authentic center of balance. Then, what you put on your body, and how you live, becomes a rich and powerful exploration of personal style.

There is even a clinical term for this. Psychologists call it self-congruity—the degree to which what you put on your body feels like an extension of your real or ideal self. When your clothes and your self-concept agree, you experience less internal friction and more emotional stability, even if no one else finds your look remarkable. In the pages that follow, we will craft the practical aspects of your aesthetic: your visual language, your signatures, and the considered choices that add up to a life that looks and feels like you.

145. BE ICONIC

Decoding Style: Reading Beneath the Surface

Most style advice points you toward people you admire and tells you to take notes. Pin outfits onto a mood board. Buy what they buy. Study what they wear. Copy the formula. This book is going to suggest something more interesting—and considerably more useful. The difference is this: instead of copying what you see, you are going to learn to read it.

It might be a character in a movie, a person you notice across the room, or an image you save on Pinterest without quite knowing why. When someone's style stops you cold, pay attention, because something significant is happening at the level of your code. Learning to identify it is one of the most powerful things you can do as you develop or refine your personal aesthetic and ethos.

Here is how to do it.

Step 1: Name the feeling before you describe a single item.Before you identify what someone is wearing, stop and register what you feel when you look at them. Not "she's wearing a trench coat"—that comes later. First, find one word describing the overall impression. Calm. Severe. Playful. Unhurried. Grounded. Dangerous. This feeling word is your first clue, because you are not responding entirely to the clothes. You are responding to what the clothes are expressing.

Step 2: This is where the secret almost always lives. Restraint is load-bearing in elegant aesthetics. Ask yourself: *what could this person be doing that they are not doing? What have they left out? What are they declining?* The gap between what is available and what is chosen is where character reveals itself.

Step 3: Find the contrast.The most riveting aesthetics are almost never a single note—they are two opposing forces held in deliberate tension. This is the principle that separates an aesthetic that looks good from one that is genuinely arresting.

Consider Carolyn Bessette-Kennedy. Style guides describe her as "effortless" or "minimalist" and tell you to find a white slip dress and call it done. But that analysis misses everything. CBK was not just about ease. She was ease against a backdrop of everything that could have been maximalist: extraordinary beauty, extraordinary wealth, the most scrutinized marriage in America, and a fashion world that would have dressed her in anything she wanted. The ease was not neutral. It was ease in direct defiance of every expectation and every available excess she could have chosen, but didn't. That tension—restraint held against enormous potential drama—is what made her impossible to look away from. The brown corduroys and the plastic tortoiseshell headband weren't interesting objects. They were interesting *choices*, and her choices were a statement about who she was and what she refused to do. That is an elegance code at work.

Or consider a Ralph Lauren advertisement from the 1990s: a man in paint-spattered jeans, an artist's afro, the unmistakable visual language of the creative outsider—and then a tweed jacket and a rep striped bow tie laid right on top of it. You saw that image and thought, *Wait. What?* That disorientation was the point. Two worlds, two vocabularies, two identities held simultaneously, resolved by neither, made more compelling by the collision. That is not a styling trick. That is a personality expressed as aesthetic tension.

Step 4: Name the underlying value in one word.CBK: ease. Audrey Hepburn: refinement. Steve Jobs: transcendence. The Ralph Lauren man: duality. That single word is the principle animating everything. It is what you are initially responding to when someone's aesthetic delights you, and it has almost nothing to do with what they are wearing.

Step 5: This is the pivot that makes the whole exercise personal. If the word that describes CBK is "ease" and that word resonates somewhere in you, the question is not *how do I dress like her?* The question is: *where does ease already live in my life, and what would it look like to let it expand into everything I do?*

What this practice gives you is something no shopping trip ever will: the ability to look at any person whose aesthetic compels you, understand what they are expressing and why it moves you. A stranger on the street, a figure in a vintage photograph, a character in a film—every one of them becomes a lesson not in what to buy, but in what to be, and in who you are, if you are willing to look.

Style books hand you a formula. This one hands you a method of thinking that you can apply to anyone, anywhere, for the rest of your life.

146. HOLD THE TENSION

Every style quiz you have ever taken has sorted you into a category. Dramatic. Natural. Classic. Romantic. Sporty. The idea is that once you know your "type," you can shop accordingly, dress consistently, and present a unified, legible image to the world.

Here is the problem with that: the most compelling people are not legible in thirty seconds. They are not one thing. They contain contradictions, and rather than resolving those contradictions to make themselves easier to understand, they have learned to hold them and to play them up. That unresolvable quality is what makes them compelling.

Think about the artist and the Ivy Leaguer occupying the same body, neither one canceling the other out. Think about the woman whose ease is so emphatic it borders on provocation. Think about the old-money family in frayed khakis who happen to own half the city. None of these aesthetics are tidy. None of them would score well on a style quiz. That is not a weakness. That is the whole point.

Your contrasts are not inconsistencies to be ironed out. They are your most interesting material.

151. DON'T LET YOURSELF BE PIGEONHOLED

The most enduring aesthetics are not built. They are deposited layer by layer and choice by choice, until a person's values become so visually consistent they read as a signature. The people we call iconic were not trying to look like anything. They were trying to be something. The look was incidental.

Artist Georgia O'Keeffe's wardrobe was minimalist, often home-made, and deeply intentional, like her art and her interiors. She did not follow the fashion rules of her time. She crafted a spare, personal elegance entirely her own, and she became more interesting with every passing decade rather than less.

Photographer Richard Avedon helped define an era's idea of visual elegance. His fashion images were sleek, modern, and full of movement rather than stiff poses. He worked in a simple uniform of shirt and jeans and heavy-rimmed glasses, because he saw himself as a working portraitist, not decoration. His elegance came from the through-line in his life: his way of seeing, his exacting standards, his pared-back aesthetic, and his refusal to pretend to be something he was not.

Steve Jobs pursued what he called "deep simplicity," stripping products down to their essence so they were clean, intuitive, and humane to use. He described this as finding "elegant solutions." His uniform of a black turtleneck, jeans, and sneakers was the same philosophy worn on a body: plain, focused, and free of the nonessential, so that attention stayed on the work rather than the person presenting it.

Jane Birkin built an aesthetic from the most ordinary pieces: jeans, striped tops, simple dresses, basket bags, and little makeup, and wore them with an unbothered individuality that made each one feel like a choice. As she aged, the silhouette loosened into oversized shirts and wider trousers, but the same essential quality remained unchanged. She was always manifestly herself.

What these four people share is a settled relationship with their values. That settledness is what we respond to when we call someone iconic. We are drawn to people who appear to have solved being human. A person who moves with precision, speaks with unhurried clarity, and wears clothes that fit their life creates a different kind of beauty—not the beauty of perfect features, but the beauty of perfect coherence. When the parts of a life are so well-aligned, it is hypnotic.

That is available to you. Not by copying any of these four people, but by doing what each of them did: deciding what you believe, what you love, and what you absolutely refuse, and then pursuing a way of living with such commitment that style is the evidence left behind.

152. THE WHOLE LIFE

Your two words do not belong only in your closet. Once you have found them, let them flow into everything: the way you set a table on an ordinary weekend, the art you live with, the travel style that suits you, the grocery store that calls to you, the garden you plant—is it a lemon tree on the patio, a bed of dahlias, or pots of tomatoes? The wrapping paper you reach for, the perfume you choose, and whether you prefer white roses or pink tulips. An aesthetic that lives only in your wardrobe is a costume. An aesthetic woven through your life is a philosophy.

This does not require more money, more space, or more time. It requires only attention. Pause before you add something to your life and ask: Does this belong here? Does it speak to one of my words? Does it earn its place? And the equal willingness to release what does not, however beautiful it may be on its own, because beauty that doesn't belong to your world surely belongs to someone else.

When your home, your table, your suitcase, your wardrobe, and your daily habits are all in conversation with each other, something extraordinary happens. You stop managing areas of your life separately and begin living in harmony. The sense of a considered life lived fully is what people respond to when they walk into a room and say, without quite knowing why, this is so *her*.

Which brings us to the most important skill of all.

153. AN AESTHETIC IS CURATED

Curating means carefully choosing what you allow into your life. It's about selecting and caring for things with intention, rather than collecting everything that looks appealing. A curator is like a steward of a collection—she decides what belongs and what has meaning, and she lets the rest go.

To curate is to say, "This I will keep and honor, and this I will release." It is a way of living with discernment and taste, knowing what fits your life and what does not. A curator is not someone who has everything, but someone who has only what she truly values.

She understands that more is not always better, and that clutter—whether in possessions, commitments, relationships, or thoughts—does not create peace. Instead, she finds richness in quality, not quantity, and takes satisfaction in knowing that what remains was chosen on purpose. When we live this way, we notice how much of what is offered to us is not really meant for us, and we see that chasing everything we admire leads to restlessness. A life of fewer, chosen things is not deprivation; it is freedom.

14

CREATE WELLNESS

I did then what I knew how to do. Now that I know better, I do better.

Maya Angelou

FOR MOST OF THE past century, we have treated health as though it lives only in the body. We measure it in numbers: blood pressure, cholesterol, weight, heart rate, scans, labs. We treat the body like a machine, a collection of parts to be fixed, tuned, or replaced as though health were only the absence of breakdown. But we know, deep in our bones, that this is not the whole truth.

A person can have a perfectly functioning body and die of grief. A person can have strong limbs and a sound mind and still be undone by depression, loneliness, or anxiety. What lives in the mind, the heart, the soul does not stay there. It travels. Fear, chronic reactivity, or relentless striving writes itself onto the body in tension, fatigue, and illness. A heart that stays closed, a mind perpetually at war with itself, a soul that feels unseen—none of these leave the body untouched. To be truly well, our inner world must be at peace. Health, then, is not only in the body. It is in the way we carry and experience ourselves in the world.

154. WELLNESS IS NOT A PRESCRIPTION

We have been told that health is a matter of compliance: eat this, avoid that, hit these numbers, log these steps, follow this plan. If you stray, you have failed. It is an exhausting way to live, and for many of us, it doesn't work. Not because we lack discipline, but because what looks like a brilliant idea on paper doesn't feel like a life. It feels like a life sentence.

Some of you love boot camps, cross-training clubs, or any fitness philosophy that considers torment a feature rather than a bug. Keep doing what you love. That is the point. But if the idea of being yelled at before dawn has never once appealed to you, the science is now firmly on your side. In 2022, a study published in Frontiers in Psychology surveying over 270 exercisers across nine health clubs found that enjoyment was the single strongest predictor of exercise habit, frequency, and intention to keep going; ahead of intensity, ahead of discipline, ahead of every external metric they measured. And the "no pain, no gain" doctrine that has guilt-tripped generations of us? In 2011, researchers at Edith Cowan University in Australia found that muscle growth and strength gains were identical whether or not participants experienced any soreness or muscle damage during training. Suffering, it turns out, is not the price of admission to progress. It has just felt that way for a very long time.

I want to be clear: I am not a health professional or medical expert, and nothing in this chapter should be taken as medical advice. Please consult your doctor before undertaking any new wellness initiative. What I can offer is companionship in exploration. As someone who has tried the rules, the diets, and the plans, and keeps arriving at the same question: What if we've been thinking about this all wrong?

155. LISTEN

What if the body isn't the problem? What if, instead of treating it as an enemy to be disciplined or a machine to be optimized, we treated it as an ecosystem to be cherished? What if the body wants to help us be well? And what if the most powerful health practice isn't a plan at all, but a skill—the skill of listening to it?

Listening when the body says I need rest, and stopping. Listening when it says this food makes me feel terrible, and choosing something better next time. Listening when it says I need to move, and playing with your dog, or dancing in the kitchen. The obstacle for most of us isn't a lack of desire—it's years spent training ourselves to override those signals in favor of rules, schedules, and the opinions of strangers on the internet. Reclaiming that inner attunement takes patience and practice, and it begins with one long-overdue act of faith: trusting that our instincts might be on our side.

Because here is what I genuinely believe: most of us don't want to neglect ourselves. Most of us like to move when it feels good—tennis, pickleball, golf, riding a bike, gardening, a long stroll with no particular destination. We enjoy natural food and can tell the difference between something fresh and clean and something that makes us feel heavy and tired. The desire to be well is there. What gets in the way is the noise.

The messaging around health and fitness is often aggressive and condescending enough that it can produce the opposite of its intended effect. I'll confess: sometimes I wonder whether I resist doing the very things I know are good for me out of sheer rebellion against the preaching. I was not surprised, then, to learn that researchers at the University of Michigan found that the traditional "exercise must be hard and intense" message doesn't just fail to motivate most people—it actively works against them, directly conflicting with their natural desire to feel renewed rather than depleted during their leisure time.

The only person harmed by that rebellion, of course, is ourselves. I didn't write this chapter because your fitness level has any bearing on your elegance. I wrote it because the clamor around food, health, and the body is so loud and so relentless that it deserves to be named for what it is—a potential obstacle to feeling at home in yourself.

156. FLOURISH

When I had a horse, I loved watching her play when I turned her out after riding. She would toss her head and run from one end of the pasture to the other at top speed, pulling up and curving around the fence, then running flat out to the other end. She did not do this because she thought, I'd better get my exercise in today. She did it because it felt good to move, because she was jazzed by the raw power of her own muscles and speed, because every part of her was awake to the joy of being exactly what she was.

She wasn't exercising; she was alive. She wasn't checking off a box or punishing herself for yesterday's indulgence. She was running because her body was strong, because the wind was in her mane, because the ground was solid beneath her hooves, because that moment called for motion and she answered without hesitation. There was no plan, no program, no counting of laps or monitoring of heart rate. There was only the pure, unfiltered pleasure of movement, followed just as naturally by stillness when she was done.

A horse does not separate her body from her spirit. She does not think about "working out." She moves because movement is woven into her being; she rests because rest is woven into her being. She grazes, she rolls in the dust, she stands and watches the sky. None of it is self-improvement. All of it is life.

To approach flourishing through play is to remember that part of us. It is to imagine wellness not as a regimen, but as a return to the wholeness that we lost somewhere along the way. Dancing because it feels good to dance, sleeping when it feels good to sleep, laughing because something is funny, eating because it feels good to be nourished, not because we are trying to earn another day on the calendar.

Flourishing, in this sense, is not about forcing the body into a plan. It is about paying attention to it as if it were a high-spirited creature that sometimes longs to gallop, sometimes to wander slowly, sometimes to nap on a warm summer day and do nothing at all. It is about trusting that there is wisdom in our impulses when they are not distorted by shame, comparison, and should.

The richest kind of health may not be found in the effort to live longer, but in the willingness to live better now—to allow ourselves, even for a few minutes, to feel as free as Bella thundering down the length of her pasture, not to become someone "better," but to be, fully and without apology, our own vivid, breathing, powerful self.

157. LIVE

All living beings want to live. Even the tiniest ant, when threatened, will fight for its life. A bird will struggle free from a predator. A plant will stretch toward the light, even in the shade. There is a deep, wordless will in every creature to continue—to breathe, to move, to be.

We are no different. But there is a danger in making living longer the central goal, the measure of a good life. When we fix our gaze on the distant horizon—on years, on decades, on how many more birthdays we can collect. We live as though life is always later. We eat not because food is a pleasure, but because it is "good for longevity." We move not because it feels good, but because it is "necessary." We rest not because we are tired, but because it is "part of the plan." We become so focused on adding years that we lose the only moment we have: this one.

What if the goal were not to live longer, but to live? Not to stretch time, but to deepen it. Not to hoard days, but to inhabit them. My horse did not postpone her joy until she had earned it. She never said, I'll enjoy this pasture when I've lost a few pounds. She was simply here — fully, in her body, in her moment. To live now, fully, is not to reject care for the body. It is to shift the center of gravity: from a machine to be preserved for some distant future, to a living thing that is already here, already worthy, already deserving of kindness and presence.

Eat

Eat because the food tastes good. Eat because the body feels nourished. Eat because a meal shared or savored can be a celebration of being alive. This is not as indulgent an idea as it sounds. A systematic review published in PLOS ONE, analyzing 45 studies, found that eating pleasure, meaning the genuine sensory enjoyment of food, was consistently associated with healthier food choices, better nutritional status, and greater overall wellbeing.

People who enjoyed what they ate made better decisions, not worse ones. Pleasure, it turns out, is not the enemy of good health. Deprivation and distraction are. A Harvard review of 68 studies on mindful eating found that slowing down, paying attention, and being present during meals improved eating behavior, reduced overeating, and increased satisfaction—no plan required.

158. ON WEIGHT

For many of us, perhaps most of us, wellness conjures the scale, and all the feelings that come with it. Weight is perhaps the most loaded subject in the entire wellness conversation because the surrounding commotion is so deafening. We have been sold plans, pills, programs, shakes, injections, and moral frameworks that treat the body's natural fluctuations as personal failures. It is, to put it plainly, a mean-spirited way to live and, as the research is increasingly showing, not an effective one.

What I have noticed in my own life is that when my inner world is calm, when I am rested, unhurried, and not running on anxiety, my body finds its best weight on its own. When it goes out of balance, the culprit is rarely a lack of discipline. It is stress, exhaustion, or the low-grade overwhelm that sends us looking for comfort in the nearest available form. The body is not misbehaving; it is communicating.

There is also our food itself. The modern food supply is laden with processed ingredients, additives, and chemical residues in our soil, in our packaging, and in things that arrive in grocery stores imitating nutritious food. Scientists have identified a class of compounds now called "obesogens." These are synthetic chemicals found in food packaging, pesticides, and processed ingredients that interfere with the hormones that regulate weight. A 2024 review published in Nature found that exposure to these chemicals is now essentially universal, and that they affect weight gain independent of diet and exercise. When the body is constantly parsing substances it was never designed to metabolize, asking it to "make better choices" is a little like asking a bee to make honey from flowers stripped of their nutrients. The instinct is there, but the raw material isn't.

What I keep returning to is this: the body's preferences are far less mysterious than the wellness industry would have us believe. When I eat food I can picture growing somewhere, my choices make themselves. Treated with consistent care and given something wholesome to work with, my body tends to know what it needs.

159. HUG YOUR FURRY FRIEND

A pet is not an accessory; it is a relationship with fur or feathers. For many of us, that relationship is one of the most stabilizing forces in our lives. Who doesn't love a creature who is visibly thrilled every time we walk into the room?

Research continues to confirm what pet owners know by experience: life with an animal can be physically and emotionally protective. Dog and cat ownership has been linked with lower blood pressure, less stress, and a reduced risk of heart disease and premature death. People who live with animals report less loneliness, more daily structure, and a strong sense of being needed.

Part of this is practical. A dog must be walked. That means you go outside and move your body even on days when you and your duvet are in serious negotiations. On average, dog owners are more physically active than those without dogs, and that shows up in better mood, sleep, and metabolic health. Even a small animal imposes rhythm: meals, fresh water, litter boxes, grooming. Someone in the house expects you to get out of bed, and that someone is, refreshingly, not your email inbox.

Part of it is chemical. Stroking a pet, hearing a purr, or being greeted at the door has been associated with changes in the body's chemistry: more oxytocin and serotonin, less cortisol. The clinical description is improved regulation of the stress response. The lived description is that, after time with the dog, you are less likely to snap at the next person who emails you a "quick question" that is neither quick nor a question.

There is another element: relief. A pet does not care about your résumé, your weight, your follower count, or the current state of your kitchen. An animal responds to your presence, your tone of voice, and your touch. For women who spend their days managing the expectations of other people, the uncomplicated loyalty of a pet can be profoundly restorative. In their view, you are perfect. Unless, of course, you are late with dinner.

The Responsibility Side

A pet is also a responsibility. Animals require time, money, training, and care. Travel becomes more complicated. Rugs are stained. Hair appears on black clothing. Allergies, limited space, and other realities mean this is not the right choice for every person in every season, and it is better to be honest about that than to romanticize it.

If you decide to bring an animal into your life, it does not have to be a puppy. Puppies are charming and demanding. They require significant time and training. There are many older, house-trained animals in shelters and rescues who need affection as much as we do and who are grateful to be given another chance. Senior dogs, dignified older cats, and bonded pairs that were surrendered together are often the last to be chosen and the most relieved to find themselves safe again.

If you are considering a particular breed, it is worth speaking with a knowledgeable veterinarian or experienced rescue before you adopt, to be certain that the animal's usual temperament, energy level, and health needs suit your real life rather than your fantasy one. There are excellent species-specific guides such as The Adopted Dog Bible for dogs and The Complete Guide to Adopting a Cat for cats, as well as more philosophical works like Patricia McConnell's The Other End of the Leash, which reminds us that our behavior is half the relationship.

Adopting Wisely

Even with research, the early days with a new animal rarely feel like a montage. Many shelters and rescues now teach a simple "three days, three weeks, three months" framework for adjustment: the first three days are often marked by adrenaline or shutdown, the first three weeks by testing boundaries and learning the routine, and the first three months by deeper trust and settling in. It is not a rigid schedule so much as permission to expect awkwardness at the beginning.

My friend Trista, who has been rescuing, fostering, and adopting animals for over twenty years, told me that if new owners can offer love and patience to their new family member, they will almost always discover their new best friend—one who loves them exactly as they are. "And really," she says, "isn't that what we are all looking for, and what we all most need?" She also reminds adopters that many of these animals come from genuinely awful situations, and that it takes time for them to rebuild trust and confidence. When you adopt through a rescue, you are not just getting a pet; you are entering into a healing process with another living being.

Trista is very direct about the number of animals that are returned for being “too high energy,” a problem that often could have been avoided if the adopter had honestly assessed her own lifestyle and done some research ahead of time. Love and patience make the relationship possible; training makes it livable. Training is not punishment, but owner and pet learning a shared language that makes life less confusing for both. There are countless low-cost and free resources: training apps, thoughtful YouTube channels, and online classes that can help you learn how to communicate clearly and kindly with your new family member.

If you love animals and your circumstances can sustain one, it is reasonable to recognize that this is not a trivial indulgence. A dog at your heel or a cat on your lap is not only “cute.” That presence contributes to your physical health, your emotional equilibrium, and your sense of not being alone.

You may think of a pet not only as a being you care for, but as a companion that, in its own way, takes very good care of you too.

160. ALIGNMENT

Some years ago, I found myself at a rather over-the-top Napa Valley resort, the kind that takes its spa menu and lemon-infused water very seriously. This was California, so the doors were open to sunshine and soft breezes, and I floated out of my treatment room in that pleasantly muzzy post-facial state. On my way out, I noticed a dragonfly trapped against a large window, flinging his delicate body again and again at the glass.

My first response was the one many of us have learned: a brisk little "Oh, it will be fine; he'll find his way out," followed by an almost physical turning away. But a few steps later, another thought arrived, annoyingly clear: If not me, then who? I turned around, went to the front desk, and asked—perhaps with a bit too much earnestness—for a plastic cup. I explained the situation in a tone that strongly implied I was not leaving until the dragonfly's problem was solved.

The staff were lovely and obliging. I suspect they could not have cared less about the insect, but they did care about helping the over-invested woman in the robe, which, for my purposes, worked just as well. One of the estheticians and I went back, gently trapped the dragonfly in the cup, slid a card underneath, and carried him outside to the olive trees. He shot up into the air, a streak of iridescence, and vanished.

For the rest of my stay, I kept seeing a dragonfly, almost certainly not the same one, but I chose to believe it was—hovering around whenever I stepped outdoors. It felt like a tiny benediction, a wink from the universe: Yes, this. This is who you said you wanted to be.

The point of the story is not that I am uniquely kind to insects. It is that, in that moment, I lived one of my values instead of merely admiring it in theory. My day was better; the dragonfly's day was unquestionably better, and perhaps the people at the spa went home with a slightly different sense of what is "worth the trouble." This is what it looks like, in miniature, to have a code: when the unglamorous opportunities appear, just take them.

Wellness is also the absence of self-betrayal. When your actions match your values, your whole body relaxes in a way no fancy spa treatment can manufacture. Acts of alignment, like stopping to save one dragonfly, can enhance your internal climate more than the most elaborate self-care routine. The afternoon at the resort reminded me of this, and of how quickly a small value-driven choice can make a day feel both calmer and more alive.

161. FORGIVE YOURSELF AND RETURN

A woman who lives by a code will sometimes fail it. This is not a flaw in the woman or the code. It is a feature of being human. No set of values, however well chosen, executes itself perfectly across a lifetime. You will be short with someone you love. You will take the easier path when the harder one was right. You will make a decision at thirty that you can see more clearly at fifty, and what you see will not flatter you. A marriage that ended. A choice made as a mother. A professional decision that had a cost. Thoughtlessness in a relationship that mattered. A failure of courage when courage was required.

What matters is what you do next. You acknowledge the failure. You apologize to whoever was affected, if that is possible and if an apology is wanted. You grieve, and then you forgive yourself and return to your code. The fourth step is the one most women skip. It is also the step that determines whether the failure becomes a lesson you carry forward with compassion for yourself and others, or a sentence you serve for the rest of your life.

Between knowing what you did and deciding to put it down, there is the work of feeling what it cost and mourning the person you hurt, the relationship that is not what it was, the version of yourself you lost in the process, and the life that did not happen because of the choice you made. That is grief, and it is different from guilt. Guilt is a vigil. Grief is a passage. One can become permanent. The other, if allowed to run its course, does not.

The Sequence Is Not a Transaction

An apology is an act of acknowledgment. Self-forgiveness is an act of return. They are separate, and self-forgiveness does not depend on the apology being accepted. You can see your mistake. You can grow. You can offer the most sincere apology of your life and have it refused. The other person may not forgive you. They may never forgive you. That is their sorrow, and they are entitled to it.

Many women stay in a holding pattern for years, sometimes decades, waiting for the person they hurt to release them. They have decided, without quite saying so, that they may not live fully until absolution arrives from outside. The person on the other end may be gone. May not be speaking to them. May be carrying their own pain in a way that makes forgiveness impossible for them.

None of this changes what is true: no one else can release you from a punishment you have given yourself. The sentence is being served in your own mind, and only you hold the key.

The Fantasy of Sufficient Payment

There is a fantasy that keeps women in this holding pattern. The fantasy is that if you suffer enough, for long enough, the debt will be paid. You will have served your time. The universe, or the person you hurt, or some internal judge, will finally agree that you have been punished sufficiently and set you free.

This is not how it works. There is no threshold of suffering that triggers release. You can carry the guilt for another ten years, another twenty, and be no closer to the exit than you were the day you began. Your unhappiness is not a payment. It is not a gift to the person you hurt. It does not restore them, soften what happened, or rebalance any ledger. It is a second loss, stacked on top of the first. You hurt them, and yourself once. Now you are withholding yourself from everyone in your present life in tribute to a past you cannot undo. You and the people who love you now are paying for a debt they did not incur.

A Return

Forgiving yourself is not a feeling you summon. For most women, the feeling comes later, if it comes at all. What you can do is decide before the feeling. You can decide that the sentence is over. You can decide to live as a woman who has forgiven herself before you have fully felt it. Elegance, in this code, has never been about how you feel. It is about how you live.

When the old guilt surfaces, as it will, you need a line you can hold. Not an affirmation. A statement. Something like: I have accounted for this. I will not account for it again. Or: I made that decision with what I knew then. I will not keep paying for it now. The line does not have to be poetic. It has to be available at three in the morning when the memory shows up uninvited.

Setting It Down

If you are a woman who has been carrying something for a long time, hear this clearly. You made a decision with the understanding and information you had at the time. You may have hurt someone who did not deserve it. You cannot undo it. What you can do is stop adding to the cost.

Your presence in your own life is not optional. The people in front of you, your spouse, your children, your friends, the woman you are still becoming, need you whole. Not the appearance of whole. Really here. A woman who has been withholding herself for years out of loyalty to a past she cannot repair is not being faithful to anyone. She is being faithful to her guilt. The guilt is in addition to, not the same as, the love she still carries for the person she hurt. It is a separate thing, and it has outlived its usefulness for everyone involved.

Put it down. Not because you have earned it. Not because enough time has passed. Not because the person you hurt has finally forgiven you. Put it down because continuing to carry it harms more people, not fewer, and because you have a code to return to, and the return is waiting for you whenever you are ready to take it.

15

CREATE WEALTH

He is free who lives as he wishes to live; who is neither subject to compulsion nor to hindrance, nor to force.
Epictetus, Discourses

TO CULTIVATE, AT ITS root, is to tend, to nurture, to draw forth growth. It comes from the ancient practice of working the soil: preparing the earth, sowing seed, watering, weeding, protecting, and waiting, so that something living can emerge and thrive. A farmer cultivates crops; a rosarian cultivates flowers; a pearl farmer cultivates oysters. In each case, cultivation is not about forcing, but about creating the right conditions for what exists in potential to grow.

Over time, the meaning of cultivate has deepened beyond the field. It came to describe the fostering of growth in a mind, a skill, a character, or a relationship. One cultivates a love of music, a taste for fine wine, a friendship, a reputation, a reflective mind. In every case, cultivation asks for attention, care, and time, so that what we touch becomes more developed, more refined, more alive.

Cultivation is not a single act; it is a steady engagement over time with what you seek to bring to life. It is patient rather than hurried, attentive rather than distracted. It honors the rhythm by which living things grow. When we understand this, we see that wealth too can be cultivated. It responds to the same devotion, the same patience, the same respect for growth that guides the tending of a garden.

162. ABUNDANCE

To live with a sense of abundance is to recognize the plenitude that surrounds us. The world is not shrinking; it is expanding. The universe itself continues to unfold, making room for more stars, more ideas, more possibilities. There is no shortage of opportunity; no need to fear that someone else will receive what was meant for you.

Abundance begins in perception. When you believe there is enough, you act with generosity and calm. When you believe there is not, you grasp and compare. These are not merely attitudes. They are strategies, and they produce opposite results with remarkable consistency.

The person who operates from abundance shares credit, makes introductions, speaks well of competitors, and refers work they cannot take. They do this not from naivety but from an accurate reading of how reputation and relationships function. Generosity circulates. It creates goodwill that returns in forms and timing you cannot predict or control, which is precisely what makes it powerful. The generous person becomes known as a source, and people return to sources.

The person who operates from scarcity hoards information, guards territory, treats every competitor as a threat, and hires beneath themselves to avoid being overshadowed. Each of these behaviors is rational within the scarcity frame. Each of them also produces isolation, stagnation, and the slow contraction of possibilities. The grasping hand signals to everyone watching that there is something worth grasping for, and that you do not trust them near it. People remember that signal.

Consider what happened in the early days of the pandemic. There was no meaningful shortage of toilet paper. The supply chain was strained but functional. What collapsed was confidence, and confidence, once lost in a crowd, produces exactly the outcome everyone feared. One person bought more than they needed. Then another saw the thinning shelf and bought more than they needed. Then someone else arrived, saw nearly nothing left, and bought whatever remained. By the time the philosophers of scarcity had finished their work in aisle seven, the shortage was real. They had manufactured it themselves, twelve double rolls at a time.

No one involved thought of themselves as the problem. Each person had a perfectly reasonable explanation. That is how scarcity thinking works: it always arrives dressed as prudence.

Scarcity thinking operates the same way at the individual level, only more slowly and therefore less visibly. Hoard your information, your contacts, your ideas, and gradually your world will shrink to reflect the smallness you feared.

The next time you feel the impulse to withhold, to guard, to grasp, pause long enough to ask what the abundant response would look like. Whether you do this because it is right or because it works, the result is identical.

Abundance is your elegance code in operation.

163. COMPETITION

There is a persistent fantasy in business, and in life, that the ideal condition is to have no competition at all. To be alone and unchallenged. Competition does several things that comfort cannot. It sets the pace. It forces precision. It tells us exactly where we are strong and where we are not. The competitor who keeps us sharp is doing us a service we did not ask for but cannot afford to be without.

Which is why what BMW did in 2019 was not merely good marketing. It was a demonstration of how a company that understands competition behaves. When Mercedes-Benz CEO Dieter Zetsche retired after nearly five decades with the company, BMW released a short film: a Zetsche lookalike hands in his badge, says his goodbyes, gets chauffeured home in a Mercedes, walks into his garage, and drives away in a BMW i8 Roadster. The closing line read: "Thank you, Dieter Zetsche, for so many years of inspiring competition." Mercedes-Benz, to their credit, fired back on social media, suggesting he had already decided to go electric with them instead.

The exchange went everywhere because it was confident, funny, and friendly. Each company acknowledged the other as worthy, which is something only the secure can do. Insecurity defaults to dominance. Elegance can afford grace.

The question is not whether your competition deserves your respect. It is what your response to them says about where you stand. The company, the professional, the institution that can congratulate a rival without flinching is sending a signal that travels further and lasts longer than any product launch or market share report.

164. SPORTSMANSHIP

Good sportsmanship is to have integrity whether we win or lose, and we teach it to children with the seriousness of a commandment. Shake hands. Win without gloating. Lose without excuses. We teach good sportsmanship as a virtue because that is the language available, but what it transmits is a set of behaviors that produce better outcomes. The moral framing is the wrapper. The content is practical intelligence.

Those who lose gracefully study. Those who rage, blame the referee, or dismiss the opponent as lucky close the feedback loop. They protect their egos at the cost of understanding. The graceful loser does something far more intelligent: they watch, file, and prepare.

Contempt for our competitors is laziness. If we convince ourselves they succeeded because of connections, or luck, or a market that won't last, we never have to examine what they did well. The opponents who beat us are our most honest advisors. They do not flatter us. They do not tell us what we want to hear. They show us, in the clearest possible terms, exactly what we still need to learn. Sometimes that is worth more than a win.

The desire to eliminate excellent competition is the desire to stop growing. In every domain where mastery is the goal, practitioners seek out the best competition available. Chess players who only beat beginners do not improve. Writers who read no one better than themselves plateau. The business that crushes every competitor and sits alone in its market grows comfortable, then slow, then overtaken.

The tradition of sportsmanship transmits all of this. The adult version looks at the mechanism directly: we treat competitors with respect because it keeps our thinking accurate, our skills sharp, and our reputation intact across a career long enough that we will need both.

There is also a practical reality: today's competitors are tomorrow's collaborators, clients, or employers. Industries are smaller than they look from the inside. The people we congratulate and treat with dignity remember that.

What we call sportsmanship is training in a specific form of attention: the discipline of taking seriously what is in front of us, rather than what our egos would prefer to see. That discipline, practiced long enough, becomes the thing that keeps us enjoying the game.

165. TIME SOVEREIGNTY

There is a model of working life so embedded in the culture that most people follow it without ever examining whether it was designed with their interests in mind. Work exhausting hours. Defer your health, your relationships, your curiosity, your pleasure. Identify completely with your role. Give the organization everything it asks for and a little more. Retire when your best years are behind you and then attempt to enjoy what remains on a fixed income with a body, mind, and relationships that were never quite maintained.

This model is not designed by people who live it. The executives who build cultures of total dedication manage their own health, their own development, and their own exits on entirely different terms. They understand something they do not teach: that the person is the asset, and assets require maintenance.

The company that benefits from sixty-hour weeks, skipped vacations, and deferred health does not reward that sacrifice with loyalty. When the burned-out employee is finally used up, the organization says thank you very much and hires someone younger and cheaper. The sacrifice is never an investment in a mutual relationship. It is a withdrawal from an account the employee does not know they are depleting.

The people who age well professionally make one foundational decision differently. They think of themselves as the asset. Not the company, not the title, not the role. Themselves. Their energy, their judgment, their relationships, their reputation, their physical and mental capacity. These are the things worth protecting because these are the things that compound. A well-managed person at sixty carries something no thirty-year-old can replicate: decades of accumulated wisdom, experience, and relationships that took a lifetime to build. And because most people their age have not maintained the mindset or the body to stay in the game; they are largely competing alone.

Bob Iger

Bob Iger understood this early and literally. Both of his parents suffered heart attacks at forty. In his twenties, before he had any status or any guarantee of where his career would lead, he changed his diet, built an exercise discipline he would maintain for the next fifty years, and decided that his body was a professional asset worth protecting. He did not arrive at health after success. He built success on a foundation of health.

At seventy, Iger is at the top of his game. He can walk into virtually any boardroom in the world and be taken seriously on sight, not merely because of his record, but because he looks and sounds like someone still at the height of his powers. Whether he wants to work at that level anymore is another matter entirely. In any case, he is not fading away on a fixed income. He has what the conventional model almost never produces: a choice.

Willow Bay

His wife Willow Bay is sixty-two. A former Estée Lauder model who built an entirely separate career in journalism, she is now Dean of USC's Annenberg School of Communication, one of the most prestigious programs in the country. She did not retire from modeling into obscurity. She built a second life of equal substance. Between them, the Igers are not winding down. They recently acquired a majority stake in Angel City FC, a women's professional soccer franchise. At a combined age of one hundred and thirty-two, they are making hundred-million-dollar investments and running institutions.

That is what the sovereign model produces at the far end: a person who is not winding down, but one who continues to unfold and expand for the rest of their life.

The conventional model was built for a world where people retired at sixty-five and died at seventy. The math worked then. It does not work now. People burn out at fifty or sixty and live another twenty or thirty years, not on the income, engagement, and purpose that a working life provides, but on savings that are never quite enough and an identity that dissolves when the role disappears. A paycheck at seventy is not just money. It is agency, structure, relevance, and cognitive engagement. The person who is still sought after at that age enjoys benefits that the retired person, however comfortable, does not have.

The Sovereign Professional

The sovereign professional does not wait for their employer to develop them. They develop themselves and bring the result to whoever is currently their best client. They protect their health because a depleted asset loses value. They build relationships beyond their current organization because they understand that organizations change and relationships endure. They do not fully identify with any single role because they know the role is temporary and they are not. You can hold a job and think like an owner simultaneously.

The question is not whether you can afford to manage yourself this way. It is whether you can afford the alternative: burning through your best years for an organization that will replace you when you are exhausted, arriving at the last third of your life with a maxed-out 401K and everything else depleted.

The people who invert this model do not work less. Many work harder than anyone around them. But they work smarter—as sovereigns—investing in themselves as deliberately and generously as corporate loyalists invest in their jobs. This allows the sovereign to arrive at seventy still sharp, still connected, still in demand, still producing. That is not luck. That is a decision made early and maintained consistently. It is available to anyone willing to make it.

Bob Iger operates from his own Elegance Code. The culture had a model for him. He had a better one.

166. THE WEALTH OF BEING HARD TO REPLACE

In any field, at any level, the person who has developed a combination of skills, relationships, and judgment that no one else precisely replicates has security that a salary cannot provide. This is not job security, which is fragile and dependent on someone else's decision. It is market position, which is built from the inside over time and belongs entirely to you.

The mistake most people make is measuring their market value by the narrowest possible standard: the specific job title they currently hold, the technical credentials they can list, the role as it appears on an organizational chart. By that measure, a great many experienced people conclude that they have nothing special to offer as they age out of the roles that defined them.

This conclusion is almost always wrong, and it is worth examining why.

What accumulates over a serious career is not a collection of tasks performed. It is something much more valuable and considerably harder to acquire quickly: the ability to read situations accurately, to make sound decisions under uncertainty and pressure, to build and sustain trust with a variety of people, to see consequences that those less experienced cannot yet see, and to know, from having lived through enough cycles, what really matters and what does not. These are not soft skills. They are rare competencies that organizations at the highest levels will pay handsomely for, precisely because they cannot be downloaded, rushed, or quickly and easily credentialed.

There is another form of value that almost never appears on a resume and is rarely calculated until it is absent: the cost of mistakes that an experienced person simply does not make. Bad hires, misread situations, avoidable conflicts, negotiations that go sideways, projects derailed by failure modes that someone with more experience would have recognized before they became problems. These are extraordinarily expensive, and organizations absorb these costs constantly without ever attributing them to the absence of seasoned judgment. The experienced professional who does not make those mistakes is not merely adding value. They are preventing loss, which is often worth considerably more. Prevention is invisible by nature. No one writes a case study about the crisis that never happened because someone in the room had seen it coming.

The variable that determines whether all of this compounds into lasting market value is currency. The experienced person who stays current, who understands the new tools, the new landscape, the new generation of competitors and colleagues, carries something that no junior person can replicate and no senior person who stopped paying attention still possesses. Depth without currency becomes dated. Currency without depth is what every entry-level hire brings. The person who maintains both does not compete with either group. They occupy a unique, highly marketable category of their own.

The person who has managed people, navigated organizations, built relationships across industries, and accumulated decades of judgment is not sitting on nothing. They are sitting on capital that a younger worker with superior technical skills cannot replicate, no matter how talented. The thirty-year-old has not yet been wrong enough times to know what being right requires. The thirty-year-old has not yet watched enough situations unfold to recognize the early signals. They have not yet built the trust that takes years of consistent conduct to establish.

None of this is automatic. The person who spends their career executing without reflecting, following without leading, or specializing so narrowly that they do not develop broader judgment may indeed find their options limited later on. But the person who pays attention, who builds relationships rather than just contacts, and develops judgment along with experience, has something the market perpetually needs.

The Elegance Code asks you to take an inventory of the full scope of your career. Not what your resume says. Not what your last title was. Security clearances are extraordinarily expensive and time-consuming to obtain, and a person who already holds them is unquestionably rare and valuable in ways that have nothing to do with age. The same applies to advanced degrees, professional licenses, certifications that require years of supervised practice, and specialized accreditations. These are not soft assets. They are hard credentials that took significant time and investment to acquire and cannot be quickly replicated. Add to that what you know, who trusts you, the mistakes you no longer make, and the insight that allows you to see what others cannot yet see. That inventory, done thoroughly, is almost always more impressive than the person conducting it believes.

If you are earlier in your career, this is not a distant concern. It is the blueprint. Every relationship built with integrity, every mistake examined rather than excused, every skill developed beyond what your current role requires, every effort to stay current while going deeper: these are deposits into your account and will define your options at fifty, at sixty, at seventy. The best time to think this way is now.

Being hard to replace is not about making yourself indispensable through information hoarding or political maneuvering. It is taking care of yourself, being your own boss no matter who you work for, and living with an elegance code, while developing capability and character. Then be confident enough to acknowledge that the market has no easy substitute for you, know your worth, and figure out how to communicate it. That is wealth. It is also, not coincidentally, freedom.

167. WEALTH LEAKS

A wealth leak is an elegance leak. Not only because of the slow financial drip, but because the nagging awareness that money is disappearing somewhere you cannot quite account for creates a background hum of unease that undermines your peace of mind as reliably as anything else we have discussed.

Wealth leaks are rarely dramatic. They are the streaming service you forgot you had, still faithfully charging you every month for content you have not watched since the pandemic. They are the gym membership held as a tribute to your future self, who, it turns out, prefers taking the dog for a walk to running on a treadmill. They are the impulse purchases, the upgrades, the spending benchmarked against people whose tax bracket you are not in—yet.

I am not a financial advisor, and nothing here constitutes financial advice. What I can tell you is this: one of the fastest ways to feel wealthier is to stop the bleeding. Once a season, or at a minimum once a year, look at what auto-renews. Look at what you have not touched in six months. Look at the recurring charges silently going about their business in the background of your financial life, confident you have forgotten them, because you probably have.

Plugging wealth leaks requires no particular expertise. It requires only the willingness to look, which turns out to be the harder part.

16

Travel Well

Though we travel the world over to find the beautiful, we must carry it with us or we find it not.

Ralph Waldo Emerson

THE AIRPORT, WITH ITS lines and security checkpoints, temperature swings and gate changes, is a concentrated test of your elegance code. Flight delays and re-routings can collapse a carefully arranged day and leave you holding nothing but what you brought: the contents of your bag, the outfit on your body, and whatever internal resources you have developed for situations like this.

Watch people in airports and you will see elegance codes, or the lack of, on full display. The traveler who is composed, organized, and moves at her own pace is not necessarily having a better day than anyone else. Her flight is just as likely to be delayed. Her bag is just as likely to be searched or lost. But she has developed a system. What you notice on the outside is her system at work.

In naval tradition, a shakedown cruise is a vessel's first serious voyage: a trial run designed to test every system in working conditions. Anything that is going to fail will probably fail on a shakedown cruise. Travel does the same thing for your code. It strips away the familiar scaffolding of your daily routine and puts your various systems under pressure. The wardrobe that works in your regular life may reveal its weak points in a Tokyo bathroom at six in the morning. The tote that carries you through a busy Monday at the office may falter when your connecting flight to Amsterdam is canceled and your checked bag lands in Omaha.

An airport combines time pressure, loss of control, physical demand, and uncertainty in a single environment. Flights do not wait. You are on your feet for hours lugging bags, often without adequate food or sleep. You know your itinerary, but regardless of whether you fly private or commercial, you do not control the events of the day. Travel presents multiple systemic pressures at once, which makes it a useful proving ground. If your code works here, it works.

168. DRESS FOR THE UNEXPECTED

A friend of mine ran into a college roommate at the airport in Paris, who invited her to dinner. My friend said yes without hesitation. She is a woman who values spontaneity, ease, and being open to whatever fun a day produces. Those are not small values, and they are worth dressing for. Unfortunately, the velour tracksuit she had chosen for travel comfort left her feeling disheveled when her roommate's elegant Parisian father unexpectedly appeared at the curb and whisked them to an upscale restaurant.

Her outfit did not betray her values, but it failed to support them. If spontaneity is important to her, her travel clothes must be able to keep up. The tracksuit made her feel conspicuous and underdressed in the exact type of situation her values embraced. She did not return from Paris and decide that spontaneity was overrated. She came home and reconsidered her travel outfit. Her values stayed. The velour tracksuit did not.

TRAVELER'S PORTRAIT: BERYL MARKHAM

Beryl Markham was the first person to fly solo across the Atlantic from east to west, fighting headwinds the entire way. She was also a racehorse trainer in colonial Kenya, a woman who effortlessly moved between rugged outdoor work and the social world of Nairobi. She knew who she was in a cockpit, at a racetrack, and at a dinner table, and her preparations reflected that clarity. Her memoir, West with the Night, reads like a woman who decided the life she wanted, then travelled accordingly.

169. TRAVEL CONTINGENCIES

Once in a while, travel goes according to plan and looks just like the brochure. It can also be hours of delay at the gate, a diversion to a city you did not plan for, and a hotel room you reach at midnight with whatever you have in your purse.

I was once stranded at a small airport in Louisiana because of storms at my destination. We were taken off the plane and told we could either spend the night in the airport or at a local hotel, but our checked bags would not be unloaded.

That experience permanently changed how I pack. When I check a bag now, my under-seat tote contains a compact but complete toiletry kit, a spare top, and lingerie. I often wear slacks or dark jeans with stretch, a blazer, and a dressy long-sleeved tee. If necessary, I can sleep in what I wore on the plane and have a fresh layer to put on in the morning. Clothing that travels with me must hold up when things do not go perfectly.

The best travel outfit is a variation on your personal style, adapted for your specific transit demands. If you are naturally tailored and spare, your go-to outfit might be slim dark trousers, a fine-knit top, and a blazer you can remove. If you lean toward ease and flow, it could be wide-leg trousers in a wrinkle-resistant fabric, a silk tee, and a wrap.

Start with what you know works. If you travel regularly, you have a mental catalog of outfits that perform well and outfits that do not. The trousers that stayed comfortable through a nine-hour flight. The blazer that still looked sharp after being crammed repeatedly into overhead bins. The shoes that got you through a gate change, two terminals, a broken escalator, and an hour-long customs line without complaint. Those are your data points.

Besides sheer survivability, also ask yourself: Will I be happy I wore this if I am surprised to be seated next to an important business contact, a celebrity I admire, or an old friend I have not seen in years? What if the flight is delayed and I have to spend the night in this outfit? Can I cart myself and my belongings down a steep flight of steps if they drop us on rainy tarmac at Heathrow instead of parking the plane at the gate? Can I step off the plane and go out for an impromptu dinner?

Test Your Travel Uniform

When you have a prospective travel outfit, wear it for a full day before you go, including the shoes. Sit for hours. Walk a little further than you think you will need to on your trip. Note how you look and feel at the beginning and end of the day. A travel outfit that survives a thoughtful trial run at home will represent you well abroad.

In the Sovereign Wardrobe chapter, we discussed uniform dressing as a strategy for reducing decision fatigue and maintaining your code under pressure. Travel is where that strategy earns its keep. A travel uniform is a formula: a combination of silhouette, fabric, and layering you feel great in, and can assemble in a flash. When your alarm goes off at four in the morning for an early flight, you do not want to be standing in your closet making decisions. If you love to travel, consider dedicating an area in your closet for your complete travel kit. This might even encourage you to travel more often.

TRAVELER'S PORTRAIT: ISAK DINESEN

Karen Blixen arrived in Africa with a European sensibility, a baroness's bearing, and ideas about land and farming that the continent dismantled. Africa did not remake her. It stripped away what was borrowed and left what was essential. The farm, the people, the landscape made demands that Europe never had, and she rose to meet them in ways she could not have predicted, because the capacity was always there, waiting for the right conditions.

The opening line of *Out of Africa*, "I had a farm in Africa, at the foot of the Ngong Hills," is one of the great first sentences in literature because it is already elegiac. She is writing from loss, and the loss gives the book its quality of knowing what something was worth only in retrospect.

But Karen's story is also cautionary for the traveler without a framework. Africa wrote on her so completely that when she lost the farm and returned to Denmark, she could not integrate what she had become. Denmark could not contain what Africa had made of her. She spent the rest of her life writing about a place she could not return to, because she had no internal architecture for folding the experience into a life that continued forward. She had been transformed, and did not know what to do with the transformation.

Your elegance code is your architecture. It does not prevent the world from affecting you. It gives you somewhere to bring what you find.

170. THE FORMULA

A travel uniform has four components: a base layer, a structure layer, a comfort layer, and shoes.

The base layer sits against your skin: a top, a bottom, and the undergarments beneath them. These must feel good for extended wear. Fabrics that itch, cling, wrinkle, or trap heat are disqualified. Look for fine knits in lightweight merino, silk blends, or high-quality stretch cotton. Solid colors are easier to travel with. Your base layer does the most work and gets the least credit.

The structure layer gives your outfit polish: a blazer, a trim cardigan, or a well-cut jacket or coat. This is the layer that takes you from "comfortable" to "put-together." It is also the layer you remove when you want to relax on the plane. Choose something that holds its shape when folded into an overhead bin.

The comfort layer adapts your outfit to temperature and climate: a scarf, a wrap, a lightweight cashmere sweater you can tie around your shoulders or compress into your bag, and for bigger weather shifts, a packable parka or trench coat.

Do not forget a packable hat and gloves in cold weather. They take up almost no space, and you will be glad to have them the moment you walk out of the terminal into weather you did not expect. These tiny considerations enrich the experience far beyond what their size suggests. Finding a thin pair of cashmere, leather, or cotton gloves in your coat pocket when your hands are cold is like finding ten dollars at the bottom of your purse—it brightens the whole day out of all proportion to the discovery. A handkerchief or a few neatly folded tissues in your pocket are a lifesaver when you need one.

Shoes are the foundation. They must be easy to remove at security when the TSA Pre-Check line is closed, comfortable for long walks, stable on wet surfaces, and presentable enough that you do not need to change them when you arrive. Flat ankle boots, loafers, well-made ballet flats, and even sophisticated sneakers are proven performers. Stilettos and brand-new shoes are not. If you cannot walk a mile in them without thinking about your feet, they do not qualify. Shoes take up significant room in your bag. One versatile pair for evening and two for day, plus the shoes you wear on the plane, should easily get you through a one to two-week trip.

Accessories earn their weight in a travel wardrobe. Pack one neutral-colored sheath dress or monochromatic trousers and a matching top, and wear each multiple times by changing the look with accessories. A silk scarf worn at the neck, tied at the waist, or used as a shawl, combined with a change of earrings and shoes, can turn one dress into three different outfits.

Seasonal Versions

Your travel uniform should have two versions: one for warm weather, one for cool. The silhouette stays the same. The fabrics, weights, and comfort layers shift.

In warm weather, your base layer might be a silk or linen-blend tee and lightweight trousers. Your structure layer could be an unlined blazer or a fine pima cotton V-neck. Your comfort layers could be a foldable Panama hat, a pashmina, and a rain jacket.

In cool weather, your base layer becomes a sleek merino knit, and wool-blend trousers or dark jeans with stretch. Your structure layer might be a wool blazer or a camelhair jacket. Your comfort layer could be a balmacaan with a removable lining, or a down vest or jacket you can compress.

Develop a formula you trust, in at least two seasonal versions, so that packing for a trip never becomes a project. Adjust your formulas for a ski trip, a beach vacation, or a tropical cruise as needed. You should be able to lay out your travel uniform in under five minutes because you have worn it before, know it works, and have it ready to go.

171. CHOOSING LUGGAGE

Luggage is part of your wardrobe, and the same standards you apply to the rest of your wardrobe apply here. Your bags should work for you. They should be easy to maneuver, simple to organize, and durable enough to survive being handled by people who do not care about them.

If you prefer not to check bags, a well-designed carry-on and a personal item that fits under the seat are your entire system. If your trips require more clothing or equipment, you need a checked bag that is distinctive enough to spot on a carousel and sturdy enough to absorb rough treatment.

Weight matters more than most people realize. A suitcase that weighs twelve pounds empty is stealing twelve pounds from your packing allowance before you put a single item inside. Lighter bags give you more capacity for the things you need. Hard-shell or soft-sided is a matter of preference and use. Hard shells protect fragile contents and resist moisture. Soft-sided bags compress, flex, and often have exterior pockets that are useful in transit.

Other Considerations

Do you need to extra security of a clamshell closure, or is a zipper closure sufficient? Will you have space at your destination for a bag that opens flat, or do you need a trunk-type case? Do you want pockets to organize small items, or do you prefer open space?

Whatever you choose, learn your bag. Know how to pack it efficiently and where to put items you need to access quickly. Your luggage is part of your travel equipment, and equipment works best when you know how to operate it.

TRAVEL SMART

Check the U.S. Department of State website for updates and specific regional warnings for your destination.

Before you book a hotel in an unfamiliar place, read reviews carefully and take a "walk" around the neighborhood with Google Maps Street View. You can also download maps and directions for your destination in Google Maps offline, so you'll have them if cell service is spotty.

E-mail yourself the combination and instructions for the lock on your check-in bag in your personal carry-on item so if you forget, you'll be able to open your bag at your destination.

Pass along your read magazines or a great novel you finish in flight to the flight attendants. Less to carry, and they'll appreciate the gesture.

Pickpockets are determined and very good at their jobs. If your valuables are vulnerable, you will lose them. Do not carry a wallet in your pants or jacket pockets; it almost guarantees you'll be a prime target. If you must carry a bag, secure your zippers and pockets. Rick Steves has said that he uses a money belt under his clothes next to his body for things he really doesn't want to lose. His website has more great tips and specific location information.

Phones are now a common target of theft. Tourists are especially vulnerable at street corners and crosswalks. Learn how to securely back up your essential documents and photos to the Cloud before you go, then do it daily on your trip.

The Under-Seat Tote

Your under-seat tote, airlines call it a Personal Item, stays with you. It is the bag you reach into during the flight and the bag that sees you through if your checked luggage does not arrive. Once you have a plan for what you need to carry in it, you can choose one that is under-seat size compliant and complements your personal style and way of travelling.

The "wings" of my black leather tote fold down and button to the sides of the bag to make it smaller or larger as needed. It contains my travel documents, phone, AirPods and charger, a compact toiletry kit, a change of clothes, my iPad or laptop, a pen, a pared-down wallet, sometimes noise cancelling headphones, and a few essentials I would rather not be without overnight. Over time, I've curated a kit that functions happily even if everything else disappears. It has a pocket on the back that unzips to allow it to slide over the handle of my wheeled bag, or zips closed to hold a magazine or newspaper.

I am a huge fan of clear zip-lock bags for organizing my luggage. This surprised a travel companion when she saw it because they are not glamorous, but they are lightweight and see-through so I can find things in a snap. I always bring extras in various sizes. A compression bag, made flat as a pancake, holds my extra tee, socks, and lingerie.

Decide what you will do with your house and car keys so they don't fall out in transit. They could be tied to a ribbon and pinned to the lining of your bag.

TRAVELER'S PORTRAIT: ISABELLA BIRD

Isabella Bird traveled alone to places that challenged the most seasoned men: the Rocky Mountains, the Tibetan plateau, the interior of Japan, and came back changed every time. What is remarkable about Isabella is that she brought herself to each place so completely that she was more fully herself there than she had ever been in an English drawing room.

At home she was frequently ill, depressed, and, by her own account, barely functional. The moment she traveled, particularly to physically demanding places, she became vigorous, capable, and alive in a way that surprised even her. She wrote about this with candor, without entirely solving it.

What Isabella's life suggests is that some people carry a self that their ordinary circumstances are too small to contain. Travel was not her escape. It was her ideal environment. The code she lived by: curiosity, fearlessness, precision in observations, indifference to what was considered appropriate for a Victorian woman, expressed itself most fully when the setting had enough scale to hold it.

You may not need the Rocky Mountains to find that out about yourself. But it is worth asking what environments bring you most fully forward, and whether you are traveling toward them or away from them.

172. TRAVEL WITH YOUR VALUES

You cannot see everything. You cannot do everything. Every destination offers more than a single visit can absorb, and the pressure to maximize every hour can turn a trip into an exhausting exercise in consumption rather than an experience tailored to you.

Your values solve this problem. They are the filter. If you value beauty, you do not need to visit every museum in Florence; perhaps you need only to stand in front of three paintings that fascinate you. If you value solitude, skip the group tour of the Amalfi Coast and hire a private guide. Or spend a morning on a terrace with coffee and the sea in front of you. If you value learning, an afternoon in a single neighborhood talking to shopkeepers may give you more than a full day racing through a checklist of landmarks.

Before a trip, ask yourself what you want to feel, not just what you want to see. "I want to feel restored" produces a different itinerary than "I want to feel stimulated." "I want to reconnect with my partner" produces a different schedule than "I want to explore on my own." You might see less, but experience more, and come home with memories that matter to you rather than a camera roll that looks like everyone else's.

The Intentional Itinerary

An itinerary built from your values has a different rhythm than one built from a guidebook. It allows open time for serendipitous discoveries. It includes meals that are experiences, not just fuel stops between attractions. It leaves room for the unexpected, which is where some of the best travel memories live.

For each day, choose the thing you most want to do or see, then build the rest of the day loosely around it. If you want to orient around a morning visit to a cathedral, the afternoon might be unplanned. If the anchor is a dinner reservation at a place you have wanted to try for years, the day can unfold at whatever pace it likes.

If you are traveling with others, the anchor system helps there too. Each person can choose the anchor for one day, which distributes the decision-making and ensures everyone gets at least one experience that feels like their own.

TRAVELER'S PORTRAIT: INDIANA JONES

Indiana Jones is fictional, but his dual uniforms are instructive. He does not have one wardrobe; he has two, and each one is a functional boundary.

In the classroom at Marshall College, he is the archaeology professor: tweed blazer, bow tie, glasses, chalk dust. The look is deliberately unremarkable. It is social camouflage, a signal to the world that there is nothing here worth disturbing. When students breach his office anyway, he exits through the window.

In the field, the camouflage is gone. Fedora, leather jacket, whip, real dust. This is the uniform of a man fully immersed in the thing he cares most about. The artifact belongs in a museum. Everything else is secondary.

He does not confuse the two. He does not wear the blazer into the canyon or the fedora into the lecture hall. Each uniform tells him, and everyone around him, where he is and what he is there to do. His travel wardrobe works because the thinking was done before he needed it. When the unexpected arrives, he is already dressed for it.

173. THE TRAVEL DEBRIEF

When you return from a trip, take a few minutes after you unpack to briefly review your system. What worked well? What did you have too much or too little of? Was there a moment you wished you had packed something different? Did your luggage work, or did you spend the trip fighting with it, hunting for items, or rearranging? Did your under-seat tote contain everything you needed when plans fell through, or were you missing something that would have made a difficult moment easier?

Write it down. Keep a running note on paper or on your phone of what worked and what did not. Over three or four trips, patterns emerge. You find certain trousers perform on every trip, that you never wear the "just in case" dress, and that your toiletry kit is missing something (tweezers? bandaids? a nail file? aspirin?) you always end up buying at a drugstore on arrival.

This is the same after-action approach from the Sovereign Wardrobe chapter, applied to travel. Small, specific observations collected over time add up to a system that gets better with every trip. The goal is not to pack perfectly on the first try; it is to learn from each experience until your travel preparation becomes second nature.

YOUR CODE NAME

17

Drafting your Elegance Code

As is your desire, so is your will.
As is your will, so is your deed.
As is your deed, so is your destiny.

The Upanishads

IN THIS CHAPTER WE will pull it all together, review the notes you made, and draft your discoveries into your personal elegance code. This is the logical next step because your code is particular to you. Putting your code into your own "dossier" makes it a useful go-to when your day is difficult, your confidence wavers, or someone asks you to be someone you are not.

Your written code also gives you something you can return to and adapt whenever you want. It will change as your life does because it is a living document. The woman who wrote her code at forty-two may revise it at fifty. The woman who wrote it when she was single may rewrite parts of it when she is married. Each revision means the code is alive and growing, right along with you.

How to Format Your Dossier

I keep my elegance code in a leather notebook on my desk. It is not framed or on display. No one has ever read it but me. Some women I know keep theirs in an app on their phone, or folded into a journal, or typed on a card tucked into a drawer. The format is irrelevant. What matters is that you know it is near, and can find it when you need it.

A friend of mine, a surgeon, told me she wrote her code on the flight home from a medical conference where she had felt, in her words, "professionally competent and personally lost." She did not write anything elaborate. She wrote five sentences on a cocktail napkin. She said those five sentences did more to reorganize her interior life than the previous two years of trying to figure things out in her head. The napkin is still in her wallet.

That is what we are after. Not an article suitable for publication, but a private document that is honest, specific, and short enough to reread in two minutes.

174. GATHER

Before you begin, gather what you have written so far:

1. Your one to two paragraph vision statement from Chapter Two
2. Your three to five core values from Chapter Three
3. Your center of balance circle, with the words you wrote in Chapter Four describing how it feels to be at your own center
4. Your two ethos words from Chapter Thirteen.
5. Any notes you made in the margins of other chapters, phras-

es you circled, images you cut out, or lists you made along the way.

Bring them to your desk, or your kitchen table, or wherever you do your best thinking.

175. YOUR VISION

Find the vision statement you crafted in Chapter Two and read it before you write anything down.

Does it still fit? If yes, copy it to the top of your card or fresh journal page unchanged. If it has shifted, if the woman you were when you wrote it has grown into a woman who wants something slightly different, revise it from where you stand today. A vision you have outgrown is usually a sign of progress; you have lived into some part of it and are ready to look further.

Below your vision, write your "one thing." That one shift, or one change in how you think, live, or spend your time, that will move you meaningfully closer to your vision.

Your vision is the compass heading. Your one thing is the first degree of correction. Without your vision, the rest of your code has nothing to orient toward. Without your one thing, your vision remains just an idea. Together, they set the top of the page in motion.

176. YOUR VALUES

You did the harder work in Chapter Three. You sat with your values, turned them over, and practiced them in your life as it is. Find that list now and read it before you transfer anything to your code.

Ask yourself, value by value: Is this still true? Some will be. Copy them onto your page. Some will have evolved, and the words you used six chapters ago may no longer capture exactly what you mean.

Go ahead and revise those. A thesaurus helps here. Sometimes the word you want is one shade over from the word you wrote.

When you have your working list, write a single sentence after each value. Not a definition, but a description of what that value looks like when it operates in your life. This is where the precision happens. "Warmth" is a word. "I treat my family with patience and warmth, especially when I am tired" is a practice. The word tells you what you value. The sentence tells you what you do about it.

Be specific. Be honest. If one of your values is independence, do not write the version that sounds best on paper. Write the version that is yours: "I earn my own money, make my own decisions about how to spend it, and do not ask permission to live the way I choose." If your value is beauty or timelessness, say what that means in practice. You are writing this for the woman who may reread this on a day when she has lost her balance and needs to be reminded where she stands.

A few things to watch for as you write.

If your values sound like they came from a commencement speech, slow down. Your code should sound like you thinking as you blow dry your hair, not you on a stage accepting an award. "Integrity" is fine if that word rings true. If what you mean is "I do not pretend to agree with people when I think they are wrong," write that.

If you are having trouble writing the sentence after a value, the value may not be yours yet. It may be something you were taught to want, or something you admire in someone else, or something you are growing toward but have not claimed yet. That is useful information. Set it aside and approach it later, or consider rethinking that value.

If two of your values seem to conflict, say, enjoyment and health, or wealth and peace, do not resolve the tension on paper. Name both. The tension between them is part of your code. A woman who values both freedom and loyalty is not confused. She is a woman whose life requires both words.

177. YOUR CENTER OF BALANCE

Draw your name or a stick figure at the center of a circle. Around it, write the words you chose in Chapter Four to describe how it feels when you are centered in your own life: the physical sensation, the ease in your voice, the way time seems to move around you.

Beneath the circle, note how you recognize the first signs of tipping off-center. Is it a tightness in your jaw? A particular hurried gesture? Over-booking creeping into your schedule? Your balance a state to return to, and you can learn to monitor it. Your earliest signs of losing it are the most useful ones to name.

178. NAME YOUR ETHOS

You did this work in Chapter Thirteen, Create Your Aesthetic, when you discovered the two words that hold your contradictions in productive tension rather than resolving them into something safer and less interesting. Find those words now and write them in next. These two words are the base of your style. They are words you would be secretly thrilled to overhear someone use about you.

Your two contrast words are touchpoints for your ethos and aesthetic, and you have been mixing these choices for years in your closet, your home, your travel habits, and your entertaining. They are the qualities that, if someone who knew you well were describing you to a stranger, would make the stranger say: I can picture her.

The ethos section of your elegance code is not limited to only these two words. This is also the place to describe, in a few lines, the quality of your presence: at a party, in a group text, a difficult afternoon, and the specific events or obstacles that you foresee. How do I maintain my ethos when it's hot, when I am traveling, when an impromptu party ends up at my house?

179. YOUR MANIFESTO

This part is new. It is the part of your code that faces the future. Your values are your *why*; they are the foundation you stand on. Your vision tells you *what* you are building. Your ethos is *how*—it tells you how you do things in your own unique way. Your manifesto is your promise. It is your commitment to yourself, and describes the way you will hold to your code when the world tries to pull you off course.

Write five to ten sentences. That is all you need. This is not a speech. It is a set of private instructions from you to yourself about how you plan to live from here.

You might begin with: "Given the world as it is, I choose to..." and finish the sentence. Or you might begin with: "Looking back from the end of my life, I want to have been a woman who..." and write from there. The first opening is a declaration. The second is a reckoning. Both are useful, and they produce different documents.

The first says: here is what I will do. The second says: here is who I will have been. Some women will write from one and feel nothing, then try the other and feel everything. Use whichever one unlocks the most passion for you.

Your manifesto should include two statements:

- What you will no longer do.
- What you will no longer delay.

This is where your manifesto plugs in and powers up. You have spent this entire book identifying leaks: the habits, tolerances, and compromises that drain your composure. Your manifesto is where you name them and decline to continue. "I will not spend my evenings in arguments that leave me shaken but change nothing." "I will not keep clothes that make me feel wrong in my own body."

"I will stop saying yes out of guilt to invitations I dread." Refusals are potent elements in an elegance code.

Then write what you will protect. Your values, your time, your attention. "I protect an hour at the start of my day." "I protect my sleep." "I protect the loving way I speak to my spouse when we disagree." Your values are the things you have said matter. Your manifesto is where you describe how you will defend them in practice.

When you are done, read your manifesto aloud. Listen for the line that makes you feel a little stronger for having said it. Underline that one. That is the line to keep in front of you when a day is not elegant at all.

180. PULL IT TOGETHER

You now have your personal elegance code as a single document. Give it a title, "My Elegance Code," and today's date. The date matters. It marks this version as belonging to this season of your life, and reminds you that you have permission to revise it when your life changes.

And it will change. The code you write at thirty-eight may not be the code you need at fifty-five. A woman who has just become a mother, a woman who has just lost one, a woman who has left a marriage or started a company or moved to a country where she does not speak the language: each of these women will need a different document. The structure stays. The content evolves.

When you are finished, resist the impulse to show it to anyone right away. Not because it is a secret, but because the moment you hand it to someone else, you edit it for their reaction. You soften a line that feels too sharp, or add a value that sounds more generous. You wonder whether your manifesto is too blunt, too personal, or too much. It is not too much. It is yours. Let it stay yours for a while before you decide whether to share it.

If you do choose to show it to someone, choose carefully. Show it to a person who wants your happiness and well-being more than your compliance. Someone who can read it without rushing to add their own edits to your life.

181. EXPECT IT TO CHANGE

Your elegance code is a working document. Revisit it once or twice a year. At the turn of a new season, on your birthday, at the start of a new year, or whenever life delivers one of those changes that rearranges the furniture in your interior. You may find that some values have deepened. Others have faded. A word in your ethos section that felt essential in January may feel decorative by October. A line in your manifesto may have been tested so thoroughly that it has become part of you and no longer needs to be written down.

That is your code at work.

You may also find that you have drifted from your intentions. Perhaps a month or a season went by in which your code sat in a drawer untouched. That is the ordinary friction of being alive in a jumbled world that does not organize itself around you. Your code is there for your return. Pick it up any time, read it, and ask: Is this still me? If yes, come back to it. If parts of it are no longer true, revise them. The willingness to revise is itself a form of elegance. It means you are paying close attention to your life.

You might begin your revisits with three questions:

• What have I outgrown?

• What has become more important?

• What have I been pretending doesn't matter, that clearly does?

182. YOUR ELEGANCE CODE

The Elegance Code was designed to help you create a way to maintain your grace, peace of mind and personal style regardless of people and events that swirl around you that you cannot control. You have done that work.

You have gone inward to your values, your vision, and your center of balance, and built outward from there. The wardrobe, the manners, the way you travel and spend and speak: all of it has been chosen by you, because it matches something true about yourself that you want to build a life on.

You have also put it in writing. You now have a document you can reference when other people's expectations blur the edges of your own.

You will not live every day in perfect alignment with your code. No one does. Some days you will rush, leak, speak sharply, ignore your own good advice, and forget what you wrote here. Those days are not evidence you have failed. They are the days when you grow, and get to practice returning.

Return as often as you want. Read your words. Remember that you wrote them in a clearer hour than this one, and trust the woman who wrote them. Then take a step that moves you a degree closer to that woman.

That is your elegance code at work, in large gestures and small: in the way you pour your coffee, answer your phone, plan and dress for the day, and speak one line at a time into the life you have chosen.

18

Everyday Expressions of Your Code

Look and you will find it—what is unsought will go undetected.

Sophocles

THIS CHAPTER IS AN opportunity to play with the possibilities your code holds for you when it winds its way through every aspect of your life. Read through, circle what makes you smile or sparks an idea, and continue to add your own. This is your life. Sink into it. Explore. Experiment. Have fun.

183. CELEBRATE YOUR CODE

Music and images can remind you of your code faster than almost anything. A song can elevate your mood at once. A photograph can remind you of your vision. This is because images and music reach the emotional brain through a more direct route than words do. Both activate the limbic system, which governs emotion and memory, faster than the analytical mind can weigh in. An image can register and shift mood in milliseconds. A few notes of a familiar song can summon a feeling before you have consciously identified the song. Words require interpretation. Music and images arrive as experience.

So it makes sense to enrich your day with both.

Playlists

I start my day with a streaming station called Morning Coffee Jazz. Three of my favorite things in one title. By late afternoon, when I am flagging, I switch to a good 1970s rock station, dance around the kitchen island with my German Shepherd Indy, pour a cup of tea, and I am back in business.

A playlist that sounds like your code does the same work as a signature perfume or a favorite cardigan. When you need a lift or to wind down, you know just what to reach for.

Build one. Name it whatever you like. Gather the songs that sound like you, and add to the collection over time. If your ethos words are Refined and Wild, you might layer old standards with 1970s rock, or bluesy jazz with something off-kilter. Miles Davis meets Fleetwood Mac meets that song from your college years you will never admit to loving. If your ethos is Soft and Electric, it might be whispery vocals and finger-picked guitar threaded through with strong synthesized beats.

Images

Mood boards are not the path to elegance, but once you have done the work of discovering your code, they become great sources of play and inspiration.

Open Pinterest or a search engine and try your values and ethos words paired with something unexpected, like luggage or silk scarves. Pair your words Regal and Bohemian with art or interiors. Serene and Dramatic with perfume. Try your values words plus gardens, jewelry, travel, ceramics, architecture, or bookshops. The pairings bring back results you may not have found otherwise, and the internet may hand you a surprising version of your own aesthetic. Search your words paired with your city, your country, or a place you love, and see what turns up. A collection of images that makes you think, *Yes, that is me,* becomes a private museum you can visit whenever you need to remember what you love most about being you.

184. WRAP IT UP

Wrapping is part of the gift. Before the ribbon is untied, the package has already said something about the person who sent it. Think of Cartier's red box, Tiffany's blue box with white ribbon, or the iconic Hermès orange and brown. Each is recognizable at a glance, a statement of the house, and a courtesy to both the giver and the receiver.

Develop your own signature wrap. Ask yourself: if my aesthetic showed up on a gift, what colors, textures, and details would it wear?

If you love gardenias, choose a floral paper with a green or brown silk ribbon, tuck a real or silk gardenia into the bow, and write the gift tag in green ink. If you are sporty or preppy, a bold rep-stripe with pink and green grosgrain ribbons is cheerful, and a monogrammed tag pulls it together. If your style is tropical, try white paper with a chartreuse ribbon and a palm-tree gift tag, or a custom calling card printed with a pineapple, crocodile, or colorful bird. If your style is natural, you might choose brown kraft paper and dress the package in a multi-wrap of twine, a sprig of greenery, a native seed packet, and a hand-tied tassel.

The easiest way to make your gift style yours is to keep it simple and repeatable. No need to have twenty random rolls of paper on hand. Pick one or two wrap colors you love, and one or two types of ribbon. Then add a signature element: a watercolor sketch of your favorite flower or bird, a lemon leaf or sprig of cedar from your yard, a wax seal, a toy or charm, a seed packet, or a handwritten tag. Use this combination for birthdays, hostess gifts, and holidays. You can adapt the colors with the seasons, but the underlying language stays the same. After a while, people will recognize your packages from across the room.

185. "HOW" IS THE FUN PART

We all do more or less the same things each day. We wake, eat, work, sleep, and put on our pants, as they say, one leg at a time. But there are countless differences in how we do things. That is a positive thing. Imagine how dull the world would be if we all liked and wanted the same things.

Be Choosy

Many people do not put a lot of thought into how much agency they have over their choices. They buy a certain toaster because their mother had that one. They paint the walls beige because a magazine says neutrals are timeless. There is nothing wrong with this, but you can also enjoy expressing your code through your preferences.

Give a bit of thought to ordinary selections: hardcover or paperback, bath or shower, stairs or elevator, stemmed glass or stemless, bound notebook or spiral. The choices themselves matter less than the fact that you have made them consciously. When you buy ivory candles instead of white, do you pick ivory because it feels warmer, or white because it seems cleaner? Do you want the window seat because you like looking out, or the aisle because you hate feeling confined? Do you prefer suede or smooth leather, silver or gold? Why?

Once you know what you like, and why, your days feel more deliberate, and trends have less power over you.

It is useful, too, to notice when your tastes change. The hardware you chose at thirty because everyone had it. The shoes you bought because your friends did. Taste becomes interesting the moment it turns conscious.

There are far more possibilities than this book could hold. If you want more, I have posted a list of 260 word pairs on my Substack at ninagates.substack.com for you to borrow from.

186. YOUR FONTS

I am fascinated by words and letters. Graphic designers have opinions about fonts, the way sommeliers have opinions about stemware, and will argue for an hour about the difference between Garamond and Sabon and mean every word. That enthusiasm is not misplaced because fonts work hard. Before a person reads a single word, the font has already told them whether the content is expensive, playful, or serious, and whether they are looking at a sign for a law firm or a candy shop.

This is because we subconsciously link shapes to traits. Rounded fonts feel soft and friendly and angular fonts feel bold or high-tech. Fonts also carry the DNA of specific eras. A typewriter font feels nostalgic and tactile. Elongated fonts feel Art Deco. A high-contrast serif can feel like a 1950s fashion magazine.

To Chisel or Not to Chisel

The first fork in the road is serif versus sans serif. A serif is the decorative stroke at the end of a letter: the little feet on a T, the finial on a Q. Serifs were common on Greek and Roman stone inscriptions, making them as old as the Western Latin writing system itself. Picture the chisel marks on Roman monuments. That is why fonts like Times New Roman, Garamond, and Baskerville feel traditional and authoritative. They were, literally, carved in stone.

Sans serif fonts (*sans* meaning "without") dropped those decorative strokes in the twentieth century, when modernist designers decided that ornament was sentimental and letters without little unnecessary thingamajigs attached were easier to read. The result is what we recognize as modern: fonts that are clean, efficient, and architectural. Helvetica, Arial, and their descendants populate airports, corporate logos, and phone screens because they read as neutral and contemporary. Coco Chanel understood this early. The house's signature font, a custom, bold, all-caps sans serif, was radical when it was adopted because it challenged the opulent, ornate, "feminine" aesthetic that defined luxury in the early twentieth century. Chanel bet that elegance could come from restraint rather than ornamentation.

Neither is better. They are doing different jobs. A serif says heritage. A sans serif says now. Some of the best correspondence uses both: a serif for a letterhead and a sans serif for the body, or vice versa, because the contrast creates the sense of a designed page rather than a default one. The writer who doesn't pick a font is using one anyway; the one her software chooses for her. Choosing deliberately is the difference between a message and your voice.

Finding Your Font

You do not need to know every font. Here are starting points organized by your desired mood for your correspondence.

If you want your writing to feel warm and approachable, try Nunito or Quicksand. Both have soft, open shapes that read as generous rather than stiff. They work beautifully for personal notes and blog posts.

For classic editorial polish, try Playfair Display. Its tall, high-contrast letters evoke a Vogue spread from the 1950s. It has the razor-thin hairlines and dramatic strokes of Didot or Bodoni without requiring a specialty license.

If you prefer something nostalgic and tactile, Courier New is on every device you own, and IBM Plex Mono is a more refined alternative if you are willing to install it. Both carry the rhythm of a typewriter. They are excellent for signature files, pull quotes, and anything you want to feel handmade.

For Chanel's brand of modern minimalism, try a clean geometric sans serif like Montserrat or Futura, headings set in all caps with generous letter spacing. Designers call this tracking, and a slight adjustment makes a significant difference. Most word processors let you increase letter spacing in the font or character settings; start with a setting of around 100 to 200 units, or whatever reads as "expanded" in your software. The extra air separates a corporate-feeling sans serif from one that feels couture.

If you are sophisticated and cosmopolitan, you might love the Art Deco glamour of Bebas Neue. It gives you tall, condensed letterforms like grand hotels and cocktail menus. It is a display font meant for headings and invitations rather than full paragraphs, but used well, it announces a point of view.

A fun reward is when a friend opens your note and knows, before reading a word, that it came from you.

187. YOUR MONOGRAM

Monograms are one of the oldest forms of personal identification in the Western world. The Chi Rho, the overlapping Greek letters for Christ, is among the most recognizable. Constantine carried it on the labarum into battle. Early Christians embroidered it on vestments and placed it over altars. It predates the modern alphabet's version of either letter.

Queen Elizabeth I had an elaborate monogram that appeared on her bookbindings, her furniture, even her glove linings. It served as both a signature and a warning: this belongs to the queen. Napoleon commissioned a monogram with an interlocking N that he used across the French Empire, engraved on silver, woven into carpets, and stamped into buildings. After his fall, royalist craftsmen chiseled it off palace walls.

In the Victorian era, monograms became part of elaborate social codes. A woman of standing had her monogram on her calling cards, her stationery, her handkerchiefs, and her trunks. The trunks were particularly revealing. When she arrived at a hotel in Paris or a country house in Scotland, porters would unload her luggage, and the monogram on each trunk, hand-painted in her chosen colors, often with matching stripes, identified her household before she had said a word. The custom has not disappeared. Houses like Louis Vuitton and Goyard still paint clients' personal monograms and stripes onto their trunks today.

The pleasure of a monogram is that it claims a thing as yours. A bath towel becomes your bath towel. A notecard becomes your notecard. A silver cup becomes a cup that will outlast you and still carry your letters long after you have stopped using it. This is what monograms have always done. They turn an object into an heirloom.

Traditionally, a woman's monogram uses three initials in the order first, last, middle, with the last initial slightly larger and centered. Plenty of women now use two initials instead, or pair a single letter with a small icon that means something to them, such as a bee, a sunburst, a fleur-de-lis, a horse, or a heart. Your monogram should express your point of view. An elegant script reads traditional and feminine. A clean block reads modern and spare. Interlocking letterforms with negative space read artistic. Any good graphic designer can create one for you, and there are free tools online if you want to experiment before you commit.

Once you have it, put it where it will please you. On your stationery. On a wax seal. Embroidered on cocktail napkins, a bathrobe, or the lining of a jacket. Stamped on the inside of a gift box. Engraved on a piece of jewelry, a silver frame, a luggage tag, or the cover of a leather notebook. A monogram that appears across the everyday objects of your life becomes one more thread of your code, visible only to you and those who spend time near you.

188. YOUR MOTTO

A motto is the shortest form of your code. It is a line you can carry with you and return to when you need to remember what you believe.

Mottos have a long history. The great houses of Europe adopted them as a way of stating what the family stood for in four or five words. The Medici used *Semper*, meaning always. Queen Elizabeth I used *Semper eadem*, meaning *always the same*, a motto she chose during her turbulent reign.

Your motto does not have to be in Latin or French, and it can be practical: *First, do the hardest thing.* Philosophical: *Nothing is wasted.* Reassuring: *You have done harder than this.* It can be humorous if humor returns you to yourself.

What are the words you want to hear, in your own voice, when you need to remember who you are?

Once you have it, you can place it where you will see it, or where no one else will. Embroidered on a pillow. Printed and framed by the bathroom mirror. Engraved inside a ring or a locket. Written on a slip of paper tucked into a wallet. Some women carry their motto on the lock screen of their phones. Others keep it somewhere no one else will ever see, because it is meant for them alone.

189. NATURE

Nature reminds us that we are part of the environment we live in, not above or outside it. Our lives depend on a healthy ecosystem, even when we do not fully understand it or find parts of it strange or a little scary. The more we learn, the more allied we feel.

An opossum visited my yard one night, and it sent me on a research tangent. I was surprised to learn that opossums eat thousands of ticks, termites, and mice. They do not dig their own dens; they borrow shallow spaces from other animals. If one visits your garden, it is eating the grubs that would otherwise destroy your lawn. A creature I might have shooed away turned out to be on my side. The more I paid attention, the more I saw this pattern. The spiders in the corners were catching flies before they could come indoors. The hawks circling the field at dusk were hunting the mice. Every creature was doing work I had not asked for and did not have to pay for.

You can participate in the conversation by adding something to it. Plant a favorite flower in drifts around your house. Many garden clubs sell yearly rose, daffodil, or lily bulb collections, and it is a pleasure to forget what you planted and watch the surprise bloom each summer. Add pollinator-friendly plants that require almost no effort and enjoy watching them support the bees and butterflies. How you treat the natural world, and how you see your place within it, is a direct reflection of your values.

190. YOUR STATIONERY

Personalized writing paper is one of the loveliest expressions of an elegance code. Your favorite colors, patterns, monograms, and motifs can all live on the page.

You might choose a particular weight or color of paper. A handful of houses have been making the best of it for centuries, and any one of them is worth meeting.

Smythson of Bond Street opened in London in 1887, when Frank Smythson hung his shingle on New Bond Street and began selling what the shop called *"stationery and fancy articles of a high-class character."* In 1908, the house created the first Panama diary, the slim, leather-bound notebook that became its signature. In 1916, Frank patented Smythson Featherweight, the pale Nile blue paper at half the thickness of ordinary writing paper, strong enough to take a fountain pen without bleeding. Each page is watermarked with a faint globe and feather, visible only when held to the light. The house has held Royal Warrants since 1964, and over the years its diaries and stationery have passed through the hands of Queen Victoria, Winston Churchill, Sigmund Freud, Grace Kelly, Katharine Hepburn, Sir Edmund Hillary, and very likely a few people you know.

Crane & Co. was founded in Dalton, Massachusetts in 1801, making it among the oldest papermakers in America. The family's papermaking tradition, however, reaches further back: the founder's father, Stephen Crane, established the Liberty Paper Mill in 1770 and supplied the paper to Paul Revere, who printed the American colonies' first currency on it. The Crane family has been making paper in one form or another ever since. Their signature Ecruwhite Kid Finish, a warm, soft, 100% cotton sheet, has been a fixture of American correspondence for more than a century and was the paper of choice for Jackie Kennedy's condolence notes, President Taft's White House invitations, and the dedications of both the Statue of Liberty and the Golden Gate Bridge.

Pineider opened its doors in Florence in 1774, when Francesco Pineider set up shop in the Piazza della Signoria, a stone's throw from Michelangelo's David. He sold the first personalized printed letters in Italy, and within a generation his shop had become a required stop for Grand Tour travelers. Byron, Shelley, Stendhal, Leopardi, and Napoleon all bought paper there. When Italy unified and made Florence its capital in 1865, Pineider became stationer to the embassies, the ministries, and the Royal Court. The house still produces watermarked cotton papers, hand-painted borders, and deckle-edged sheets in the traditional way, and still holds the original engraved plates and dies for centuries of its customers' monograms in its Florence archive.

Your envelopes could carry your icon or signature color, or be lined in your favorite pattern. A wax seal, a carefully chosen stamp, or a small drawing in the corner makes the letter feel like a special event when it arrives in someone's mailbox.

A friend of mine brightens my days by sending handwritten notes in creative cards, many of which she makes herself. I adore them, and keep them tied with ribbon and reread them on flat days.

191. YOUR HOBBIES AND PASTIMES

Are you a diver or a snorkeler? Do you like to go deep and learn everything you can about a subject, perhaps mastering it? Or do you prefer to skim along the surface, dipping in when something catches your interest and then swimming on to whatever draws you next?

Your hobbies can reflect your values and your vision for your life too. If you value creativity, you might take a painting class, keep a sketchbook in your purse, or spend weekends making something by hand with your children. If you value learning, you might volunteer at a library or museum. If you value connection, choose activities that bring you into community, such as serving at a food pantry or joining a book club. If you love growing things, start seeds for friends and give the seedlings away.

192. AN EDWARDIAN INTERLUDE

If you love the historic series that have found their way onto Netflix — *Downton Abbey*, *The Gilded Age*, *The Crown*, *Belgravia* — you have already been studying a particular kind of life. The Edwardian lady's day was a masterclass in shaping hours, and her hobbies are instructive even now, when almost none of us have a lady's maid or a gong at eight.

Her day was not idle. It was organized. She woke late by our standards, was dressed by her maid, and breakfasted around nine-thirty. Then she went to her morning room and began her work. The housekeeper arrived first, to consult on the day's plans, any expected guests, the state of the linens, the condition of the house, any minor crises below stairs. Then the cook came up, and together they settled the menus for luncheon and dinner, often for several days in advance. A great house of that period was an enterprise, and the lady ran it. Add in the household books and accounts, the correspondence with tradesmen, the thank-you notes, the letters of introduction, the letters of condolence, and the letters to friends and relations scattered across the country and the Continent, and her morning was filled.

By late morning she might change and take a walk in the garden, or ride, or practice at the piano for an hour — not for an audience, but because music was part of how she was taught to think. A great many Edwardian ladies were seriously accomplished on the piano, the violin, or the harp. They sketched. They kept watercolor boxes and botanical notebooks. They pressed flowers and learned the Latin names for them, and identified birds by ear.

After luncheon came the rituals that shaped the social fabric: morning calls (which, confusingly, were made in the afternoon), afternoon tea at five, and the art of receiving visitors with ease and grace. A well-kept drawing room, a well-chosen cake, a conversation held lightly and with wit. These were not small things. They were the currency of a woman's social life, and she gave them real attention.

Evenings were for reading, for needlework, for embroidery so fine it could be an heirloom. French was expected. Novels were devoured and discussed. The better sort kept a commonplace book — her personal anthology of quotations, ideas, and observations worth saving. Before bed she wrote in her journal. Virginia Woolf, a child of this period, kept diaries from girlhood; so did countless of her countrywomen whose names we do not know.

193. NOBODY DID IT ALL

Each woman chose what suited her, and the rest she let alone. When Lady Catherine de Bourgh interrogated Elizabeth Bennet at Rosings on the subject of her accomplishments, Elizabeth confessed to scarcely any of them. No governess. No drawing. No serious command of the instrument. *Those who chose to be idle,* she observed, *certainly might* — but such as wished to learn had always been given the means. Elizabeth had not wished to learn the harp. She wished to read, to walk, and to think, and these she did prodigiously. She crossed three fields in bad weather to reach a sister she loved, and arrived with her petticoats muddied to a degree that scandalised the ladies of Netherfield and interested Mr. Darcy more than he had planned to be interested. Her accomplishments were her own. She had assembled them on her own terms.

This is the argument concealed within the daily round. A lady's life was not dictated. It was composed. The frame was given by the period — morning for business, afternoon for society, evening for the private pleasures of the mind — but the furnishings of each hour were her own concern. One woman embroidered; another rode to hounds; another read Greek for pleasure; another kept a menagerie of finches and wrote letters to the botanical society. The form was common property. What filled it was entirely hers.

194. A ROOM OF HER OWN

What made much of this dignity and creativity possible was something we have mostly forgotten: her day was shaped not only in time but in space. Different rooms for different activities, different rooms for different degrees of privacy. The morning room for the business of the house. The drawing room for receiving callers. The library for serious reading. The boudoir, her private sitting room, often adjoining her bedroom, for the hours that belonged to her alone. The word *boudoir* is from the French *bouder*, to pout or to sulk, and the original sense was telling: a room to which a woman could retreat when she wanted to be left alone. She was entitled to it, and the household knew it.

A room claimed by the lady of the house was understood by everyone to be hers. Servants entered only when called. Husbands knocked. Children came in only when they were called for. The door could be closed, and when it was, the world paused at the threshold.

Jane Austen knew this, and she gave us a poignant portrait of a woman arranging her spaces in *Pride and Prejudice*. When Elizabeth Bennet visits Charlotte Lucas after her marriage to Mr. Collins, Charlotte leads her into a parlor at the back of the house that she has claimed for her own particular use, where she can read and think and receive friends without being disturbed. Charlotte, newly married to a man she does not love, has walked into her modest parsonage and performed architectural surgery. She has given Mr. Collins a small room at the front of the house as his study, placed so he can spend his days watching the lane for Lady Catherine's carriage. She has claimed a different room at the back for herself. The result, engineered entirely by her, is that husband and wife spend much of the day in separate rooms, and Charlotte has her private hours, thoughts, and her friendships to herself.

Charlotte is not a great lady with a country estate. She is a clergyman's wife in a small parsonage. She had no wealth, no title, and no servants to speak of. What she had was the willingness to look at her situation and rearrange it to suit her needs and desires.

That is the takeaway lesson.

Many of us now live in houses or apartments where every room is available to everyone at all times. We answer email from bed, take calls in the kitchen, and try to read a book in a living room with a television on. The Edwardian lady would have found this chaotic beyond belief. Her life worked because her spaces were designated, and the people around her knew the rules.

Almost no one has the architecture for a full separation of uses anymore. But the principle is portable. Even one corner of one room, claimed and defended, changes what is possible in your day. A writing chair that is understood to be yours when you are sitting in it. A reading nook where no one will ask you a question. A section of the dining table that holds your sketchbook and your watercolors. A desk in a guest room that is your personal desk, and is not to be disturbed.

What you are doing when you claim a space is giving your attention somewhere to rest. You are making an important physical agreement with yourself and with the people you live with: this is where I do this thing, and when I am here, I am doing it. The room may be grand or casual. What matters is that it or a portion of it is designated, and that you and the household both agree.

What is interesting about the Edwardian lady's day is not that it was elegant, though it was. It is that it was built. Her mornings were working mornings. Her afternoons were social in a way that required preparation and sometimes nerve. Her evenings were for long-form pleasures that reward sustained attention. Nothing in her day was accidental. Even her idleness she arranged.

You do not need a country house or a retinue to borrow from her example. What she models is an older idea of how to live: that a day has its hours, and each hour is given to its proper occupation. A morning for the business of your life. A middle of the day for people. An evening for the things that feed your mind and hands. A little time at the end for the page.

The costumes are charming, but what those series offer is the image of a life lived in its proper orders of time and space, with each attending to its own business. You can have that life now, in whatever century you happen to occupy.

195. YOUR PLACES

It is perfectly fine to have preferences about the places where you spend your time.

The shops and markets where you run errands can either drain your energy or lift it. I find that certain grocery stores make me want to be more inventive about how I cook. It is clever of them to use attractive lighting and display fresh food in appealing ways. I enjoy the experience, and I suspect they sell more because of it. Other stores make me want to get in and out as fast as possible.

Someday, retailers will fully recognize that people are visual, sensory, and tactile. We notice beauty. If we just want convenience, we can order online. When we take the time to walk into a shop, it should be worth the walk, whether it is a clothing store, an auto parts shop, an office supply store, or a hardware store.

When you think about where you *want* to spend your time, and then make the effort to support those places instead of the ones you do not enjoy, you help create more of the world you prefer, and less of the world you do not. We vote with our feet. Find places you enjoy being in. Become a loyal patron, and let the owners know you appreciate the warmth they have built.

196. FOOD AND PREP

Jean Anthelme Brillat-Savarin, the French gastronome and magistrate, wrote *The Physiology of Taste* in 1825. One of its most famous lines: *Dis-moi ce que tu manges, je te dirai ce que tu es.* In English: *Tell me what you eat, and I will tell you what you are.* It is the ancestor of the modern *you are what you eat*, but the original is both more elegant and more philosophical. Brillat-Savarin was making a civilizational argument, not a nutritional one.

Food is part of your daily experience, and the way you approach it reflects your preferences and your values.

What you eat matters. So does how you prepare it. Chopping vegetables, heating a pan, brewing coffee. These can feel like chores or pleasures, depending on your approach.

A pantry reveals more than almost any other part of a house. What is on the shelves shows what we believe about our own hunger, our hospitality, and our wellness. The places we shop matter too, and so do the people we buy from.

197. YOUR MORNING AND EVENING RITUALS

The way you begin and end your day sets the frame for everything in between.

A morning ritual can be brief or leisurely, depending on your life. Some women make the coffee before they look at their phones. Some stretch, write a page, walk the dog, sit with the cat, or simply stand at the window while the kettle heats. The ritual is the agreement with yourself that the first few minutes of the day are yours.

Evenings are the reverse. The ritual is how you close the day and signal to your body that it is time to move from doing to being. Wash your face with intention. Change into something you love to sleep in. Place a decanter of water by your bed. Read a few pages of a book that has nothing to do with work. Some women keep a one-line journal by the bed and record only what they are grateful for from the day.

I set aside about an hour before bed to wind down. You might make sure the kitchen is clean, the counters are wiped, and the dishwasher is running. A friend of mine walks around her house tidying and fluffing the sofa pillows so she can wake up to a peaceful scene. You might dim the lights, run a bath, and turn down the bed. I set a mat beside mine like a schmancy hotel, so I can step into bed without a coating of German Shepherd hair on my feet. I sometimes listen to an uplifting book while I do my skincare routine.

Create a relaxing, centering routine that you do the same way each night. Sleep researchers have found that a consistent pre-sleep routine, especially one that begins with soft light and ends with a calming activity, helps the body shift into deeper, more restorative sleep.

198. YOUR COFFEE AND TEA ORDER

How do you take your coffee or tea?

You can walk into a cafe and order a grande half-caf flat white with three pumps of sugar-free hazelnut and two Splendas, and no one blinks. They just ask for your name and get on with it. You are allowed to be that specific.

Strong, black, and scalding. Iced with extra cream. Weak with a lot of milk and exactly one sugar. Your order is a mini statement that says, *This is what I like.*

How do you take yours? Do you order what you actually want, or do you default to whatever is easiest?

199. YOUR PAJAMAS

In my novel *The Gilded Talisman*, the heroine Maren sighs with relief when she takes off one of her beautiful outfits and pulls on her old Harvard sweatshirt. It means the day is done and it is time to relax and dream.

What signals that moment for you?

Do you love your husband's old shirts like a 1970s film starlet? Do you reach for a dramatic silk kimono, a loud caftan, a simple cotton nightgown, or matching cotton separates that make you feel like Audrey Hepburn? Are you long or short, pants or gown? Think of your ethos words. Could your evening wear and pajamas reflect your style as clearly as your daytime clothes do? You do not have to look presentable for anyone else. You can still choose to look like yourself.

200. ON A HIGH NOTE

None of what is in this chapter is required. Not one word of it. You do not need a motto or a monogram or matching pajamas to have an elegance code. What you need is the willingness to treat your life as yours and to let your own preferences show up in the ordinary hours.

The font you choose, the way you wrap a gift, the flowers you plant, the ritual that opens your morning: these are not decorations on top of a life. They are the life. They are where your code becomes visible, not to anyone else particularly, but to you. Every time you catch a detail that is unmistakably yours, you are reminded that you are the one living here, and that the living is being done on purpose.

Pick what delights you. Leave the rest. Come back in a year and pick something else.

That is what a life of your own design looks like, lived one well-chosen day at a time. Enjoy every moment.

Bonus Chapter: Mise en Place

You will do foolish things, but do them with enthusiasm.

Colette

SOME OF MY FAVORITE authors tuck a bonus chapter at the end of their books. Fiona Ferris does this, and I have always loved the feeling of receiving a little extra gift when I thought the book was done. What follows is one such gift for you. The concept, *mise en place*, has shaped more of my daily life than almost any other idea I have picked up, and I hope it will do good work for you as well.

I hated cooking. It was a confusing mess of ingredients, heat, tools, equipment, instructions, pans, timing, temperatures, expectations, a ridiculous amount of math, and oh, yes, flavor. You know, how things tasted at the end of that nightmare.

Enter a brilliant chef, friend, and in this case a savior, and the concept of *mise en place*. In French it means *put in place*, or *everything in its place*, and to a chef it is a way of working, a way of life, and to my friend, practically a religion. In culinary school he had it tattooed on his arm.

"Look," said he, in that careful, kindly way one might speak to a lost puppy or the insane, "you already do this in your studio. Think about the complex steps involved in painting. You do not start until your tools are laid out. You have chosen your materials. You think about the quality of the paint, canvas, and supports. You prepare your space. You think through the steps beforehand to help avoid the things you know can go wrong."

"Cooking," he said, "is the same."

The Meese

Chefs call it *the meese*. In essence, *mise en place* means deciding what you want to create, then organizing everything you need before you begin, and arranging the steps in the order you will follow them. Ingredients are washed, chopped, and measured. Tools are set out. The order of steps is clear. Instead of reacting as you go, you are ready. When mastered, it is an art.

When you use this in daily life, you stop hunting. You stop reacting. You work with what is in front of you, at the pace you choose. Both life and dinner feel less like an emergency.

A simple checklist for any complex, multi-step task:

Read the recipe all the way through.

Gather every ingredient.

Do the chopping and measuring first.

Set out the tools and pans you will use.

Keep your workspace tidy. Clean as you go.

It takes a few extra minutes at the beginning, but it saves many more later.

Everyday Expressions

The way you prepare shapes how you experience what comes next.

When you take a few moments to set things up, whether it is making a meal, beginning your day, or starting a project, you bring something of your own code into the doing of the thing.

Laying out your clothes the night before. Setting up your workspace before you write or pay bills. Gathering what you need before errands. Thinking through the steps ahead of time. These are all forms of *mise en place*.

Elegance Audit: Mise en Place

Choose one domain, such as your kitchen, your desk, your wardrobe, your morning routine, or your car, and consider:

Where do I experience havoc, delay, or friction?

If this were a recipe, what would count as my ingredients and tools?

What would it look like to have those ingredients in place before I begin?

What specific practice could I introduce to prepare in advance as a matter of habit?

It is a habit worth developing: prepare first, then begin.

Over time, this builds order and ease. What once felt overwhelming becomes deliberately manageable. You spend less time correcting mistakes and more time enjoying the process. We do not have to tattoo it on our arms for *mise en place* to become part of how we do things. That is how it becomes part of your code, one more everyday expression of elegance, and one whose value you only notice once you have lived without it.

Author's End Note

You cannot get through a single day without having an impact on the world around you. What you do makes a difference, and you have to decide what kind of difference you want to make.

Jane Goodall

It never once occurred to me to wonder whether we would continue. Lately, an image comes to mind of humanity sitting on a tree limb we are busily sawing off. The world isn't likely to end in the years I have left, yet it's hard to ignore the direction of travel. At our current pace of conflict and consumption, it isn't melodramatic to imagine that unless something shifts radically in how we think about ourselves, one another, and the planet we inhabit, the full reckoning will come after we're gone. We may not live to see the worst of it, but the people we love might.

That knowledge feels like watching a beautiful, complicated relationship you've spent decades nurturing turn toward a heartbreak you can't prevent. You mourn not only what may be lost, but all the potential that might never be lived.

My answer is simple: I can't decide the fate of the world in this century, but I can decide the quality of my days and make my brief years here as sane and beautiful as I know how. If our branch breaks one day, I want my part of the story to have been conducted with care and elegance.

That is what this book is about—not pretending the world is fine, but living well in it anyway. When you don't know what else to do in any given moment, pause, breathe, and turn toward happiness. Then turn toward it again in the next moment, and the next. And if enough of us do that, steadily, routinely, with kindness, gentleness, and heart, the future may find its footing after all.

With love and peace,

Nina Gates

Reader and Book Club Discussion Questions

Satisfaction of one's curiosity is one of the greatest sources of happiness in life.

Linus Pauling

A word before you begin.

These questions are offered in the spirit of continued conversation, either with yourself, with a book club, or with one close friend. There are no correct answers, and there is no particular order you need to follow. Take what is useful. Leave the rest.

A book club meeting for *The Elegance Code* can go in many directions. Some groups may want to discuss the philosophical framework the book builds. Others may want to share the elegance code they have written. Still others may want to pour a good cup of coffee and talk about how they wish to live.

If you are reading alone, these questions are just as much for you. Sit with one at a time, in whatever order suits you, and write your answers in a journal or the margins of this book. A solitary conversation with yourself, carried out over a stretch of weeks, is one of the more useful practices a woman can develop. Whatever shape your conversation takes, I hope it is illuminating.

QUESTIONS FOR DISCUSSION

1. How did this book surprise you? What did you expect when you picked it up, and what did you find?

2. The author argues that elegance comes from the inside out—from values, vision, and a sense of one's own center—rather than from clothes or accessories. Do you agree? Have you found this to be true in your own life?

3. When you think of a woman who strikes you as truly elegant, what qualities does she have that you find most captivating? How much of it is what she wears, and how much is something else?

4. The book introduces the idea of an "elegance leak"—a small drain on your composure that you may not even notice until you start looking. What leak did you recognize in your own life as you were reading?

5. The author talks about having a "signature"—a small, consistent choice you keep returning to that anchors you. What is your signature? Or, if you haven't quite identified one, what choice are you most often drawn back to, or what signatures have you admired on others?

6. The chapter on the Sovereign Wardrobe asks you to consider whether your clothes are working for you or you are working for them. After reading, did anything in your closet suddenly seem like it belonged to a different version of yourself?

7. The book makes a case for choosing your two "ethos words"—two words in tension that describe how you want your life to feel and look. Did you land on yours? Were you surprised at all to discover them? What were they, and what did you uncover about yourself in the process of choosing?

8. The Self-Forgiveness section in the Wellness chapter argues that

"guilt is a vigil; grief is a passage." Did this distinction land for you? How did the chapter change the way you think about something you may have been carrying?

9. The author writes that the airport is "a concentrated test of your elegance code." What environment in your own life works the same way? Where does your code get tested, and how does it hold up?

10. The book closes with the author's belief that we cannot decide the fate of the world but we can decide the quality of our days. How did the End Note land for you? What will you carry with you from this book?

Further Reading

Adam, H., and Galinsky, A. D. "Enclothed Cognition." *Journal of Experimental Social Psychology* 48, no. 4 (2012): 918–925.

Anderson, Clinton. *Clinton Anderson's Downunder Horsemanship: Establishing Respect and Control for English and Western Riders.* North Pomfret, VT: Trafalgar Square Books, 2004.

Anon. *How to Shine in Society; or, The Art of Conversation: Containing Its Principles, Laws, and General Usage in Modern Polite Society.* Glasgow: G. Watson, 1860.

ASPCApro. "Pet Adjustment Periods: The 3 Days – 3 Weeks – 3 Months Guide." *ASPCApro,* September 16, 2024. https://www.aspcapro.org/resource/pet-adjustment-periods-3-days-3-weeks-3-months-guide.

Aurelis. "What Is Elegance?" Ghent: aurelis.org, 2018. [VERIFY AUTHOR AND PUBLICATION DETAILS]

Aurelius, Marcus. *Meditations.* Translated by Gregory Hays. New York: Modern Library, 2002.

Barroso da Silva, André, Diogo S. Teixeira, Luís Cid, and Diogo Monteiro. "Enjoyment as a Predictor of Exercise Habit, Intention to Continue Exercising and Exercise Frequency: The Intensity Traits as Moderators." *Frontiers in Psychology* 13 (February 17, 2022): 1–11. https://doi.org/10.3389/fpsyg.2022.780059.

Barry, Barbara. *Barbara Barry: Around Beauty.* New York: Rizzoli, 2012.

Barzel, Baruch, et al. "Why Are There Six Degrees of Separation in a Social Network?" *Physical Review X* 13, no. 2 (2023): 021032. https://doi.org/10.1103/PhysRevX.13.021032.

Beccari, Pietro. *Dior: The Legendary 30, Avenue Montaigne.* New York: Rizzoli International Publications, 2022.

Bédard, Andréanne, et al. "Can Eating Pleasure Be a Lever for Healthy Eating? A Systematic Scoping Review of Eating Pleasure and Its Links with Dietary Behaviors and Health." *PLOS ONE* 15, no. 12 (December 20, 2020): e0244292. https://doi.org/10.1371/journal.pone.0244292.

Blackstone, William. *Commentaries on the Laws of England: A Facsimile of the First Edition of 1765–1769.* Vol. 1, *The Rights of Persons.* Chicago: University of Chicago Press, 1979.

Blumberg, Bruce, et al. "Obesogens: A Unifying Theory for the Global Rise in Obesity." *International Journal of Obesity* 48, no. 4 (April 2024): 449–60. https://doi.org/10.1038/s41366-024-01460-3.

Cassiday, Laura. *The Complete Guide to Adopting a Cat: Preparing for, Selecting, and Caring for Your Rescue or Shelter Cat.* Independently published, 2021.

Chapman University. "New Research Shows Most Women Report More Body Dissatisfaction Directly After Seeing Fashion and Bikini Models." Orange, CA: Chapman University, 2017.

Cockburn, J., Collins, A. G. E., and Frank, M. J. "A Selective Role of Dopamine in Information-Seeking." *eLife,* 2020.

Dariaux, Geneviève Antoine. *A Guide to Elegance: For Every Woman Who Wants to Be Well and Properly Dressed on All Occasions.* London: HarperCollins, 2003.

Doyle, Laura. *The Empowered Wife: Six Surprising Secrets for Attracting Your Husband's Time, Attention, and Affection.* Dallas: BenBella Books, 2017.

Ebenstein, William, and Alan O. Ebenstein. *Great Political Thinkers: Plato to the Present.* 4th ed. New York: Holt, Rinehart and Winston, 1969.

Ferris, Fiona. *The Peaceful Life: Slowing Down, Choosing Happiness, Nurturing Your Feminine Self, and Finding Sanctuary in Your Home*. Independently published, 2020.

Flann, Kevin L., et al. "Muscle Damage and Muscle Remodeling: No Pain, No Gain?" *Journal of Experimental Biology* 214, no. 4 (February 15, 2011): 674–79. https://doi.org/10.1242/jeb.050112.

Gates, Nina. *The Gilded Talisman.* Austin: Boheme Eclat Press, 2025. http://www.amazon.com/dp/B0FTPPN3HK.

Gates, Nina. *The Roses of Ainsworth Manor.* Austin: Boheme Eclat Press, 2025. http://www.amazon.com/dp/B0G5J8PKBQ.

Gladwell, Malcolm. *The Tipping Point: How Little Things Can Make a Big Difference.* New York: Little, Brown, 2000.

Goddard, Molly Claire. "Cindy Crawford Does Not 'Offer Unsolicited Advice' to Adult Children Kaia and Presley: 'I Really Try Hard'." *Morning Honey.* New York: MorningHoney.com, 2024.

Greene, Robert. *The 48 Laws of Power*. New York: Viking, 1998.

Gruber, M. J., Gelman, B. D., and Ranganath, C. "States of Curiosity Modulate Hippocampus-Dependent Learning via the Dopaminergic Circuit." *Neuron* 84, no. 2 (2014): 486–496.

Hall, Kevin D., et al. "Ultra-Processed Diets Cause Excess Calorie Intake and Weight Gain: An Inpatient Randomized Controlled Trial of Ad Libitum Food Intake." *Cell Metabolism* 30, no. 1 (July 2, 2019):

67–77. https://doi.org/10.1016/j.cmet.2019.05.008.

Harper's Bazaar. "Kaia Gerber Says Mom Cindy Crawford Raised Her 'Without Shame'." New York: Hearst Magazines, 2026.

Holden, Edith. *The Country Diary of an Edwardian Lady: A Facsimile Reproduction of a Naturalist's Diary for the Year 1906.* London: Michael Joseph/Webb & Bower, 1977.

HuffPost Editors. "Miranda Kerr: Models Are Some of the Most Insecure People I've Ever Met." *HuffPost.* New York: HuffPost, 2013.

Iger, Robert. *The Ride of a Lifetime: Lessons Learned from 15 Years as CEO of the Walt Disney Company.* New York: Random House, 2019.

Kraus, Michael W., and Bennett Callaghan. "People in Higher Social Class Have an Exaggerated Belief That They Are Better Than Others." *Journal of Personality and Social Psychology,* 2019.

Lauren, Ralph. *Ralph Lauren: A Way of Living: Home, Design, Inspiration.* New York: Rizzoli International Publications, 2023.

Locke, John. *Essays on the Law of Nature.* Edited by W. von Leyden. Oxford: Clarendon Press, 1954.

Locke, John. *Second Treatise of Government.* Edited by C. B. Macpherson. Indianapolis: Hackett Publishing Company, 1980.

Markus, Hazel, and Paula Nurius. "Possible Selves." *American Psychologist* 41, no. 9 (1986): 954–969.

Martin, Judith. *Miss Manners' Guide to Excruciatingly Correct Behavior.* Illustrated by Gloria Kamen. New York: Atheneum, 1982.

May, Matthew E. *In Pursuit of Elegance: Why the Best Ideas Have Something Missing.* New York: Currency/Doubleday, 2009.

McCarthy, Carrie, and Danielle LaPorte. *Style Statement: Live by Your Own Design.* New York: Little, Brown and Company, 2008.

McAdams, Dan P. *The Stories We Live By: Personal Myths and the Making of the Self.* New York: Guilford Press, 1993.

McConnell, Patricia B. *The Other End of the Leash: Why We Do What We Do Around Dogs*. New York: Ballantine Books, 2002.

Michigan State University Extension. *Animals Can Help Our Health.* Michigan State University, February 28, 2025. https://www.canr.msu.edu/news/animals_can_help_our_health.

Milgram, Stanley. "The Small World Problem." *Psychology Today* 1, no. 1 (1967): 60–67.

Molloy, Louise. "Even Supermodels Hate the Way They Look." *Ravishly.* Oakland, CA: Ravishly.com, 2014.

Montaigne, Michel de. *The Complete Essays.* Translated and edited by M. A. Screech. London: Penguin Books, 2003.

Müller, Florence. *Christian Dior: Designer of Dreams.* New York: Rizzoli International Publications, 2021.

Neimeyer, Robert A. "Meaning Reconstruction in the Wake of Loss: Evolution of a Research Program." *Behaviour Change* 25, no. 3 (2008): 135–145.

Oettingen, Gabriele. *Rethinking Positive Thinking: Inside the New Science of Motivation.* New York: Current/Penguin, 2014.

Pressfield, Steven. *Turning Pro: Tap Your Inner Power and Create Your Life's Work.* New York: Black Irish Entertainment, 2012.

Pryor, Karen. *Don't Shoot the Dog!: The New Art of Teaching and Training.* New York: Bantam Books, 1999.

Roehm, Carolyne. *At Home with Carolyne Roehm.* New York:

Clarkson Potter, 2001.

Rohn, Jim. Quoted in Canfield, Jack, and Janet Switzer. *The Success Principles.* New York: HarperCollins, 2005.

Russell, Cameron. "Looks Aren't Everything. Believe Me, I'm a Model." TED Talk. New York: TED Conferences, 2013.

Segar, Michelle L., et al. "The Secret Life of All-or-Nothing Thinking with Exercise: New Insights and Implications for Health Promotion." *American Journal of Health Promotion,* forthcoming, preprint 2025. https://doi.org/10.1177/08901171231234567.

Simionescu-Panait, Andrei. "On Elegance." *Daily Philosophy.* Vienna: daily-philosophy.com, 2021.

Slepian, M. L., Ferber, S. N., Gold, J. M., and Rutchick, A. M. "The Cognitive Consequences of Formal Clothing." *Social Psychological and Personality Science* 6, no. 6 (2015): 661–668.

Sommers, Susan. *French Chic: How to Dress Like a Frenchwoman.* New York: Villard Books, 1988.

Sommers, Susan. *Italian Chic: The Italian Approach to Elegance.* New York: Villard Books, 1992.

Spade, Kate. *Style.* New York: Simon & Schuster, 2004.

Stoddard, Alexandra. *Creating a Beautiful Home.* New York: William Morrow, 1992.

StudyFinds Staff. "Seeing Fashion Models Makes Women Feel Worse about Their Bodies." *StudyFinds*. April 12, 2022. https://studyfinds.org/seeing-fashion-models-women-feel-worse-bodies/.

Swami, Viren, and Martin J. Tovée. "Body Image Concerns in Professional Fashion Models." *Psychiatry Research.* Amsterdam: Elsevier, 2013.

Tasca, Giorgio A., et al. "Increased Eating Disorder Frequency and Body Image Disturbance in Fashion Models." *Journal of Eating Disorders.* London: BioMed Central, 2024.

Taylor, Ina. *The Edwardian Lady: The Story of Edith Holden*. Devon, England: Webb & Bower, 1980.

Tocqueville, Alexis de. Democracy in America. Translated and edited by Harvey C. Mansfield Jr. and Delba Winthrop. Chicago: University of Chicago Press, 2000.

VanSonnenberg, E. "Enclothed Cognition: Put On Your Power!" *Positive Psychology News,* 2024.

Viala, Maud, et al. "Fashion Models' Experiences of Aesthetic Labor and Its Impact on Body Image and Eating Disorders." *Eating Behaviors.* Amsterdam: Elsevier, 2023.

Ware, Bronnie. *The Top Five Regrets of the Dying: A Life Transformed by the Dearly Departing.* Carlsbad, CA: Hay House, 2012.

Weingarten, Gene. "Pearls Before Breakfast." *The Washington Post,* April 8, 2007.

Weinschenk, Susan. "The Dopamine Seeking-Reward Loop." *Brain Wise* (blog). *Psychology Today*. February 27, 2018. Accessed your access date. https://www.psychologytoday.com/us/blog/brain-wise/201802/the-dopamine-seeking-reward-loop.

White, E. B. *Charlotte's Web.* New York: Harper & Brothers, 1952.

Winston, Patrick Henry. "How to Speak." *MIT OpenCourseWare*, January 2018. https://ocw.mit.edu/how_to_speak.

Zeelenberg, Marcel, and Rik Pieters. "A Theory of Regret Regulation 1.0." *Journal of Consumer Psychology* 17, no. 1 (2007): 3–18.

About the Author

Nina Gates is the author of *The Gilded Talisman*, *The Roses of Ainsworth Manor*, and *Be an Artist (or Just Live Like One)*, which debuted at number one on Amazon in Art Study and Teaching. She holds a degree in political science, and is a U.S. Army veteran. She lives in Texas.

Connect:
On Instagram @NinaGatesAuthor
On Good Reads at https://www.goodreads.com/ninagates

Also by Nina Gates

The Gilded Talisman

The Gilded Talisman sweeps readers into an opulent world of history, intrigue, and romance as gifted art restorer Maren Bennett's unconventional life is upended by tragedy and a single cryptic message: "Come to Venice as soon as possible—trust no one." Drawn into the city's shadows, and the secrets surrounding a mysterious ring, Maren is tasked by the enigmatic Marquise de Saint-Clair to recover Roxelana, a legendary sixteenth-century Ottoman talisman necklace lost to history. Her pursuit becomes a globe-spanning race between those who would protect the talisman's legacy and rivals willing to kill for its power, carrying her from the legendary Orient Express, where luxury masks danger, to Parisian designer salons and glittering Istanbul ballrooms. Complicating her mission is a man who is devastatingly handsome, impossibly wealthy, and bound to the talisman's dark past in ways he refuses to admit. Blending old-world glamour with the heart of romantic suspense, The Gilded Talisman is a novel of bravery, obsession, and the transforming power of self-discovery.

ABOUT BOHÈME ÉCLAT PRESS

Bohème Éclat Press publishes books for readers who would rather think than be told. Founded in 2025, the press takes its name from two principles its books are made to honor: the freedom of bohemian self-direction and the radiance of clear thought. Each title is designed and produced with the conviction that the form of a book should match the seriousness of its argument.

A NOTE ON THE TYPE

The text of The Elegance Code is set in Caslon Libre, a contemporary revival of the eighteenth-century English typeface designed by William Caslon. Caslon's letterforms have been associated with serious printing since their first cutting in the 1720s and have been used by everything from the Declaration of Independence to the works of Benjamin Franklin's press. The face is admired for its even color, its quiet authority, and its capacity to disappear into the act of reading.

The headings are set in Roboto, a contemporary sans-serif designed by Christian Robertson. Its geometric clarity provides a structural counterpoint to the warmth of the Caslon body text.

Playfair Display appears only at the section openings, where its formal elegance signals that the reader is crossing into new territory.

BOHÈME ÉCLAT PRESS

www.ingramcontent.com/pod-product-compliance
Lightning Source LLC
LaVergne TN
LVHW090556110826
845146LV00001B/155